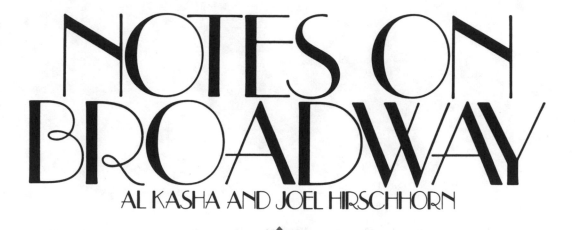

NOTES ON BROADWAY
AL KASHA AND JOEL HIRSCHHORN

INTIMATE CONVERSATIONS
WITH BROADWAY'S
GREATEST SONGWRITERS

A FIRESIDE BOOK
Published by Simon & Schuster, Inc.
NEW YORK • LONDON • TORONTO • SYDNEY • TOKYO

Copyright © 1985, 1987 by Al Kasha and Joel Hirschhorn

All rights reserved
including the right of reproduction
in whole or in part in any form.

First Fireside Edition, 1987

Published by Simon & Schuster, Inc.
Simon & Schuster Building
Rockefeller Center
1230 Avenue of the Americas
New York, NY 10020

Published by arrangement with Contemporary Books

FIRESIDE and colophon are registered trademarks
of Simon & Schuster, Inc.

Manufactured in the United States of America

10 9 8 7 6 5 4 3 2 1 Pbk.

Library of Congress Cataloging-in-Publication Data

Kasha, Al.
    Notes on Broadway.
    Originally published: Chicago: Contemporary Books,
c1985.
    "A Fireside book."
    Includes indexes.
    1. Composers—United States. 2. Lyricists—United
States. 3. Musical revue, comedy, etc.—United States.
I. Hirschhorn, Joel. II. Title.
ML385.K25 1985   782.8'092'2   87-16340
ISBN 0-671-63508-5 Pbk.

Permission acknowledgments and photo credits appear on pages
347–49, which are to be considered an extension of the copyright
page.

With loving thanks to my wife, Ceil, and my daughter, Dana.

Al Kasha

With love and gratitude to my wife, Jennifer, and my parents, Evelyn and Irving Hirschhorn.

Joel Hirschhorn

CONTENTS

FOREWORD

THE BROADWAY MUSICAL is America's cultural gift to the performing arts. The Viennese may have given us the form, but we have taken the musical and made it an international art. The sounds of American musical comedy and drama are heard throughout the world.

The Broadway musical began as purely unpretentious entertainment, designed to divert the average family or the tired businessman. It also mirrored America's emotional climate. Look at our musical heritage, and you will find satire, history, drama, even social commentary—all dressed in song and dance, all devised to entertain.

Our nation's history has taken many unexpected turns; our musical theatre has kept pace with the changes. We roared musically through the twenties, escaped frivolously in the thirties, marched patriotically in the forties, came home to prosperity in the fifties, experimented in the sixties. As we hit the seventies, we were still growing, finding new forms of musical expression, working with deeper content. In the eighties, we are developing a more diverse theatre, ranging from rock operas to intimate musicals. As always, the goal is to entertain and enrich audiences.

Time has taken its toll on the librettos of these wonderful shows, but the melodies linger on. The hit parades of the twenties through the sixties were filled with five decades of Broadway show tunes. Sometimes three and four theatre songs were in the hit parade's Top Ten, and every year the music business looked to the theatre for a new batch to add to its list of standards.

Artists juggled their recording sessions to get in on the newest Broadway show tunes prior to their New York debut. And Hollywood found that the familiar songs brought record-breaking audiences across the country to cinematic adaptations of musicals.

Without the songwriters, of course, there never would have been a Broadway. With their music (jazz, low-down, pop, or operatic) and lyrics (romantic, satiric, comedic, or polemic), they have reached out to communicate with us, and they have succeeded. We have fallen in love listening to their songs; we have rebelled with them; we have found escape through them. The great songwriters have told the world where we stand—where we could be, should be, or would like to be. They have made us laugh and made us cry. Their impression is indelible.

With *Notes on Broadway*, we can add to our knowledge of the musical theatre through firsthand conversations with some of these musical giants. As Al Kasha and Joel Hirschhorn—award-winning songwriters themselves—talk to these gifted composers and lyricists, they present us with an interchange that gives us insight into the development and evolution of many beloved shows and songs. How lucky we are to have this one-on-one dialogue as part of our great American gift to the world, our national treasure—the Broadway musical.

Lawrence Kasha
Tony Award-winning
producer of *Applause*

ACKNOWLEDGMENTS

Special thanks to the following friends for their invaluable help: Karen Sherry and Michael Kerker, ASCAP; Allan Becker and Dave Fulton, BMI; Bob Altschuler, CBS Records; Peter Brown, Brown and Peters Public Relations; Jimmy Brochu; Allan Carr; Brent Carter; Kevin Carter; Terrie K. Curran; Lord Bernard Delfont; Dorothy Dicker; Bert Fink; The Fred Nathan Public Relations Company; David Geffen; Brenda Generally; Hannah Gilman; Happy Goday; Ray Golden; Charles Harmon; Herb Helman, RCA Victor Records; Sylvia Herscher, Seymour Herscher; Bob Jani; Lester Katz; Gene Kelly; Irwin Kostal; Marvin Krauss; Miles Kreuger; Michael Lloyd; John McClure; Maureen McGovern; Richard Mills; Jay Morgenstern; John Newman; Dottie Phillips; Ben Perlis, Warner Bros. Records; David V. Stuart; Lou Tracy; Jerry Weintraub; Ed Yoe; Craig Zadan.

In memory of E. Y. (Yip) Harburg,
our friend and mentor,
a shining rainbow in the theatre.

INTRODUCTION

NOTES FROM JOEL

My love for musical theatre started in a typical way, with childhood piano lessons, and came to full fruition as a student at Manhattan's High School of Performing Arts. Let loose in New York at 13, I ran to every Broadway musical that came into town.

• The theatre bug took further hold in 1971, when Al and I collaborated with Charles Aznavour and wrote lyrics to many songs in his one-man show—including "The Old-Fashioned Way" and "I Have Lived." Charles pored over every line, emphasizing that "each word must tell a story"; he made the words his own. How much emotion did the lyrics contain? Were they universal? Were they believable? He paced the floor of his Sherry Netherlands hotel suite, mouthing each syllable, visualizing future audiences and how they would respond when we opened on Broadway.

I thought of Charles while having a drink with close friend Carol Hall in 1977. Carol had written *The Best Little Whorehouse in Texas*, scheduled for an opening run-through at the Actor's Studio that same night. Carol was breezy and talkative, but I heard the trumpeting chorus of unspoken prayers—let the actors be at their best, let my songs work, let the comedy elicit laughter, let the critics picture a full physical production beyond a bare stage and some tables and chairs. Let the show move from a workshop production to Broadway.

She needn't have worried. *Whorehouse*, even in its most primitive form, had the look and sound of a crowd pleaser. But she did worry, because Carol, like all theatre writers, cared consumingly about her project. Theatre is not a world for the moderately involved, the dilettante, the dabbler. It demands an ever-burning search for excellence.

Stephen Schwartz, composer of *Godspell* and *Pippin*, is another friend. He had originally produced an album on RCA Victor featuring my then-wife Jill Williams (later the author of book, words, and music for the Broadway musical *Rainbow Jones*). The qualities that made him a boy wonder on Broadway were already evident in his studio work as a record producer. He made sure each of Jill's songs were character songs. He wanted lyrics respected and plausibly acted when she performed. He carried these attitudes to *The Magic Show* and *Working*, which he also directed. "You don't know what it's like," he remarked cryptically after a particularly tense afternoon of rehearsal. I instinctively realized that it wasn't a complaint as much as a cry of frustration, because the birth of a show, stimulating as it can be, is fraught with what Sammy Cahn calls "labor pains." Not one theatre writer in *Notes on Broadway* manages to avoid them, nor would any choose to. These gut agonies are an integral part of the creative process which, at its best, yields shows as varied as *Gypsy*, *March of the Falsettos*, *Fiddler on the Roof*, and *Jesus Christ Superstar*.

Through this book, readers will vicariously experience, as we did, the panic of an out-of-town opening (Jerry Herman with *Hello, Dolly!*), the tension of a writer supporting himself through odd jobs (William Finn), the startled reaction of a writer who conceives a so-called "black show" and encounters prejudice when her friend elects not to see it (Micki Grant), and the courage of a composer directly defying a critic (Cy Coleman).

The shows written by the songwriters in *Notes on Broadway* speak to everyone—to children with imagination (*Peter Pan*), actors fighting for a job (*A Chorus Line*), homosexual couples coping with unexpected crisis (*La Cage aux Folles*), and women seeking a strong, independent identity (*I'm Getting My Act Together and Taking It on the Road*).

Their unique perceptions spoke to the child and the grown-up in me, and I know they will be as moving and meaningful to you.

NOTES FROM AL

"I did Sammy Cahn's nails today. Such a nice man. He gave me a big tip too."

Those words were spoken by my mother, Rose Kasha, in the spring of 1946. I was accustomed to the idea of my mother doing manicures; she worked as a beautician at the Vitagraph Studios in Brooklyn, directly across the street from the apartment house where we lived. But I remember a surge of rare excitement when she mentioned Cahn, because he was a songwriter and I had already developed an interest in writing. He stood apart in my mind from the various actors—Jack Haley and others—who had had their nails trimmed by my mother.

Cahn never returned for a second manicure, but I saw his Broadway hit,. *High Button Shoes*, in December of 1947, and relived the incident. I held on tightly to the playbill in my lap, happily enslaved by love for the musical theatre, a love heightened by my recent appearance as a child actor in Irving Berlin's *Annie Get Your Gun*. My brother, Lawrence Kasha, shared this passion. Larry became a producer in 1960, when he mounted an Off-Broadway production of Jerry Herman's review *Parade*.

At the Greenwich Village rehearsals of *Parade*, I got to know Jerry; and he turned out to be a warm, approachable human being. He not only encouraged my composing; he invited me to sing demonstration records of his songs, letting me into his life, granting me an opportunity to watch him work. I saw his joys and struggles firsthand, the commitment required, the drive toward perfection that marks all the fine composers and lyricists in this book.

My brother introduced me to other outstanding writers—Jerry Bock and Sheldon Harnick, for example, who wrote a show Larry co-produced with Hal Prince, *She Loves Me*. By then I was doing well as writer and staff producer for CBS, and I cut "She Loves Me" with one of my artists, Steve Lawrence. I also did songs by John Kander and Fred Ebb, the creators of *Cabaret*. Other songwriters who dropped by my CBS office regularly with material were Burt Bacharach and Hal David, and Charles Strouse, who later fashioned the melodies for my brother's Tony-award winning hit, *Applause*.

Repeated contact strengthened these friendships and increased my admiration for musical theatre writers. I listened intently when Charlie Strouse talked to me about songs that created characters, told stories, highlighted subtle shadings of human emotion. "Pop writers only write *song* songs," he said. "You have to get below the surface, get to that secondary level."

Jule Styne was another composer who sought out that secondary level, as I observed when attending rehearsals of *Funny Girl* as the guest of CBS Records President Goddard Lieberson. "Show writing is a collaborative effort," he said over and over. Styne was always feverishly willing to rewrite, polish, and alter numbers for the good of the show.

That point, above all, defines the authors whose words and attitudes populate *Notes on Broadway*. What is right for the show? From Jule Styne to Tim Rice, these great talents, who span a fifty-year period of Broadway history, all stress the importance of creative collaboration among directors, choreographers, stars, writers. They know the artistic interplay needed to build a cohesive, fully realized musical.

Notes on Broadway is a labor of love, a tribute to friends like Jerry Herman, mentors like Alan Jay Lerner, inspirational figures like Leonard Bernstein, and the other luminaries who spoke so personally and passionately to us. Jule Styne said, "This will be fun. I'll be speaking to fellow writers. You guys will know what I'm saying. You've been there." Jule and everyone else we visited recognized that, as songwriters, Joel and I have experienced many of their ups and downs, and they trusted us to understand their special peaks and problems. We want to thank them for sharing their insights and giving so generously of their time. Their genius wrote the words and played all the beautiful chords that make up theatre history, and we're grateful that they gave us all these memorable musical "notes on Broadway."

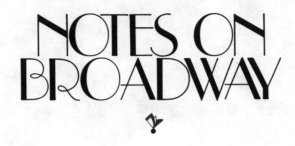

NOTES ON BROADWAY

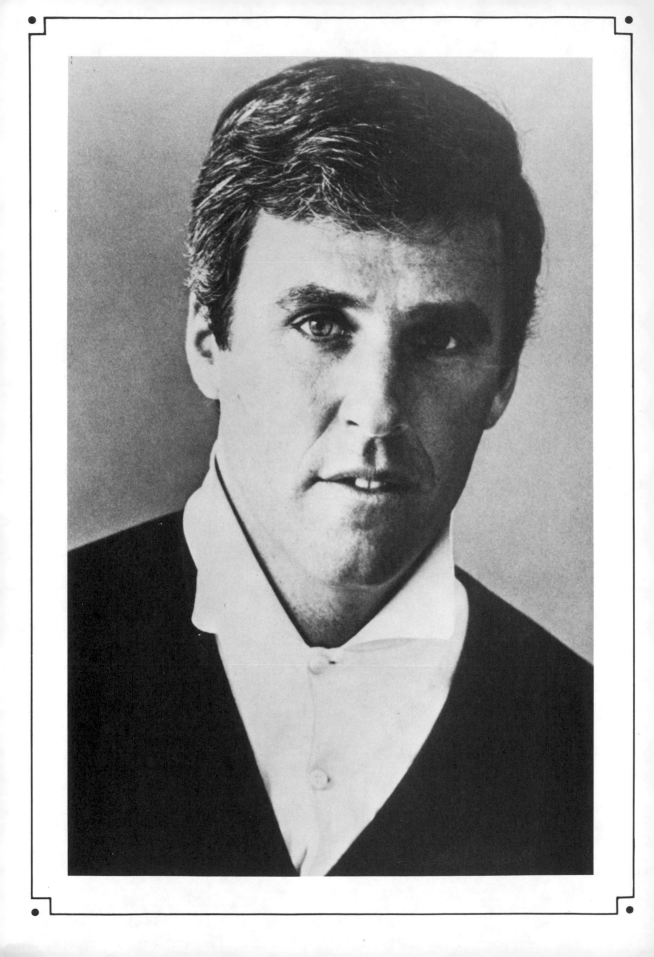

CHAPTER ONE

BURT BACHARACH

BURT BACHARACH'S PRODIGIOUS OUTPUT OF HIT SONGS would suggest that writing comes easily to him.

"Not so," says the handsome silver-haired composer whom critics have called the Cole Porter of his generation. "I battle over songs and work. It takes me a long time. I don't write easily now, and I didn't write easily at the beginning. I like to write and then look at it the next day, then a week later, and see if I come up with something better than I've already got. Often I'll wind up back where I was."

Bacharach's painstaking creative effort has yielded a remarkably varied group of pop smashes and standards. They range from the classically oriented "Only Love Can Break a Heart" for Gene Pitney, to the patriotic sing-along "What the World Needs Now Is Love." He and former collaborator Hal David lifted Dionne Warwick to superstardom with "Don't Make Me Over," "Anyone Who Had a Heart," and "Alfie." He has won three Academy Awards: one for the score of *Butch Cassidy and the Sundance Kid*, one for the song "Raindrops Keep Falling on My Head" from that score, and one for the title tune to *Arthur*. He conquered Broadway in 1968 with *Promises, Promises*, supplying imaginative music that enabled leading man Jerry Orbach to win a Tony as Best Actor in a Musical. "That's What Friends Are For" netted him a Song of the Year Grammy in 1987.

"I studied music with Henry Cowell, Bohuslav Martinů, and Darius Milhaud," says Bacharach, who was born in Kansas on May 12, 1928. "I thought at one time I wanted to be a so-called serious composer, writing

1

modern classical music. But pop was always a real influence, even before I had started studying in a serious vein. I thought I might want to take a shot at it."

Economic considerations led him away from a full-time classical focus.

"The fact is, if that's what I had really wanted to do, I would have done it. There's nothing worse than somebody sitting in a room or a bar, saying, 'Well, I could have written that great American symphony if I'd taken that direction.' My roots were jazz and pop, and you can really go broke being a classical composer. You teach at a college, function on grants. If I had wanted to do it, I'd have done it. I believe in fate, and this is what I was supposed to do. No regrets."

As he grew up, Bacharach attended the theatre and enjoyed it, but he didn't always envision himself as a Broadway composer.

"When I was getting successful with pop songs, and having hits, there wasn't something burning inside me that said, 'Boy, I want to write a Broadway show; I need to write a Broadway show.' I wasn't searching for it or looking for it. I was quite content being in the studio and making my records, writing the songs and thinking, 'Maybe I'd like to do a movie down the line'—things like that."

Bacharach's extensive classical knowledge helped him develop into a well-schooled, intelligent craftsman.

"Maurice Ravel affected me," Bacharach says. "I didn't actually like classical music too much at first. I didn't like Sunday afternoons in the car with my mother and father, driving back from Philadelphia or the shore, wherever we were coming from, and listening to the Philharmonic on the radio. It just felt sort of depressing. Then I heard Ravel's *Daphnis et Chloé* one day and, oh, that was a different kind of music. And the French impressionists, Eric Satie and Debussy, as well as the romantic Russian school represented by Rachmaninoff. Great melodies, great melodic content."

Jazz influences exerted equal fascination for Bacharach.

"There was this ray of light going from the big band era in music that was very attractive to me when I was growing up. Like Harry James, the Dorsey band. Suddenly, out of the blue, there was Dizzy Gillespie, Thelonious Monk, Bud Powell, Charlie Parker, Charlie Mingus."

All these influences had been absorbed and were building into a unique style when Burt met Hal David.

"I was making the rounds of the Brill Building—1619 Broadway—and Hal was very active at that time. He'd been writing with a couple of different people. So we started to write some songs. We didn't have immediate success. But then we had two hits together that happened at the same time: 'Magic Moments' by Perry Como and 'The Story of My Life' by Marty Robbins.

"We'd work together in a room with a window that didn't open and a kind of beat-up piano, an upright—smoking. You know, your real typical picture of how songwriters wrote, in a room at a music publishing office. We'd work together, he'd work by himself at home, I'd work by myself away from him, and we'd come in, having done some things separately. It seemed to be a good process to operate that way. I don't remember too many songs that we just sat down and, bang, wrote from top to bottom. He'd want to do some research by himself, and I'd want to do some of my own at home, working at night. I liked working by myself as well."

Together and separately, they came up with hit after hit: "Walk On By" for Dionne Warwick, "What the World Needs Now Is Love" for Jackie De Shannon, "Blue on Blue" for Bobby Vinton, "The Look of Love" for Dusty Springfield. They were firmly established as one of the top writing teams internationally when their Broadway show *Promises, Promises* opened on December 28, 1968.

"*Promises, Promises* was kind of put in my lap—or presented to me by David Merrick, who came to me because Neil Simon had this property, *The Apartment*, the Billy Wilder movie, and thought maybe Bob Fosse was going to direct it. It sounded very exciting, and I talked to Hal about it. It was certainly enticing to have a chance to work with Neil Simon. This property was a very attractive one. It turned out to be a marvelous success. I kind of went through the whole thing like I didn't know what I was doing, you know?"

Promises, Promises was a musical version of Billy Wilder's Oscar-winning 1960 film *The Apartment*. Librettist Neil Simon followed the original plot closely, in narrating the tale of a young executive who offers his apartment to superiors for their extra-marital trysts in exchange for raises and promotions. Eventually the executive gains moral fibre, rescues a young woman from her thoughtless married lover, and walks off with her into the sunset.

The show, which received excellent reviews and ran for 1,281 performances, was a fairy tale with a few dark modern twists. Bacharach was delighted with Neil Simon's libretto, and found working with Simon a stimulating experience.

"Neil is so incredible. He wrote this terrific book for *Promises*, and set up places where songs might appear. He even set up some dummy titles.

"The bulk of *Promises, Promises'* songs were written with lyrics done first. I mean, Hal and I had worked sometimes with the lyric first, sometimes with the tune, or part of the tune or part of a lyric first. But in *Promises, Promises*, to stay as literal and faithful to the tone of the Neil Simon script as possible, we tried to have all the songs evolve right out of the book. So Hal, I'd say, in general, wrote most of the lyrics first. Maybe it wasn't word for word, then set to notes, but enough of it was done that way that we had a pretty good lunge into a song.

"As things evolved, we did move songs," Bacharach notes. "Maybe took

Bacharach hopes to collaborate one day
on a show with his wife, Carole Bayer Sager.

Jerry Orbach *(top, in derby)* celebrates Christmas Eve at his favorite bar in this scene from *Promises, Promises.*

out a page of dialogue and moved a song up earlier, things like that. But it started out with a designation where Neil thought a song should come. Hal also felt some songs should maybe go in a different place. I guess it's everybody's thoughts and determination that decided where a song was put in.

"The rehearsal period," says Bacharach, "was *very* exciting, watching choreographer Michael Bennett working with the dancers, working with the singers. An interesting thing was that, once the show was cast, those songs we'd written before for an unknown cast didn't quite fit as well. We didn't know who was going to be the lead or the second lead, and once they became real people and we saw them on stage—saw what they looked and sounded like—some songs we'd written before didn't work. With Jill O'Hara, we started making changes. Her voice, the sound of it, kind of motivated me to go different musically from this cardboard figure in my imagination that I'd been writing for.

"So, once we saw the actual cast members, what they could sing, there had to be adjustments. I know we rewrote some songs. But those were exciting times."

Bacharach was pleased with the overall *Promises, Promises* score, but he doesn't have a single favorite song in the show.

"The simplest one," he says, "is 'I'll Never Fall in Love Again.' That was the fastest song we wrote. I got out of the hospital in Boston. I'd been there with pneumonia. I guess that's where Hal got the lines 'What do you do when you kiss a girl? You get enough germs to catch pneumonia. After you do, she'll never phone ya. I'll never fall in love again.' It's not a great feeling getting out of a hospital and going to work immediately to write a song that will go into the show that night. It was the simplest song, the most successful song. I like it. It seems to hold up well.

"I also like 'Knowing When to Leave,' though it's a mouthful to sing, as 'Promises, Promises' is a mouthful to sing. But I really didn't think it had pop considerations at that time. I was just thinking that what I wanted from the song was a certain urgency. If I had to do 'Promises' now, I'd make it a little easier. But that's the way the song felt at the time. It also had a certain anger to it, what Jerry Orbach's character was describing when he sang, 'Promises, promises, I'm all through with promises, promises now.' It was a mouthful, and it was spat out onstage, had a lot of different time changes, a restlessness. Hey, it was good. It was what it was supposed to be."

Promises, Promises turned out to be tuneful, witty, and, above all, entertaining. "I like musicals that entertain," says Bacharach, "that make people feel a sense of well-being upon leaving the theatre, having a good time. I think things that can happen on the stage are just wonderful—you know, the movement, dance combined with songs. I think it's hard to do a small musical. It's hard to do a two-character show. That would be, I think, a bitch to bring off; but whatever, the show should entertain, and it should *sing*.

"I guess it would be a bummer for me to have some real limitations of singing ability onstage. You know, somebody who's got like a five- or six-note range. But on the other hand, that could be a great challenge for me."

Another challenge to Bacharach is being faithful to the medium he's writing for.

"I don't think there's one song or one instance in *Promises, Promises* where I felt, 'Let's write it this way, because if we do we'll have a better chance for a hit record.' My fidelity and intent were toward the property, what would work onstage. Then, in turn, it would come and have a life of its own and be able to be sung and performed on records, television, away from the show. But you have to be faithful to your first premise, and the same goes for a film song.

"With film songs, I never take something out of the drawer. Never did that, never in my life took an old tune and had a lyricist hang some words on it so it became a title song. Never.

"With a pop song, you know, you just go for it all. If you can guess what the market is out there, then you try not to go against the grain of the market, but I never had much luck saying, 'If I write it this way, it will be more commercial than if I write it that way.' You just try to make it as good as possible. I do believe you have to stay in touch with what's happening around you. You can't isolate yourself and not listen to the radio. You gotta hear what's happening. You can't be living in a vacuum."

Bacharach and Hal tried to make the score of *Promises, Promises* "as good as possible" and succeeded.

"I like to think we had an innovative score, innovative at that time, with a pretty fresh sound coming from the pit. Phil Ramone, producer of Billy Joel, designed that pit, so we had some separation, isolation—not overlapping, blurring into each other. And girls down in the pit sang 'Digging for Coal.'

"We had some pretty good sounds coming out of there. We were trying to get a kind of split. I mean, I don't like to hear an orchestra in a pit playing, and you don't hear anything coming from the center of the theatre; you just hear it coming from the speakers on the side. That's a real unsatisfying feeling for me, you know. Sometimes, though, it can't be helped.

"What I like best of all is getting at least forty percent live coming from the center, which would be coming live from the pit, and the rest coming from speakers on the side."

Bacharach knows what he wants to hear, and show, pop, and film audiences worldwide have come to recognize his particular style.

"I can't define the Bacharach style. They used to call it the Bacharach sound in England, and I don't quite understand it. Maybe it's the orchestration. Maybe it's got something to do with certain sounds that I used, like the flügelhorn, or things like that, or certain rhythm patterns. I mean, a song like

'What's New Pussycat?' is far removed from 'Walk On By,' so I never quite got what they meant by the Bacharach style. But I'm flattered that they refer to it. It doesn't make me angry; it pleases me."

The Bacharach style clearly accounted for much of the success enjoyed by *Promises, Promises*, but Bacharach is quick to give credit to the other individuals who helped create it.

"Another element of the show was that it had a wonderful script by Neil. Michael Bennett did some wonderful stuff, moving people around. Bob Moore directed it great. There were terrific performances—Jerry Orbach and Jill O'Hara. It entertained. You had the audience rooting for the people onstage. Very important. You wanted them to wind up together. You wanted Chuck to get the girl. You have to get the audience rooting. They had a rooting interest here."

Promises, Promises had critics as well as audiences rooting. But there are disappointments in every composer's life, and when Bacharach experiences them, he compares the sensation to owning racehorses that don't win—an apt comparison, since he owns horses.

"You just have to remember, you don't win all the time. That's all. Nobody does. It's a very cyclical thing; goes in cycles. Say you write what you feel is a terrific song and somebody makes a terrible record of that song. Or you make a terrible record of that song yourself. Or the singer goes in and records it in another city with another producer and changes the melody. For the worse. Well, that's not great.

"So anyway, you write as well as you can. You go through periods where you're writing with a higher degree of energy and are more productive, and you go through shallow periods. But the main thing is to stay in touch with your music just about every day. If you can, go to the piano, even if you're not on a project, even if you're not recording an artist—with nothing at all, you have to write. No assignments. Play freely. Stay in touch. Have contact with your music. Just go to the piano even if you have to improvise."

Improvising at home is one thing. But sometimes substitute players will be called in during the run of a musical when regular musicians are unavailable. They may not know the music and play, unintentionally, as though they're improvising.

"It used to drive me crazy on *Promises*. There would be eight subs in the orchestra, including the drummer. My music is not that easy to play. I mean, I know that first Saturday matinee after *Promises* opened, I got called from Palm Springs. David Merrick called me and said, 'Eight subs in the orchestra, including the drummer,' and guess who was in the audience. Richard Rodgers! It made me feel just terrible, because our drummer was sight-reading. A song like 'Promises, Promises' changes time signature in almost every bar. And he's saying this great, great composer, Richard Rodgers, is coming to judge our show and judge my music—and of course I want him to like it. And I've got eight subs with a drummer who's never played it before. The drummer's very key, you know. When a trumpet's a sub, OK, the other two trumpets will help him.

"So the live nature of Broadway is kind of exciting, but in a nail-biting kind of way. The impermanence gets to you because everything shifts from night to night. I mean with a film, if you've got it right, it's embedded forever. It's there, you know. A great take is there. If you've got a great take on a record, it's there. Theatre lives. It's exciting. But it keeps shifting."

Trends should keep shifting too, in Bacharach's view. "As for current music video and film used in theatre—great. It should open up. The more inventive, the better; I'm all for it. With theatre, all kinds of things are possible; they just cost money. I mean, you could turn the whole theatre into part of the stage. Look what *Cats* is like. You've got to keep in touch. You want to touch the audience; you've got to get them involved too, you know. They're used to seeing things that are so incredible on MTV. I don't know that you can do a show where somebody just goes from dialogue and opens his mouth and starts to sing a song, like you could in the past. Credibility, you know. And as for rock—well, there's *Dreamgirls*. That was more like R&B than rock and roll. I can't see rock dominating the theatre, but it will certainly have a growing place, and it should have. Revivals and all—there'll always be a place for that too.

"As for where the theatre is heading, I just don't know. It can grow and become more interesting and more dazzling to the senses. You've got to be careful of the audio level in a theatre too. You have older people who go, and you can't beat them and assault their ears with overly loud sound."

Bacharach's sensitivity to his audience doesn't smother his creativity, his desire to hear unusual sounds in the theatre. "I do imagine that you could be sitting with four or five keyboard players in a Broadway pit, off to the side, probably in the pit, playing different synthesizers. Wonderful sounds. It's just unfortunate, you know, that a young man or woman goes to school, to Juilliard, and plays a great violin or reed instrument or a horn and is replaced because you can get a great French horn stop on a synthesizer and that French horn will sound like a French horn, if you want to make it that way. It will never make a mistake, unless you make a mistake with your fingers playing it. But the happiest solution would have to be real instruments combined with synthesizers in the pit. I mean, on a recording these days you just wonder if you should go into a studio with strings, synthesizers, whatever. There's nothing to replace violins, the way they sound, soaring up there and making a beautiful noise, you know? Sound is important. I mean, if I do another show, even if it's a period piece, if it's set in the fifties, the forties, whatever, I would definitely think in terms of having one or two keyboard players playing different synthesizers in the pit."

In describing his development as a composer, Bacharach
points to a wide variety of influences, from classical to jazz—
among them Ravel, Debussy, and Dizzy Gillespie.

Whatever types of sound are featured, Bacharach feels a score is hard to absorb fully at one sitting, yet that's what critics have to do when reviewing one.

"They've got too much to do on the first night," Burt claims. "They have to review the sets. They have to review the show, the actors, and the singing and clothing and a score they're hearing for the first time. It's a little unfair. I always felt it was a little unfair.

"I thought it would be great if the music came out a couple of months before, on a record or cassette, so they would have some familiarity with the work. Listen, I've written things I didn't like the first time—or the second or the third time—like a record I'll hear on the air. And I'm in the music business! I didn't like *Hair* the first time I heard the music, and I said so publicly. It was a bad mistake, to be quoted as saying I didn't like *Hair*. So if I can't discern it and separate it the first time, I don't think critics can. I don't think their ears are going to be necessarily better than mine. Being able to do justice in really evaluating a score the first time out of the bag—difficult."

The inability of those who make or break a score to hear it fully the first time around is one disadvantage in writing for the theatre. What others has Bacharach encountered?

"It takes a lot of time," he says. "You get a big shot. Maybe somebody wraps up his life for four or five years giving attention, devotion, energy to a show. Maybe someone wrote a great score and got rapped by a bad book. Maybe the book was OK, and the score was very good, and the director killed it. Maybe they waited for four or five years to get one star, and the star didn't come through. I mean, it's just tough. You're putting in a lot of your time, energy, creative flow. And then you go out, and you're at the mercy of theatre critics. It could be one, two critics, and if they don't like it, over and out. Four or five years down the drain. Tough. If you're making or producing a record or writing songs, you can write a couple a week, something like that. Your output could be greater; that's what I'm trying to say."

In spite of the built-in hardships, Bacharach is looking for another property to do.

"I want to do a show with Carole," he says, referring to his wife, lyricist Carole Bayer Sager. "Carole had a big hit with *They're Playing Our Song*—also with Neil Simon—and I had a big hit too. It just wouldn't be right not to give it another shot and write something together. We tried writing something with Neil Simon about a year ago, a property of Neil's that was a movie, *The Heartbreak Kid*. From our standpoint, the three of us, it just didn't work as a musical. We wrote about seven songs, and it was better to find out at that stage that it wasn't working. Terrific script. Terrific movie. The songs just seemed to kind of interrupt the flow of the book, the humor of it. It has to be the right property. So we haven't found anything quite right yet, but we will."

CHAPTER TWO

LEONARD BERNSTEIN

L EONARD BERNSTEIN, AS ALL LOVERS OF MUSIC KNOW, is a vibrant, theatrical personality. His passionate movements and brilliantly intense eyes single him out in any recording studio, on any stage, or at any podium.

This theatricality was relatively subdued when we interviewed him in his Central Park West co-op on a rainy afternoon. He wore slippers and a white pullover sweater, and his voice rarely rose above a whisper due to a nagging sore throat. Yet, surrounded by floor-to-ceiling bookcases and pianos in nearly every room, the maestro remained a commanding presence.

Bernstein's inherent magnetism is an accident of nature. But there's nothing accidental about his greatness as composer of light and serious scores, as pianist, teacher, and conductor. Since the age of ten, when he began piano lessons, through years of study under Fritz Reiner at the Curtis Institute of Music in Philadelphia, he has continued to refine his natural gifts. In 1943, he replaced Bruno Walter on short notice as guest conductor of the New York Philharmonic and drew raves, as well as a front-page *New York Times* story.

Bernstein's list of award nominations—an amazing total of fifty-four—is worthy of front-page attention too. This kind of peer recognition is due largely to his open-mindedness about new trends. He was an early champion of Lennon and McCartney, when "serious" musicians discounted the Beatles as a passing fad. And he felt special pride after receiving a 1985 Grammy Award for Life Achievement.

"I was terribly moved, yes," he says, "a few weeks ago on my way back from Brazil, when I stopped in Hollywood for this award—and all the rock and roll people knew my music and said they loved it. Cyndi Lauper and Lionel Richie, Tina Turner, Michael Jackson."

Admiration for contemporary rock stars is consistent with the personality of the man who wrote *West Side Story*, an innovative trend-setter itself. Although the *New York Times*, after noting the show's "wildness, ecstasy, and anguish" dubbed it "horrifying," *West Side Story* became a classic. We wondered what prompted Bernstein to choose such an unusual property.

"I choose whatever feels right, whatever seems heaven-sent, whatever has the right timing. It's not that I just sit around waiting for these ideas to appear. I lead such a complicated life that I can't just concentrate on that. And when something seems right, that's when I do it. In the case of *West Side*, it wasn't my idea at all; it was Jerome Robbins's idea. And the timing turned out to be wrong, because when we started a project about Romeo and Juliet in the slums, the East Side was what we had in mind—a story about kids fighting in the streets on the Lower East Side of New York. We took the story from Shakespeare to that setting. We—Jerry Robbins, Arthur Laurents, and I—all got excited. This was 1949."

Originally, the plot was to center on a Jewish girl and a Catholic boy. "Arthur wrote a couple of scenes," Bernstein says, "and we all began to see at a certain point that the show was dated. There was a faint odor of *Abie's Irish Rose*. So we gave it up. Five years later, the right time came."

During the interim Bernstein honored a commitment to create *Candide*. It opened December 1, 1956, and played for only 73 performances. A revival on March 10, 1974, with additional lyrics by Stephen Sondheim, was destined to do much better, achieving a run of 740 performances.

Candide musicalized Voltaire's tale of a young man searching for goodness and honesty. His journey exposes him, instead, to malice and greed, and he is cheated and beaten. In the end he returns to his home town, stripped of his illusions, and marries his childhood sweetheart.

The show was nominated in 1957 for a Tony as Best Musical, but it labored under the weight of Lillian Hellman's talkative book. The melodic "Glitter and Be Gay" was a standout, and "The Best of All Possible Worlds" vibrated with wit. Bernstein's eclecticism showed again in the variety of influences *Candide* displayed—ballads, waltzes, music-hall rousers, jazz.

When he rejoined Stephen Sondheim and Arthur Laurents to complete *West Side Story* in 1957, Bernstein composed a classic score even more distinguished than that of *Candide*.

The breakthrough happened at the unlikeliest place, given the subject matter of the show.

"I was at a Beverly Hills pool with Arthur Laurents. I think I was in California scoring *On the Waterfront*. And we were talking ruefully about what a shame it was that the original *West Side Story* didn't work out. Then, lying

COCONUT PECAN PIE

3 eggs, beaten
1 1/2 cups sugar
1/2 cup butter, melted
2 tsp. lemon juice
1 tsp. vanilla
1 can (3 1/2 oz) coconut
1/2 cup pecans
1 unbaked 9" pie shell

Preheat over to 350 degrees. Thoroughly combine eggs, sugar, butter, lemon juice and vanilla. Stir in coconut and pecans.

Pour into pie shell. Bake for 45-50 minutes. Cool, put whipped cream or cool whip on top. Decorate with additional nuts if desired.

next to us on somebody's abandoned chair was a newspaper with a big headline, 'GANG FIGHTS.' We stared at it and then at each other and realized that *this*—in New York—was it. The Puerto Rican thing had just begun to explode, and we called Jerry, and that's the way *West Side Story*—as opposed to *East Side Story*—was born."

Bernstein walked an artistic tightrope when composing the *West Side Story* score, particularly in ballads like "Maria" and "Tonight." "The important thing," he notes, "was keeping it from ever getting too poetic or too realistic." "Somewhere" was a delicate dance sequence, in which the two principals play-act a marriage in a bridal shop where Maria works. The store dummies served as witnesses, and Bernstein's music achieved a touching honesty while preserving the dreamlike mood. "Tonight" had a subtle rhythmic pulse that pumped tension into the sentimental surface of the melody.

The *West Side Story* score hit every key, from the harshly competitive "The Dance at the Gym," showing a choreographed rivalry between gang members of the Sharks and the Jets, to the romantic ballad, "Tonight," sung by leads Larry Kert and Carol Lawrence on a fire escape.

The musical also featured unusual comedic numbers, such as "Gee, Officer Krupke." When asked why that number has so few chords, Bernstein explains, "The song was based on vaudeville, on burlesque shows. The chords are very subtle, but they don't change much. They don't impede the rhythm." Bernstein also kept the music simple so that audiences could hear the satirical words of Stephen Sondheim. Bernstein did what all fine composers should remember to do—made his music unobtrusive to serve his lyricist.

Despite this beneficial meshing of talents, the *West Side Story* score underwent its share of revisions. Originally, the production opened with a number called "Mix."

"That was a very exciting song, but you couldn't understand anything the players were saying because it was too fast, too complicated, too canonical, too contrapuntal. So we wrote another one, called 'The Jet Song.'

"But the opening of *West Side* was always the prologue. The prologue, which you may not know, was originally sung material, rather than strictly danced. But it couldn't be understood either, so we made it all instrumental."

Bernstein's hectic, feverish rhythms caught the restless, antagonistic spirit of slum youth. We asked how he managed to convey so successfully a world he was not part of.

"We did *some* research for *West Side*," Bernstein says. "We went to a gym in Brooklyn where there were different gangs that a social organization was trying to bring together. I don't know if too much eventually got into *West Side*, but everything does help. However, I generally do research *inside*. I look for the tone, the notes, the flow."

West Side Story was not the first show to prove the efficacy of his approach.

The cast of *Candide* rehearses. The musical, based on Voltaire's classic satire, was nominated for a Tony as Best Musical in 1957.

Carol Lawrence and the cast of *West Side Story* record a song for the musical's original-cast album.

"The Dance at the Gym," from *West Side Story*. In composing the score to this 1957 smash hit, Bernstein walked an artistic tightrope. "The important thing," he notes, "was keeping it from getting too poetic or too realistic."

Bernstein's career in popular theatre was launched at age 26, when he teamed with old friends Adolph Green, a former Greenwich Village roommate, and Betty Comden, to write the 1944 show *On the Town*. Comden and Green were part of a nightclub act called the Revuers, which also featured Judy Holliday. Bernstein, Comden, and Green had a common respect for one another, and as Comden puts it, "When Leonard works on something, he works very much from a base of trying to get an entire concept or one clue that's going to make the whole score fall into place for him. He thinks in terms of the whole show; there's a kind of texture to his music that's unmistakably his."

The music for *On the Town* was unmistakably his, but as Bernstein points out, "There's a popular misconception that, musically, *On the Town* was based on my ballet *Fancy Free*. There isn't a *note* of *Fancy Free* in *On the Town*. It was just the idea of the ballet that struck people as a great idea for a show—three sailors with twenty-four hours' leave. So we decided to do a show with Jerry Robbins under the guidance of George Abbott, bless him. It was the first time out for Adolph, Jerry, Betty, and me. We were all in our mid-twenties. So, thanks to the great Mr. Abbott, we made it. We were absolutely just off the boat. But we were excited, and we had something to say."

What they said in *On the Town* was simple and appealing: love will find a way. Three sailors on a one-day leave meet their dream girls and have to solve all romantic complications before reporting back to their ship. One falls for an elusive girl he first sees in a subway poster, Miss Turnstiles; another is captivated by an anthropology student; and the third is pursued by an amorous and determined female taxi driver.

With memorable songs such as "New York, New York, A Helluva Town" and "I Get Carried Away," Bernstein became the toast of Manhattan, living up to Stephen Sondheim's later evaluation of him: "It's astonishing, his facility, his invention."

The next Bernstein collaboration with Comden and Green occurred almost nine years later, in 1953, in the sparkling form of *Wonderful Town*. The score was written under extreme pressure, because Leroy Anderson and Arnold Horwitt had been hired first. When they departed, Bernstein stepped in at Comden and Green's request. He was delighted to write another theatre piece, admitting later, "This town still gets me—no wonder I keep writing about it. It's so dramatic and alive."

Wonderful Town told an amusing tale of two sisters, played by Rosalind Russell and Edie Adams, who experience culture shock when they leave Columbus, Ohio, for Manhattan's Greenwich Village. Bernstein turned out a score that included a wistful mock-ballad, "Ohio," and a comedy number called "Conga!" that featured a group of Brazilian soldiers dancing. The lively opening dance was characterized by Brooks Atkinson of the *New York Times* as "organized bedlam." Bernstein hit a peak with "Conversation Piece," centering on five people making awkward self-conscious conversation.

Over the years Bernstein has collaborated with a number of different Broadway personalities. Here he is shown *(from left)* with Nancy Walker, Adolph Green, and Betty Comden.

"The background is pure theatre music," Bernstein said at the time. "Not with an eye to 'Tin Pan Alley' and not to create a memorable tune, but something that is an integral part of the story.

"I treasure that experience," he says with a nostalgic smile. "I love collaboration. I'm used to collaborating very closely and strongly."

We mentioned his later collaboration with Stephen Schwartz on *Mass*.

"Well, Steve got into it rather late. I had been working alone on the project for some years, and it was more or less there, but there were millions and millions of words still to be written. Steve Schwartz was a serendipity. He came in at just the right moment, when I was almost abandoning *Mass*. I couldn't finish it by myself; it was too big. So he was a refreshing newcomer in my life."

Mass opened at the John F. Kennedy Center for the Performing Arts on September 8, 1971. It was danced powerfully by the Alvin Ailey Company and featured a marching brass band and a boy's choir. Bernstein's rock-flavored score made various statements about life, peace, and God, touching on then-burning issues such as ecology and draft evasion. The overall work was underrated, though again it showed Bernstein's willingness to test himself, to push in new directions.

Another collaboration, *1600 Pennsylvania Avenue* with Alan Jay Lerner, proved disappointing.

"The show didn't materialize as we both conceived it. For one reason or another, a lot of them commercial reasons, the show emerged a mere shadow of what it was originally intended to be. I didn't want to open it in New York at all, but I was not successful in closing it out of town."

1600 Pennsylvania Avenue attempted to be a history of every president and every first lady in the White House. Ken Howard played all the presidents and Patricia Routledge represented every first lady. The score had some colorful numbers: "Forty Acres and a Mule," "The Red White and Blues," and "President Jefferson Sunday Luncheon Party March." Critic Martin Gottfried praised the music as "ambitious" and *New York Times* critic Clive Barnes admitted "there is quite a lot of good, strong Bernstein music," but he also criticized its runthrough of American history as bleak and patronizing. Barnes quoted one of Dolly Madison's lines as an example of the show's witlessness: "I must go and feed my parrot; his language is becoming scandalous."

Bernstein regards the whole experience as "humiliating, embarrassing. The show ran for four days."

Still, Bernstein's track record is remarkable—four hits out of five. He has written only five full-length shows (six, if 1950's *Peter Pan*, not really a full-size musical, is included) in thirty-two years. In between, he has contributed serious works: *Age of Anxiety* (Symphony No. 2, 1949), *Kaddish* (Symphony No. 3, 1963), *The Mass* (1971), and *Halil* (1981).

Such breadth and depth of experience has given Bernstein a unique perspective on trends in musical theatre. Indeed, he has been credited with creating some of those trends through his willingness to try something new. Considering the rock basis of such shows as Steve Schwartz's *Godspell*, and the many other rock-oriented Broadway shows that have followed, does Bernstein feel that rock and roll is taking over more and more of the theatre?

"If you'll explain what rock and roll music is, I can answer your question." Bernstein's eyes flash indignantly. "Rock and roll is various styles of Afro, Cuban, Latin music, blues, which have been electronified, technologically turned into something called *rock*. It's *not* something else. It's simply highly dependent on its electronic abilities, out of which all the advances come. Take away the microphones, the electric guitars, and the synthesizers, and you have the same pop music you've always had."

He warms to the topic. "It's just that, in order to sell records, people make up words. Words like *funk* and *hard* and *easy rock*, *acid rock* and *R&B*, *new wave*, *old new wave*—and it's all *hype!* When I read rock critics, I can't believe what I'm reading: 'This album is more *rock* than the last.' What it gets down to in the end is, it sounds more white or more black."

Bernstein shakes his head sadly. "The technological emphasis has gone way out of proportion. It breaks my heart. But it has the hype."

If rock is not the trend of the future, where does the composer think the theatre is headed?

"If we survive as a decent, cultured people, we'll go in the direction of decency and culture. And if we survive as the maniacally commercial people we are now, then the American theatre will survive and grow in the direction of only commercial stuff."

He raises his hand to make a point. "I don't include myself, or else I wouldn't be writing operas. And believe me, I'm *not* against commercial success. The theatre has always had that aspect, whether Shakespeare or Bizet or Wagner, or Rodgers and Hart or Offenbach or Verdi. Music is always about being successful. Verdi and Puccini cared just as much about commercial success as Rodgers and Hammerstein and Jerry Robbins and I. But it's a question of intention. When you write the work in the first place, and you write it only to make money, chances are that's what will come out— a work written to make money, rather than a work written because one had a vision or a concept or something that had to be said."

Obviously troubled, Bernstein continues: "What has happened, I think, in the past decade or more, is a real retrogression in the American musical theatre toward infinitely more commercial work. One of the great exceptions is Steve Sondheim. He bucks the current admirably. But there aren't many others who do. Most of the stuff you see around on Broadway is lamentable—one commercial nonsense after another."

Bernstein's own solution is to concentrate on opera. He is presently writing with Stephen Wadsworth. Bernstein met Wadsworth through his daughter, Jamie Bernstein. A gifted librettist and director of operas, Wadsworth suggested to Bernstein that they collaborate on a sequel to *Trouble in Tahiti*. The Maestro answered facetiously, "Have it on my desk—have an outline on my desk tomorrow morning." A day later, Bernstein had his outline.

"I wrote my last opera with Stephen, *Quiet Place*. We collaborated day and night, and it's an extraordinary collaboration. I have a feeling he wrote every note with me and I wrote every note with him. That's ideally the way collaboration should work. We've begun our new one, and we're doing it differently this time, spending many hours together addressing the format, the scenario."

Bernstein's manner softens. One can feel his emotional dedication, an involvement so different from the write-it-for-money mind-set he deplores. "The work is a sequel to *Trouble in Tahiti*, what happens to the people in *Trouble in Tahiti* thirty years later. *Trouble in Tahiti* is a very short work, a forty-minute one-act play; and we incorporated it into this much larger three-act opera in the form of two flashbacks. So, in a sense, the new opera looks back at the old one. We as audience see them both in perspective, thirty years apart "

Over the years, theatregoers have been treated to more and more dance-oriented productions. What does Bernstein think of the recent rise of choreographer/directors?

"It's not a vogue. I think it's a historical necessity that arose out of the very nature of our musical theatre—and the existence of somebody called Jerome Robbins. Also, our musical theatre has become highly choreographic, and it needed somebody of his vision and energy to combine the functions."

Bernstein sighs. "I miss working with Jerry. I haven't worked with him for a long time, but when we did, we worked very closely."

Regardless of whom he collaborates with, Bernstein the composer faces an unusual problem when writing music: the conflict between composing and conducting. "When I conduct," he says, "I am, for instance, Brahms. That's the ideal way to conduct anyone's music—*become* that person. When I begin my composing period, it takes at least two, if not three, weeks to get everyone else's notes out of my head—Stravinsky's, Brahms's, Mozart's."

Yet an examination of the *West Side Story* music, or any of Bernstein's other scores, proves conclusively that the style, the personality, the energy are distinctly his own. "I don't have a stamp of any sort," he says. "The works come out differently. *Wonderful Town* is completely different from *On the Town*, or *Mass*, or *Candide*."

Bernstein's reviews over the years have also varied widely. Does he feel he has been treated fairly by the critics?

"Some. It depends on what you mean by fair—fair by their own lights, perhaps."

Yet one senses disappointment. The victory of *The Music Man* over *West Side Story* at the 1958 Tony Award ceremony was, in the opinion of many, a ludicrous injustice. *The Music Man* is traditional, and Bernstein has always resisted formula. He takes risks that often frighten people at first, but it also means theatregoers can look forward to delightful innovation in the Maestro's future works.

He's not only innovative; he's deeply, intensely passionate. "In the performance of music I can do things that would land me in jail if I did them on an ordinary street corner," says Bernstein. "I can fume and rage and storm at one hundred men in an orchestra and make them play this or that chord."

Designer Gail Jacobs, a friend of Bernstein's, sums up the passion Bernstein feels, the passion that he transmits to audiences. "With Leonard Bernstein," Jacobs says, "everything emanates from the heart."

CHAPTER THREE

JERRY BOCK

THERE ARE, AS THE CLICHE GOES, TWO KINDS OF WRITERS—those that love to write and those that love to have *written*. Jerry Bock, composer of *Fiddler on the Roof, Fiorello!*, and *She Loves Me*, belongs to the former group.

"The act of *doing* has always been more important to me than the results," says Bock. "I've always found the results anticlimactic, even if they were very successful. I've always had a letdown, and of course I know why. It was because it was over. I didn't care if it was over with flying banners or whether it was over the next morning. It was *over*. And depression in one form or another would ultimately reign, no matter what people thought of the show. So I could never judge anything by triumph or failure, since my rewards came from the *process* of working."

The love of work—without one eye always trained on the result—accounts for Bock's musical skill and warmth. He has humor too—a quick, affectionate wit, coupled with boyish curly hair and a teddy bear grin. A devoted family man with two children, he's exactly the composer you'd visualize writing about the close-knit family depicted in *Fiddler on the Roof*.

The road leading to the creation of this undisputed classic began in New Haven, Connecticut, on November 3, 1928.

"I came from an instinctive musical household rather than a scholarly one," says Bock. "My parents loved music. My mother played by ear, as they say, and she loved the theatre as well. In terms of formal studies, I was the first person in the immediate family to go after that with piano lessons."

Bock's love of music was evident throughout his adolescent years. "I stayed with it by having friends who shared the love of big band and swing, and I played at high school functions. I did jazz and the popular music of the day.

"As for early influences, this was the early forties—it was big band music along with classical. My music was sustained beyond formal piano lessons. I loved it in every way, but my career was evolutionary. I went to the University of Wisconsin to become a journalist. But a funny thing happened on the way to journalism. I heard some sounds from the music school, literally as I was walking up the hill to register, I interrupted myself and went into the school to make basic inquiries about how to become a music student. Evidently, I was unsure at that moment—and that moment became a turning point, because I decided to audition at the music school. They hesitated, and then I began, brazenly, to play something strange for them. I did army bugle calls in the styles of various composers, such as Rachmaninoff, Tchaikovsky, Bach, Beethoven—a reveille such as they might have composed. I couldn't sight-read well, and I had no repertoire. These were rather dusty old professorial music instructors from the old school. Obviously they were disarmed for a moment because they said, 'Well, if you promise to start all over again in terms of formal studies, we'll admit you.' That really began a serious consideration of committing myself to a career in music. I accepted the idea of being more properly trained. Journalism was abandoned for good."

Bock left the University of Wisconsin in 1948, before graduating, with lyricist Larry Holofcener, who had been a fellow student.

"We'd been writing various things, and we amassed four or five songs and brought them to New York on the promise that we'd be able to meet producer Max Liebman. Max was then doing 'Your Show of Shows' with Sid Caesar. He liked our songs, and we were practically hired on the spot to write special material. I got to know Mel Brooks, Danny and Neil Simon, the whole gang. 'Your Show of Shows' eventually became 'Sid Caesar Tonight,' the 'Sid Caesar Show,' the Sid Caesar whatever. We went, I think, from about 1949 or 1950 to about '53. That was during the regular season."

Off season, Bock and Holofcener spent their time at Tamiment, a summer camp for adults in Pennsylvania's Pocono Mountains.

"We had a full resident company to write original material for their auditorium, which was usually a Wednesday night entertainment by the performers who did their own stuff, then a Saturday and Sunday show. The show was the equivalent of a one-act revue, songs and sketches. We worked that for three summers. The training was irreplaceable, enormously valuable. Our alumni were Dick Shawn, Jack Cassidy, writers Neil and Danny Simon—Woody Allen was before us. Marshall Barer, Mary Rodgers—so many talents."

Bock and Holofcener signed with a major music publisher, Tommy Valando, in 1954, and "began to dream about the musical theatre. What did it was BMI, Broadcast Music, Inc., the society that, in addition to ASCAP, logs performances for writers. BMI had a contest for the best original college musical, and they covered schools throughout the country. We decided to take them on and wrote a show called *Half as Big as Life*, the story of Paul Bunyan. I had been writing at that point in time with a fellow named Jack Royce, who became a psychiatrist. Dave Pollock wrote the book, I did the score, and we toured the state of Wisconsin and other places. The big highlight was one night in Chicago at the Blackstone Theatre. We came back and eventually received notice that we'd won the BMI competition, and they published five of our songs.

"So," Bock claims, "I was hooked."

He was hooked enough to sign with Tommy Valando "for a very modest stipend. We signed exclusively. Our first moment—Larry's and mine—was *Catch a Star*. The show was a two-week smash."

Fortunately, songwriter Jule Styne, who was producing *Mr. Wonderful*, turned up on the opening night of *Catch a Star*. He liked one of Bock's songs, "Fly, Little Heart."

"Some columnist mentioned Styne's reaction, and that was the greatest moment of our lives—not that we had had many great moments before that. Jule decided to try new writers, rather than established ones, for *Mr. Wonderful*, so Larry and I got to do it with George Weiss."

Mr. Wonderful, which opened March 22, 1956, told the story of a small-time performer (Sammy Davis, Jr.) who is encouraged by his fiancée and friend to try out his act in Miami Beach. He does, with great success, and the show's second half was a repeat of the act Davis did in real life with his father and uncle. *Mr. Wonderful* ran for 383 performances, and featured the hit song "Too Close for Comfort."

"*Mr. Wonderful* wasn't an overwhelming assignment, because in a sense Sammy Davis, Jr., did his act in the second half. We did the book songs."

Again, someone in the audience—this time Hal Prince with Robert Griffith—saw Bock's *Mr. Wonderful* work and liked it. Prince and Griffith asked Bock and his new partner Sheldon Harnick to write the score for an upcoming show, *The Body Beautiful*.

How did he meet Harnick?

"To the best of my memory, Jack Cassidy introduced us. He was in the show *Shangri-La*, which came into town in June 1956, and he and I knew each other from Tamiment. He knew Larry Holofcener and I weren't writing anymore, so he did some matchmaking, and Sheldon and I hit it off."

The Body Beautiful, which opened in 1958, turned out to be, in Bock's words, "a sixty-day smash," though George Abbott, like Prince, Griffith, and Styne before him, singled out the Bock music for praise.

The Body Beautiful was a musical comedy about prizefighters. We wondered what research Bock did for such a subject.

"The book writer, Joe Stein, who later did *Fiddler on the Roof*, was a sociologist, and it wasn't a boxing story as much as a story of a guy who wanted to do something better than boxing. It had social overtones. It was a human story. We didn't get into the book that much. In terms of maturing as writers, it wasn't until *She Loves Me* that Sheldon and I got into the book more and more. Up till then we departmentalized: you do the songs, you do the book; occasionally you get together, try out both, and the director will take over. That was our assumption at the start. *Mr. Wonderful* was, in a sense, my first book show, but I treated it, I think, like a revue—songs, scene, songs, scene, not working close together. Same with *The Body Beautiful. Fiorello!* was actually the beginning of my curiosity as to what the other guy—the author—was doing."

Fiorello!, the musicalized life story of New York Mayor Fiorello La Guardia, had a libretto by Jerome Weidman, author of the best-selling *I Can Get It for You Wholesale*.

"We did a lot of talking with Jerry Weidman, much more than we had with the authors on our previous shows. Since *Fiorello!* wasn't a preestablished form in terms of having been a book or film or whatever, we literally had to do our own research. We shared history, we shared anecdotes, we went to New York City, heard Fiorello's speeches and talks on some original tapes, and saw a lot of newsreel coverage. We delved into it historically."

Bock's musical approach was to write "approximately two-and-a-half hours' worth of music and commentary—composing musical moments that I heard characters possibly singing, with no words or even title. I put in my two cents along the way, bringing Sheldon's attention to the fact that I thought this might be good for so and so."

Summing up their working style, Bock says, "Overall, I'd figure that in half our stuff music came first and half our stuff lyrics came first."

Backers' auditions came next, since "nothing was ever financed when we became involved. We would do backers' auditions for twenty-five, thirty-five, or forty people. We'd see how many friends and relatives could get into the living room to start with, and when we didn't receive our funding completely, we'd go out of town."

When asked which show was the most difficult to raise money for, Bock says, "I wouldn't even begin to guess at it. That was a province we were not at all interested in. It was the producer's problem. We were delighted to play our score for as many people as would listen. In terms of how long it took to raise the money, though, my impression is that Hal Prince and Bobby Griffith had a loyal coterie of backers that would invest in their shows. They could count on X amount of money. *Fiddler* was probably as difficult as any show to raise money for, since the time frame of it had to be close to four years before we got it off—from the time we began until the time it went into rehearsal."

Prerehearsal, the different production talents—set designer, costume designer, lighting man—have to be chosen. Did he have much say in these selections?

"Less than the director. The beautiful part of the musical theatre is, however—and this is unique among all other arts—its collaborative nature. It doesn't function well if it's not collaborative. So everybody assumes input is going to come from everybody else."

Fiorello! was a huge success. It brought Bock a Tony for Best Score and also won Tonys for 1959's Best Musical, best book (Jerome Weidman and George Abbott), best producer (Griffith and Prince), and best supporting actor (Tom Bosley). It also collected a Pulitzer Prize for Bock, Harnick, Weidman, and Abbott.

Tenderloin, the tale of a do-gooder minister trying to clean up New York's notorious Tenderloin District, followed *Fiorello!* a year later, opening October 17, 1960.

"We picked *Tenderloin* in the flush of *Fiorello!* We had all enjoyed working together so much that we said, 'Kids, let's do another musical.' We started talking about that project while we were ending up *Fiorello!* We were hopeful, but the show didn't really work. There are varying opinions as to why. What happened was simply that our main character was less interesting than our subsidiary character. The minister that Maurice Evans played was less attractive than the kid who clashed with him, the role Ron Husmann played."

She Loves Me, which opened in April 1963, was artistically stronger and critically applauded. It was a touching musical version of the 1940 Ernst Lubitsch film *The Shop Around the Corner*. The conflicts of two music store clerks who fall in love through letters while maintaining a real-life animosity gave Bock and Harnick many opportunities to write fine music. Some of the memorable songs include "She Loves Me," "Dear Friend," and "Will He Like Me?"

It wasn't, despite superiority in every area and a fierce cult following, the box office smash it should have been. We asked Bock what the problem was.

"There was no problem with the show. I mean, it was everybody else's problem. Sometimes you do the best you can, and you think you've done well—you *know* you've done well—and other people don't agree with you. So be it."

The construction of *She Loves Me*—the integration of story and songs—is admirable. Writer Stanley Green said, "It will stand as a model in its use of songs as an indispensable adjunct to the plot." But Bock achieves this unity of song and plot spontaneously, relying on instinct rather than a set approach.

"Some people work in order," says Bock. "Sheldon and I are skippers. The

Shown here relaxing in Puerto Rico after the success of *Fiorello!* are Patti Bock, Jerry Bock, Hal Prince, and George Abbott.

Jack Cassidy and Peg Murray rehearse a song for the musical *She Loves Me*.

opening number, naturally, is very important, extraordinarily important. The opening is the key that opens the door to the show, so you have to be wise and tell your audience what's going to happen, tell them, in Jerry Robbins's words, 'what the evening is about.' "

There were occasions, says Bock, when the audience responded to something, but he and Sheldon didn't feel it worked. When that happened, they changed it.

"Our general pattern was to play it first for our author, because we knew he would be sympathetic. Then we played it for our director and/or producer, because they tended to be more objective, which is very good. You have to trust these people. Hal Prince, for example, is a very creative producer. Even when he couldn't articulate something that bothered him, we went back to our room and analyzed it, asking, 'Why didn't our message get through?' "

The best example of collaboration on a musical number came with the opening of *Fiddler on the Roof*—"Tradition."

"That's a case in point of working ass backwards. 'Tradition' accumulated, a bit here, a bit there. We must have written twenty versions of it, and we worked with Jerome Robbins. As I look back, it was exciting. During it, it was painful. We didn't know how the hell to open the show, really, so we tried things. Some things worked; some didn't. We'd have to draw it out. That opening was perhaps the best example of collaboration on a number in a musical."

"Tradition" wasn't the original opening.

"We began with something we were *sure* was going to be the opening, because we got such great applause and our backers loved it. 'Sabbath Tonight,' like 'Comedy Tonight.' It was terrible. Robbins kept asking that question over and over: 'What is the show about?' It took us a long time to define that and get close to it. Once we did, whatever we did had to contribute to the main theme. Our first attempts at an opening number plunged right into the story too quickly, without orienting the audience. Many people didn't know what the hell was going on, and we had to give them a sense of the spirit, the tone, the feel, the look, the movement—everything. Jerry Robbins's persistent, relentless question provided us with an enormous amount of rewriting."

Looking back, Bock feels that *Fiddler* was more comfortable to write than any of his other shows. "I could still be writing it today," he admits. "I'm not sure of the reason, but I think it has everything to do with my background. I'm a Russian-Hungarian-German Jew, mostly Russian."

Was it a show he had dreamed of writing?

"No. It was like it was inside of me and somebody opened it up. I didn't know it was there, and I couldn't stop writing once I had started. I didn't have to do any musical research, but we all had to do a lot of historical research."

How did Bock feel about the translation of *Fiddler* to the screen?

"I understood that *Fiddler* was a theatre piece and girded myself not to expect a duplication, thank God. And I thought the screen version was excellent." He laughs. "The roughest part of it was getting an invitation to the opening. Once they bought the project, they started from scratch—everything that started from that day is an original film. They had their own family and their own collaboration, so it didn't occur to the film's producers to invite the people connected with the theatre production.

"Norman Jewison, who directed the movie *Fiddler*, was fine. In fact, Joe Stein went to Zagreb, where they did location shooting. Joe did the screenplay as well as the show, so he was more involved. We wrote one song for the picture on assignment, but they didn't use it. They shot it and recorded it and then decided not to put it in."

After *Fiddler*, Bock and Harnick worked on *The Apple Tree*, with Mike Nichols directing. Jerome Robbins originally had been set as director, but prework took so long that he departed to honor other commitments. *The Apple Tree* was a musicalization of three short stories—Mark Twain's "The Diary of Adam and Eve," Frank Stockton's "The Lady or the Tiger?" and Jules Feiffer's Cinderella story, "Passionella."

"Writers will sometimes take a wonderful tale, and because they believe they're bound to fill a certain amount of time, like two hours, they take that story and stretch it as much as possible. We thought we'd like to try to do the stories in the amount of time they should take, and if it was forty minutes for one, twenty for another, a half hour for another, so be it. We'd still fill the evening but give each story its rightful due. And it was tremendously exciting. It was among our favorite writing quests."

Director Mike Nichols, whom Bock greatly admired, helped make the 1966 *The Apple Tree* one of the composer's favorites.

"He's a delight. He's perhaps more subtle in terms of criticism than either George Abbott or Hal Prince. I believe Nichols works harder with actors than writers. It's funny; we were more in awe of Mike than of any other person we'd worked with previously."

The next Bock-Harnick creation was *The Rothschilds*, the 1970 show that brought the team Tony nominations for Best Score. Hal Linden won a Best Actor Tony for his role. In spite of that, dissenters accused Bock and Harnick of trying to do another *Fiddler*, simply because the production dealt with a Jewish family—in this case, bankers.

"I think it was a problem," Bock says. "It certainly didn't help. Musically, I went to a whole other direction in terms of what I heard. I listened to a lot of classical music for that show, a lot of eighteenth- and nineteenth-century sounds. I heard more Mozart than I'd ever heard before. I had the sense that it should sound like an eighteenth-century piece."

Why did they choose *The Rothschilds*, considering the problem of comparisons with *Fiddler*?

The dancing chorus of daughters in *Fiddler on the Roof*.

 Zero Mostel sings in *Fiddler on the Roof*. Bock feels that *Fiddler* was more comfortable to write than any of his other shows. "I could still be writing it today," he says.

Sheldon Harnick, Barbara Harris, and Jerry Bock gather to record the original cast album for *The Apple Tree*.

Hal Linden won the Tony for Best Actor of 1970 for his performance in *The Rothschilds*. Pictured with him is actress Leila Martin.

"We were partly badgered into it by producer Hilly Elkins. I mean, he broached it to us two years before we eventually got into it. He showed us a number of versions by English book writers. As a last shot, he handed us a script before Sheldon and I flew to California, and Sherman Yellen had done a treatment. We loved it, and all our hesitation suddenly vanished. Maybe that's the best answer of all. It's important to know what it means when you say yes. You don't call the next day or the next week or the next month and say, 'Oops, no' because, once you've committed yourself, you may have committed yourself for a long time."

Has he written other shows since *The Rothschilds?*

"Yes. I've written two, and other projects, nontheatrical projects. A few years after *The Rothschilds*, I worked with Evan Hunter and Stuart Ostrow on a show called *Caper*, which was intended to be—and which everyone wants to try once in his life—a murder mystery musical. And Evan, being a very deft writer of that genre—he wrote *The Blackboard Jungle*—seemed like a wonderful choice. I confess, also, to the enjoyment of trying words and music for the first time. Only my dear friend Ostrow would give me that chance, and it was a tremendous personal experience as a writer for me. It was abandoned, unfortunately, because Evan and Stuart didn't see eye to eye on what the material should be."

And after *Caper?*

"After *Caper* I started another one with Stuart, which was total insanity, called *Stages*. It should have been a straight piece. It was about the four stages of dying, beginning with denial."

Despite these more recent tribulations, Bock says *The Body Beautiful* was a greater disappointment.

"It was our first effort. The first time a show fails is the most painful. It probably ran two months. We were in front of the theatre every day, praying, urging people in, giving out hot coffee, doing *anything* to keep this baby open. It's your first job. So that, in terms of an emotional response, if nothing else, was our greatest disappointment."

Bock refuses to dwell on failures, though.

"I don't think in those terms. I never philosophize about this. The closest I can get to thinking of triumphs versus disasters is to remember some of my most rewarding moments outside of writing. They come when I'm able to talk to writers who are looking to write for the theatre. They call me and want to rap, and occasionally I think I've been helpful to them during the conversation. I like to feel I pass the tradition on."

CHAPTER FOUR

SAMMY CAHN

P EOPLE ASK ME WHAT IT'S LIKE TO DO A BROADWAY SHOW," says Sammy Cahn. "I'll tell you. It's the closest a man comes to understanding childbirth—literally. Only you have labor pains twice: once out of town and once in New York."

Labor is hardly the word to describe Sammy Cahn's attitude toward his work. Some writers, such as Adolph Green, refer to writing as agony, and others, like John Kander and Fred Ebb, view it as sheer fun. Cahn belongs with the Kander and Ebb group. He radiates gleeful enthusiasm, as though creating a new lyric is as carefree and joyous as attending a party.

This going-to-the-party optimism has resulted in four major shows (*High Button Shoes, Skyscraper, Walking Happy, Look to the Lilies*); his own one-man Broadway smash, *Words and Music*; plus four Academy Awards for Best Song: "All the Way," from *The Joker Is Wild*; "High Hopes," from *A Hole in the Head*; "Three Coins in the Fountain," from the film of the same name; and "Call Me Irresponsible" from *Papa's Delicate Condition*. Cahn has also written lyrics for countless hit songs, such as "I Should Care," "Day by Day," "It's Magic," "My Kind of Town," and "The Tender Trap."

His awards seem to fight for room in Cahn's comfortable office in his Beverly Hills home. Sheet music lines the walls, along with scrolls and nomination plaques. Yet Cahn himself acts completely unpretentious, speaks softly, and toys with the rhyming dictionary on his desk while answering questions.

The Sammy Cahn saga began June 18, 1913, in New York. He attended Seward Park High School in Manhattan and studied violin. Awareness of lyrics came gradually.

"It evolved from a series of small incidents," he says. "I played violin, and on sheet music in those days the violin part had lyrics on it. So I became aware of them. Mostly the lyrics were rather banal. 'Mary Lou, Mary Lou, Cross my heart, I love you'—that kind of stuff. 'I could do that,' I thought. And I did."

In those early years and throughout his career, Cahn was quick to spot a catchy lyric.

"I found the work of Mack Gordon very attractive to my ear. He wrote 'Time on My Hands' and 'You'll Never Know.' One line of his, in particular, I remember vividly:

> I've got a lot of plans for
> A place that you won't need pots and pans for

"That's enough for me," Cahn says. "I've always said that a lyric writer earns his stripes, establishes his credentials, with one line. Take Rodgers and Hart's 'My Romance':

> My romance doesn't need a castle
> Rising in Spain
> Or a dance to a constantly surprising refrain

"That's enough: those pictures and the unexpected word."

Cahn smiles. "I tend to oversimplify, but you know what I mean.

"At one point in my life, when I was feeling very low, I wrote a song with Saul Chaplin, and I came up with one of those special lines. The song was called 'You're a Lucky Guy,' and the line went:

> You're a lucky guy
> When you consider the highest bidder
> Can't buy the gleam in your eye

"That turn of phrase had what I mean—the freshness, the originality."

Cahn looks back with pride on the occasions when he has come up with inventive lines. "I always seek out the touches of what I call 'a turn of phrase.' And your mind gets sharpened to those turns of phrase by listening to lyrics. When people ask me, 'Do you know all your lyrics?' I answer, 'All of mine and everyone else's.' I have an incredibly retentive memory for lyrics."

It was inevitable, given his delight in bending words, that Cahn would turn to the theatre, a medium that prizes clever wordplay. His first venture, with

Phil Silvers *(on stage)* and Joey Faye *(below stage)*
in a scene from *High Button Shoes*. The show
ran for 727 Broadway performances.

Jule Styne, was less than earthshaking. It was called *Glad to See Ya*, a sentiment audiences didn't share when it opened in Philadelphia. The problem was director Busby Berkeley's unwillingness to cut the show.

"It had an hour and a half of music," says Cahn. "Berkeley insisted that, if the show was good, it could run 'til 2:00 in the morning. It did, in fact, run till 12:15."

Then, in the style of hokey 1930s musicals, the leading man, Eddie Davis, was injured in a car crash and couldn't go on.

"All of a sudden, on a Monday night in 1944, I played the part," Cahn recalls.

Despite an encouraging article in *Variety*, which proclaimed that *Glad to See Ya* had a better commercial chance than two other musicals trying out, *On the Town* and *Carousel*, it closed in Boston on December 31, 1944, without ever making it to Broadway.

"A horrendous comedy of errors," Cahn says. "Error after error after error. We were supposed to have Phil Silvers, who was not allowed to leave 20th Century–Fox, and therefore we should not have done *Glad to See Ya*. But we did.

"Now it's 1947, and I'm living in Holmby Hills. Jule Styne lives in Beverly Hills, at 611 North Elm Drive. And I pick up the *New York Times Book Review*, and there's an ad for a book called *The Sisters Like Them Handsome*, by Stephen Longstreet, and on the cover of the book there's a family in a Model T Ford. I went with this thing to Jule Styne and said, 'That's our musical.' Jule Styne said, "Would you like to meet Stephen Longstreet?' and I said, 'If we're going to do this musical, I suppose we should.' Jule stepped out of his front door, walked in a straight line from his front door across the street to 612 North Elm Drive, knocked on the door, and said, "Sammy, this is Stephen Longstreet.' That's the story of *High Button Shoes*."

High Button Shoes opened October 9, 1947, and turned out to be the only long-running musical produced that year. The story was set in 1913 New Jersey and depicted the manipulations of a con man, Harrison Floy, who attempted to sell useless swampland to the gullible Longstreet family. Phil Silvers stole the show as the comically conniving Floy, and Nanette Fabray balanced his broad antics with charm as Mama Longstreet. Cahn and Styne furnished a rousing, likeable score.

The Keystone Kops Ballet also added to the merriment in *High Button Shoes* and is now regarded as a classic theatrical moment. "It was the only scene Jerome Robbins did," Cahn says. "We had some very powerful people involved—George Abbott, Jerry Robbins. Jerry Robbins made that ballet the highlight of the show, but I remember when I did 'Papa Won't You Dance with Me' for him, and he said, 'Anybody could stop the show with that.' 'I Still Get Jealous' stopped the show too. He had nothing to do with any of those things. He focused on choreographing that ballet.

"As for George Abbott, he's a total theatre general. That's what he does. I called him 'Mr. Abbott' when I was very put out with him, which was most of the time, because he was such a rigid, robotlike man, and 'George' when I was feeling very friendly. I said to him that *High Button Shoes* was a good show, and he surprised me by saying, 'This is a *great* show.' And we went to New York and opened, and on opening night I discovered what a New York opening is. Where I'd been hearing laughs for three weeks straight in Philadelphia, I now heard silence. Don't ask me why I heard silence.

"Funnily enough, Phil Silvers, the star, is an old, old, dear friend of mine. I've known him for more than forty years. I knew him from vaudeville days. And one of the lines I heard him utter in burlesque was when he got into a fight with a fellow, took his glasses off, and turned to someone else, saying, 'Point me at him.' And this moment, in our show, *High Button Shoes*, he got into the same kind of quarrel with a football hero, took his glasses off, and said, 'Point me toward him.' He opened the show, and we romped away."

High Button Shoes ran for 727 performances, and Cahn looked forward to writing another show, but success in Hollywood kept him too busy. He wrote dozens of hits for Frank Sinatra, including "Love and Marriage," "All the Way," and "Hey, Jealous Lover." He persuaded Doris Day, a band singer unknown to Hollywood, to audition for 1948's *Romance on the High Seas* and launched her career with "It's Magic.' In 1955, he gave her another hit, "I'll Never Stop Loving You."

"Then I got the Broadway itch again," Cahn says. "So Jimmy Van Heusen and I decided to do *Skyscraper*."

Skyscraper was based on an Elmer Rice play, *Dream Girl*, and starred Julie Harris as the daydreaming heroine, Georgina. In the Cahn–Van Heusen update, Georgina was angry because a skyscraper was being built around and over her small brick house. Her other concerns were romantic ones: daydreams of Charles Nelson Reilly, who showed up in her fantasies as a southern gentleman, a toreador, and an FBI agent. Real, live love was represented by Peter Marshall as a handsome architect.

The show contained an amiable score, including the hit "Everybody Has a Right to Be Wrong," which Frank Sinatra recorded.

"But the way it started," says Cahn, rolling his eyes upward. "I came to do a show with producers Feuer and Martin, two giants of the Broadway theatre, and we opened in Detroit—Jimmy Van Heusen and I—to the single most *disastrous* set of reviews it could ever have been anyone's misfortune to receive. They were just devastating. Then came that inevitable meeting after opening night out of town. Feuer and Martin, to their everlasting credit, said, 'Well, we've got no show.'

"We had a fellow by the name of Peter Stone—a very, very super-talented man—and he kept rewriting the first act. Suffice to say, we closed Detroit with a first act, and we limped into New York. Instead of opening, we went

Skyscraper, starring Peter Marshall and Julie Harris, received a 1966 Tony nomination for Best Musical.

into previews there and opened to audiences who paid to see a show that was together. We were still running previews, fixing things up. Needless to say, the audience was coming out devastated, because we were trying to put together a second act. I'm telling you, Jimmy Van Heusen and I were writing a song a day, two songs a day. And that was, for me, the crux of the difference between writing for films and writing for the theatre. You can't take a song out and put a song into a film. When a song is in a film, it's locked into the sprocket—you can't take it out. You can take out theatre songs.

"So there we were, writing as hard as we knew how to write. Three nights before opening—*finally* we were opening—the word of mouth continued to be as devastating as the out-of-town reviews. People were paying one hundred dollars a ticket to see a show in flux. Columnist Dorothy Kilgallen came to see one of the Thanksgiving benefits and came out to announce, 'I had my turkey early this year.'

"She did the most horrendous review—so horrendous it backfired to our benefit. Everyone took exception to a columnist reviewing a show before it opened. She had no right to. It wasn't her domain. She had a nightclub cabaret gossip column. What was she doing reviewing a show?

"We wrote a song called 'Haute Couture.' We put the song in, and it started to work, started to land. When you get a song that's landing, it's like gold, you know. One song that lands can make the difference between a hit and a failure for you. And then, the man who was singing the song just couldn't bring it off. He went through three-quarters and then fell apart. And on opening night we called a rehearsal of the orchestra—this is all very expensive—and he couldn't do it. We opened without the song.

"Jimmy Van Heusen, I must say, didn't show up at the opening. *I* say, you show up, and you take the blows. I'll tell you in all candor, at that point I went to opening night feeling as if I was going to the guillotine. But there I went, standing in the back, and I'll tell you, the show caught fire. If anyone told me that I would walk into Sardi's later and they would stand up and applaud, I never would have dreamed it, even *remotely*. I never would have thought that Howard Taubman of the *Times* would write of me in the high praise he did: 'The Felicitous Rhymings of Sammy Cahn.' I was close to Cole Porter, he said. The whole thing turned around. So that has been the most rewarding of my shows."

Cahn's next show, *Walking Happy*, again written with Van Heusen, opened November 28, 1966. It was also nominated for Best Musical by the Tony committee, in 1967, and had a book by Roger O. Hirson (of *Pippin* fame) and Ketti Frings.

Walking Happy was an adaptation of a play, *Hobson's Choice*, and dealt with a domineering Dickensian-type father who attempts to keep his defiant daughter in line. There were good songs, especially a duet, "I Don't Think I'm in Love," and fine performances by George Rose as the father and Louise

Troy as his rebellious offspring. Walter Kerr of the *New York Times* pronounced the show "easygoing and unpretentious," a lighthearted mood considerably enhanced by Cahn's pleasing lyrics.

Cahn was also in strong form when he reteamed with *High Button Shoes* collaborator Jule Styne for *Look to the Lilies*. The show, which opened March 29, 1970, was an adaptation of William E. Barret's novel *Lilies of the Field* and had an engaging premise: a handyman meets a group of nuns and helps them build a chapel in New Mexico.

"Sidney Poitier won an Oscar for the movie," says Cahn, "but we had Al Freeman, Jr., and they kept telling us, 'He's an *actor*.' But I said, 'I want to hear a record of him. Can he sing?' And Jule Styne said, 'What good is a show if the book doesn't come off? He'll bring it off.' But I figured this way: let the book writer handle the book, I'll handle the songs."

Freeman, according to Cahn, balked at every line and challenged director Josh Logan throughout. *Look to the Lilies* did not achieve hit status and ran for only twenty-five performances.

"I never dreamed I'd do a show without one successful song coming out of it," Cahn says. Yet Clive Barnes of the *New York Times* praised his "effective lyrics" and said "the music is particularly welcome in a season where so many Broadway producers seem to have gone tone deaf, stone deaf, or both."

Broadway's loss was Hollywood's gain from 1970 forward, though Cahn didn't lose his interest in the stage.

"That's why I picked *Bojangles*. I got involved with it in the late seventies because, first of all, it's *musical*—it has an inherent musicality. I was called about it, originally, by a man I respected. He's no longer involved with *Bojangles*, curiously enough, but I knew him. *Bojangles* was done up off Harlem—kind of a workshop—and had gotten very creditable reviews, and I often said, 'Why don't we put the songs to the reviews?' We had a young book writer who was a *researcher*—a man who was an absolute fan of Bill Robinson, could tell you when he was born, why he was born, everything about him. And he wrote a book that was research instead of a book. Research, not a libretto. I mean it. I kept saying, 'We have research, fellas; we don't have a book.' For three or four years. It wasn't until Marty Charnin came aboard that we had a musical book. I couldn't make them understand we had *reading*, but we didn't have *writing*. Happily, now we do."

Cahn knows a great book and a great score when he hears one.

"I remember, I was in Philadelphia the opening night of *Guys and Dolls*. And when the fellow stepped up and said, 'I've got a horse right here, his name is Paul Revere,' I turned to a friend and said, 'This is the biggest hit that ever happened.' He said, 'What, are you *crazy*?' and I said, 'You don't understand. This is the biggest hit, because in the kernel of that line is the whole magic of the show.

"*Any* great show," he continues, "starts off with the simplest of stories. That's the first cardinal rule of a great, great evening. It has the simplest plot—you can tell a child of six to eight years old, and he'll sit there and understand, in *My Fair Lady*, for instance, that this man is taking a girl out of the gutter and saying that, by improving her language, he will make her a lady. That is simplicity, beautiful simplicity."

Just as Cahn instinctively knows when a plot and lyrics are working in a show, he instinctively knows when something *doesn't* work.

"I'm a creature of instinct in my writing, in my approach to everything I do. I don't write a song as much as a song writes me. I start a song, that's my contribution. I start it. And then I'm very pleased to be present, to see what the results are. And I never, *ever* stop writing—or rewriting.

"You can't be so in love with your work that you refuse to rewrite. I tell every writer, 'Don't quarrel about rewriting. Don't fall in love with every-thing you write.' There are many songs in *Bojangles* that I've written two lyrics for. One of our big ballads in the show was called 'What Does She See in Me?' It's now called 'When Do You Walk Away?' Same tune. That's marvelous. Think of the joy and fun of rewriting."

His pleasure in rewriting is useful for theatre work, since rewriting is the lifeblood of the medium.

"Say somebody's out on the stage singing a song of mine, and the singer doesn't give it the proper inflection. I can say, 'No, do it this way.' Then, of course, if the person does it every way possible and doesn't make it work, I have failed, and I write another line. I change it to what it needs to be or take the song out.

"The very moment a line fights me, I'll get up and walk around. Then I come back and start to type again, because there's no doubt in my mind that it's there. I think applying yourself to what you do is so much fun. That's the main thing. When I listen to other people's songs, I can tell you whether they were written with joy."

Cahn is deservedly proud of his professionalism. "I tell everybody, 'I don't know if I've written a hit, but I promise, if you sing it, it won't embarrass you.' And I'm very, very proud of a number of achievements, particularly that I've written so-called hit songs with many people—not just one fellow or two fellows. That gives me a great sense of achievement, because I don't write with the personas as much as I write with the music. The music talks to me.

"You know, if I write with a fellow who plays, as I call it 'fetchingly,' I could write five or six songs a day as easily as you go for a walk. And the people I've worked with will tell you. I start to type, I put the paper in, and out comes a lyric. Unquestionable, no doubt about it. People ask, 'How does he do that?' but that's what I do. Then the music is writing the lyric."

One of the shows Cahn takes tremendous pride in was written for TV, rather than the Broadway stage—*Our Town*, which starred Frank Sinatra and Paul Newman.

"I had special affection for 'Look to Your Heart' from that show," says

Sammy Cahn and Jule Styne at work, 1943.

Cahn, "when Emily has to go back to the graveyard, and Sinatra has his shining moment:

> Speak your love to those who seek your love
> Look to your heart
> Your heart will know what to say
> Look to your heart today

"I was very pleased with those words, and I wish everyone would think about them in their daily conduct."

He was also pleased with an unexpected success as performer in his career. It began when he appeared at Manhattan's 92nd Street Y, in a series called *Lyrics and Lyricists.*

"These were one-man or one-woman evenings by people like Alan Jay Lerner, Yip Harburg. Then, at the end of 1973, Alexander Cohen told me I'd be opening on Broadway at the Golden Theatre. He put the thing together, and there I was."

On April 16, 1974, Cahn opened to rave reviews. The first notice, from Channel Five's Stewart Klein, called it "one of the most delightful shows of the year," and all other critics followed suit.

"Know what I remember most of all? I won the Broadway Newcomer of the Year Award, and I mentioned my idol, an old vaudeville performer, Jim Barton—my absolute, absolute champion. One day there was a rap on my door, and it was Kay Barton.

"She said, 'I want to thank you for all the wonderful things you're saying about Jim.' And she brought me something—she brought me Jim's St. Genesius medal, the patron saint of performers.

"I always remembered everything he represented," Cahn says "And I tell this to every performer I meet: 'Take stage eagerly; leave it reluctantly.' If you watch a performer who can't wait to get off stage, I'll show you a performer I can do without."

CHAPTER FIVE

CY COLEMAN

C Y COLEMAN'S VERSATILITY DEFIES BELIEF. He is an outstanding jazz pianist, as his numerous Cy Coleman jazz trio albums prove. His hit songs, including "Witchcraft" and "I'm Gonna Laugh You Right Out of My Life," have been recorded by such artists as Frank Sinatra, Barbra Streisand, Nat King Cole, and Diana Ross. Film credits range from *Father Goose* to *Blame It on Rio*.

We caught up with the tireless Coleman in his music publishing office on West 54th Street in Manhattan. The name of the firm, Notable Music, defines his career. Coleman is notable as a creative force; beyond that, he serves on the board of directors of the American Society of Composers, Authors, and Publishers (ASCAP). He's also a governor of the television academy and of the Dramatists Guild council.

"I was the youngest of five children. My parents were immigrants from the small place between Romania and Russia called Bessarabia. And all I can tell you is, the reason I started playing piano was that my mother owned and was the landlord of a building. Somebody skipped on the rent and couldn't get the piano out, so it went to our house. At four years old, because of that piano, I was on my way to becoming a child prodigy."

The circumstances make an entertaining anecdote, but it's probable that the brilliantly gifted Coleman would have given his life to music without the aid of a runaway neighbor. Another neighbor—the milkman's son's school teacher—found a woman to give Coleman lessons. "Constance Talerico, who gave my mother a very good deal. My mother had a talent for business, obviously. There were two free lessons and one she paid for. So I became a prodigy and played at Steinway Hall, and I was in competition at Town Hall too. I even played Carnegie Hall at the age of seven."

Coleman was encouraged in his musical endeavors, except for one direct act of opposition from his father.

"My father was a carpenter and a cabinet maker; his occupation later served us well because we landed up in the Catskills, and he built all the houses. I was very young, and I practiced about six or eight hours a day. I was really intrigued by the piano. My father couldn't take it anymore, and he nailed the piano shut!

"He wasn't a bad man," Coleman adds. "A very sweet man, but he had just had enough. I don't want to paint this picture of a villain. He was quite nice, though browbeaten by my mother. It took a lot for him to do that. It didn't phase me a bit. I went to his toolbox and found a screwdriver and pried the piano open. The music continued, and he never tried to do anything more about it."

Coleman's teacher had him slated for a concert career, but it was not to be. "I can't tell you *why* I didn't want to be a concert pianist. Maybe it was a kind of perversity of teenage. More likely, it was a desire to do something of my own in the creative field as opposed to being a recreative artist."

By the time he graduated from high school, he had taken eight years of counterpoint and studied orchestration.

"I was already overqualified for college, at least for the career I had chosen, so I had to go and decide what to do with myself. I went and auditioned for some nightclubs, and I was an instant success in that area."

Coleman built a reputation as a darling of society. The Astors and Vanderbilts would come to hear him, and so did Colonel Sergio Blesky, who had once run the Chez Netherlands.

"I had to ask myself, 'do I want to spend the rest of my life smiling over a piano and becoming the new whoever-it-was at that moment?' The new Carmen Cavallaro or Eddy Duchin, depending on which age bracket you came from. So I gave Sergio Blesky an ultimatum. I said 'You can turn the room downstairs into a jazz room, and I'll start a jazz group,' because I thought it was more creative; but he didn't like that idea. He said he wanted me to play for dancing."

Jazz nonetheless became—and remained—a potent force in Coleman's life.

"At first I played at some of these places with little bowls on the piano. Since I was very young—I was about 17, and I looked 12—I attracted a lot of tips. I got a job accompanying a woman named Adrienne, who sent me to E. H. Morris Music—Jack Robbins was the vice-president."

Coleman had written a classical work—Sonata in Seven Flats—slated for a performance, later cancelled, in Carnegie Hall. Coleman showed the sonata to Robbins.

"He decided I was the new Gershwin. He gave me a commission to write three piano preludes, just like Gershwin. I wrote them over the summer. I was up in Monticello when I did them, while I was working at this Catskills' hotel. And after that, Robbins decided I should write songs."

The music publisher introduced Coleman to a songwriter named Joseph McCarthy.

"Joe was about ten years older than I. He was fiendish about pop songs because his father was a famous songwriter. I thought at first that it was a ridiculous pursuit. I had written sonatas and everything, so the idea of writing songs, while it attracted me from a monetary viewpoint, didn't have the same significance it did to Joe."

Nonetheless, McCarthy pounded away at Coleman, and they co-wrote "Why Try to Change Me Now," which Frank Sinatra recorded.

"It didn't get played much, but it became somewhat of a modern standard. Then we wrote 'I'm Gonna Laugh You Right Out of My Life,' and Nat Cole cut it."

During the early fifties, the Coleman-McCarthy team also wrote for Mabel Mercer."

"As a matter of fact, up until she died recently, most of the songs she did were by Joe and me."

The work process proved frustrating, however. "It took Joe days and days, and I hated songwriting because you had to *sit* with Joe! I didn't think it was a very nice profession, where I had to write the melody and then sit with him while he contemplated. I couldn't see why he couldn't do it all by himself. But he didn't want to, and I'd watch him go through this torturous ritual with every song."

These experiences provided a pop training ground, and Coleman went on to collaborate with other lyricists. "Bob Hilliard was one. Another was Hal David. Then Carolyn Leigh came around, and we bumped into each other in the Brill Building."

The woman who eventually wrote *Little Me* and *Wildcat* with Coleman became a steady partner.

"We wrote a song called 'A Moment of Madness' in one day. And then the next day we had a record with Sammy Davis. We were on our way."

Collaboration with Carolyn Leigh was a more satisfying arrangement than his former association with McCarthy.

"With Carolyn it was more of a collaboration than a night watch! We worked a lot together. Then she'd go her own way, and I'd go and polish my tune. And we'd come back and spend more hours together. Even when we'd get tired or something, she came up with strong things, like 'Witchcraft.' "

During the mid-fifties, Coleman acquired his own club, The Playroom.

"The guy who had the Italian restaurant downstairs from where I lived offered me a deal that I should have resisted, but didn't think I could. He gave me half the club, which meant I could work for half my usual fee and take half the profit of the club. So what I ended up doing was working for half my fee and getting heavy on the food that was being wasted."

The Playroom proved "not a terrific experience," says Coleman. But he loved writing, and contributed some sketches for *John Murray Anderson's Almanac*, which opened December 10, 1953, and ran 229 performances. Other contributors to the show included Sheldon Harnick and Harry Belafonte.

E. H. Morris Music was impressed and offered Coleman money each week just to write.

"I'd grown tired of eating just at my club, and I was tired of having the cash register raided by my partner. So Carolyn and I made the deal. We wrote a score for *Gypsy*—we were asked to submit four songs. We didn't get the show, but we did get a hit song out of it, called 'Firefly.' Tony Bennett cut it."

They also tried for *Skyscraper*, without success. Then director/choreographer Michael Kidd contacted the Coleman-Leigh team and asked them to write *Wildcat* for Lucille Ball. It opened December 16, 1960, and told the story of Wildcat Jackson, a woman who drills for oil and finds it, along with the love of her foreman.

"The hardest song we had to write was the first one, which was 'Hey, Look Me Over,' because we were nervous and the song was for Lucille Ball."

What kind of research did he do?

"At the time, I was naive enough to think that research didn't matter," he laughs. "I don't feel that way today. Now I research everything. I buy all the records and find I use none of it. But still it's just a way to get me into the actor's clothing or the composer's mouth. Research focuses me on that project. I remember the wise words of Jerome Kern. When he was asked to do a score about Marco Polo, the producer said, 'Well, this is a score about an Italian in China and narrated by an Irishman. What kind of music are you going to write?' And Kern said, 'I'm going to do the same thing I always do. I'm going to write a nice Jewish score.'"

Through easy jobs and difficult ones, Coleman polished his craft. "The breakthrough for me was when I learned to write dramatically and still to entertain—to keep the show moving, get an idea of pace, and be true to myself at the same time."

Being true to himself is important to Coleman. "I'm an individualist, I feel, my own kind of man. What created Cy Coleman? It's all the things I've told you. It's playing in jazz clubs, doing the society bit, accompanying people, being a concert pianist. I think you'd have to put it all in a Cuisinart and mix that up, and out would come Cy Coleman."

This wealth of individuality and background enhanced the 1962 show *Little Me*. The musical had a zany Neil Simon book that permitted star Sid Caesar to play six characters, suitors in the life of one Belle Poitrine, formerly Belle Schlumpfert. Caesar ran the gamut from Mr. Pinchley, a rich lustful banker, to Prince Cherney of Rosensweig, ruler of "the only country ever defeated by Luxembourg." "Real Live Girl" was one of the highlights of the score and later became a pop hit. Other notable moments included "I've Got Your Number," "Goodbye," and the hilarious "I Love You" ("as much as I'm able— considering I'm wealthy— considering you're poor").

"Carolyn Leigh and I almost didn't do *Little Me*," says Coleman. "We were furious with producers Feuer and Martin. They tried to screw us up on *Wildcat*. So we turned *Little Me* down, and then Bobby Fryer came to us with a project called *The King from Ashtabula*. Gore Vidal was trying to write the book. He was an important writer, so we said yes. But Vidal decided afterward he didn't like the musical theatre and the people who write in it, so he dismissed the project. We had to go hat in hand to Feuer and Martin and say we wanted to do *Little Me*. We did it and lost a part of the percentage for that little maneuver."

Little Me was creatively stimulating, but far from smooth.

"Carolyn and I had our legendary battles. We were well known for battling."

About what?

"About everything," says Coleman. "Carolyn very much liked the book to go her way." Leigh was a perfectionist, but also stubborn and unyielding. Her perfectionism resulted in brilliant, intricate rhymes, such as those featured in "Real Live Girl":

> Pardon me, Miss
> But I've never done this
> With a real live girl
> Right off the farm with an actual armful
> Of real live girl

Little Me emerged as a joyous romp and betrayed no evidence of behind-the-scenes tension. A revival in 1982 delighted audiences again and contained two new Coleman songs: "I Wanna Be Yours" and "Don't Ask a Lady."

Coleman's show *I Love My Wife* (book and lyrics by Michael Stewart), which opened in 1977, went more calmly. The agreeable mini-musical about two couples contemplating a ménage a quatre featured an outstanding performance by Lenny Baker as one of the husbands and a tuneful Coleman–Michael Stewart score. "Hey There, Good Times" was one of the many rousing numbers, and "I Love My Wife" was bittersweet and gentle, humanizing the farcical plot twists dealing with infidelity.

The intimate nature of the production also gave Coleman a chance to test out a new theory about opening numbers.

"They don't necessarily have to be big productions," he says. "In *I Love My Wife*, everybody kept saying, 'go for the big opening number.' We said no, because the construction of the show, lyricist Michael Stewart and I felt, was set to start small. We'd have no place to go. The opening number in *Little Me* was a thing called 'The Truth.' I rewrote it fifteen times! Bob Fosse and I used to kid about it—because he redid the ending to a song in the second act, called 'Goodbye,' at least twenty times. We used to say we did thirty-five rewrites and wasted all our time on the two numbers in the show that didn't give us the best results. 'Goodbye' *sort* of worked, but it never gave us what we wanted. The opening was nice, though it never fulfilled my hopes. Still, you have to try things. You have to experiment."

Coleman likes flexibility and demonstrates this point with an anecdote: "I found a guy who was very promising for a project I had in mind. We talked. And then he gave me his theories about theatre and his rules and regulations, and somehow I lost my entire taste for the project. You can't be that rigid. I don't have that rigidity, and I don't believe anybody else should."

"If I have a song that becomes a hit, chances are I won't go and write that song again. A lot of people continue along the same style and milk it, and people will ask you to do that. Somehow that perversity in me remains, and I'll go off to the other side of something."

Perversity is one Coleman trait; perfectionism is another, which is why he orchestrated his own music in *I Love My Wife*.

"Look, I don't want to sit there and let rehearsal pianists tell me what to do. I don't want the dancing to come from another source, because I need it as a whole cloth. I don't want the vocal arrangements to come from another place either. So I'll do all that, and I'll sit with my director, like Neil Simon, and I'll prompt and pull the show together in my own way. I can always take an orchestration and turn it around. I'm very fast at an orchestra rehearsal."

He was fast in dismissing a critic from an orchestra rehearsal when the critic interfered.

"He asked to be invited to one of the orchestral readings. And he went over to the drummer and said, 'What do you think of this score?' And I threw him out. He said, 'Why are you asking me to leave?' and I said simply this: 'Because you're not equipped to be here. Because had I known you were going over to the drummer to ask him about the score, I'd have given him a sixteen-bar solo, and he would have *loved* the score."

Coleman doesn't let people intimidate him, especially when it threatens the effectiveness of his work. He admires directors who defend their artistic vision and care deeply about doing the best possible job. In that context, he mentions Hal Prince, Bob Fosse, and Michael Bennett.

"When you deal with top guys they have integrity. They don't let anything get in the way of their goal—to make sure the show is in top shape. When we brought *On the Twentieth Century* to Hal, he loved it and understood it. He was very supportive when we approached the show as a comic opera."

Coleman, shown here preparing for his musical *Seesaw*, admires a proclamation in honor of George Gershwin.

Cy Coleman.

This comic opera approach was ideal for the theatrical, comically over-blown story of a Broadway producer and his wife, and their marital conflicts aboard a luxury train. Prince's direction, the stylish performances of John Cullum and Madeline Kahn, and the Coleman-Comden and Green score kept *On the Twentieth Century* (which opened February 19, 1978) firmly on track through 449 performances.

"There's a kind of energy and enthusiasm that Hal gives you, which I find inspiring. I'm kind of an energy person too, and I'm optimistic. Hal and I are alike."

The difference between Prince and Bob Fosse, according to Coleman, is "Bob will approach it in a kind of very, very intellectual, thoughtful manner. And Bobby's ultimately fair. He's just—he will just talk to you about everything. There's an excitement that happens, that builds and constructs, and is very focused."

Coleman likes that. "Every time I'm finished, I want the show to be the best I can do. I can argue with myself about certain things—maybe I wasn't ballsy enough or gutsy enough to stand up at one point or another—but I like all my shows."

He has a special fondness for *Seesaw*, which opened March 18, 1973, and ran for 296 performances. *Seesaw* was a musicalization of William Gibson's two character play *Two for the Seesaw* and focused on the romance between the streetwise, New Yorky Gittel and a straight, conventional Midwestern attorney.

"Michael Bennett's work on that was exciting. Michael pulls in a lot of people. He's like chairman of the board, you know. He pulled in three choreographers besides himself—Bob Avian and Tommy Tune, who also starred—and co-choreographer Grover Dale. There was an aura of excitement about that show. It was a terrific experience."

He regrets that *Seesaw* didn't become the smash it deserved to be.

"We should have stayed out on the road for two more weeks, but we didn't have the money. I think the negative rumors influenced New Yorkers—firing the director, Ed Sherin, and replacing him with Michael Bennett; firing the star, Lainie Kazan, and bringing in Michele Lee. The show turned around, and they weren't ready for it yet. That's my opinion."

His opinion was obviously accurate. Clive Barnes called it "the second, or maybe third, best musical of the season." Barnes then wavered: "The dance numbers come over with an assertive charm" and "the book is literate and interesting," but the show suffers from "a bland but efficient slickness." It appeared that Barnes was afraid to commit himself fully in the face of what he himself referred to as "notorious trouble in preview."

Six months after, when *Seesaw* was in financial trouble, Barnes rereviewed the production, calling it "a love of a show." He finally gathered up the courage to speak out—too late.

Barnum, which premiered April 30, 1980, had more commercial success. It featured the multitalented, magnificently agile Jim Dale as Barnum, and showed him walking a tightrope, conducting a marching band, leaping from a trampoline, and singing his heart out. "The Prince of Humbug" proved a perfect character to belt out songs by Coleman and collaborator Michael Stewart.

"Michael Stewart called me up and said, 'I think we can do this.' A lot of people had talked about doing Barnum's life in the past, but that was all. I thought there was something intriguing about a circus show. Then I called Michael, after a sleepless night, and said, 'If you can put this show in the middle of a circus ring, I can bring in all kinds of chases to keep it going, and I love to write chases.' Michael bought the idea. David Merrick was the producer, and he dropped out to do *42nd Street*, so I said, 'let's produce it ourselves.' Then Michael dropped out too, and there was this girl, Judy Gordon, who had been talking about doing a show—an evening with Cy Coleman, that kind of thing—and I resisted. I said everybody was doing shows about composers, and I didn't see myself there yet. But what about *Barnum*?"

He and Gordon eventually went to St. Petersburg, Florida, where the circus was playing, and they played for Irving and Kenneth Feld, sat around with the circus people and got the needed money. "So that's how I became a producer," says Coleman, "although I'd been a producer prior to that on television. Judy and I produced *Barnum*."

Television productions included the 1974 TV special "If They Could See Me Now" for Shirley MacLaine, which he conceived and wrote in addition to producing. He also produced MacLaine's 1976 musical "Gypsy in My Soul," which brought him an Emmy for Best Musical Show.

We asked how he enjoyed working with stars.

"Stars have particular talents. And some have certain limitations too. It depends. With Lucille Ball, obviously I wasn't getting Joan Sutherland, but I had certain great comic values. She was right for the show. When I did *Twentieth Century*, I was looking for voices for our chorus, and I found ones that were magnificent. With Sid Caesar it was a comic role. I had good singers in *I Love My Wife*. And Gwen Verdon can certainly project a song."

Verdon proved that brilliantly in *Sweet Charity*, which opened January 29, 1966. A song and dance version of Fellini's *Nights of Cabiria*, *Charity* followed the love affair between an accountant and a dance hall hostess. In its depiction of a free, slightly tarnished girl and a convention-bound man, the show resembled *Seesaw*, and it had a downbeat ending as well.

Nonetheless, public reaction proved positive, and songs like "Big Spender" became popular. Backstage, however, a problem had arisen that created chaos shortly before opening night.

"In *Sweet Charity*, Irene Sharaff walked in with her costumes for "Big

The cast of Coleman's
1966 musical *Sweet Charity*
does a rousing version of
"I Love to Cry at Weddings."

A scene from *Sweet Charity*.
The musical comedy was
nominated for a Best
Musical Tony in 1966.

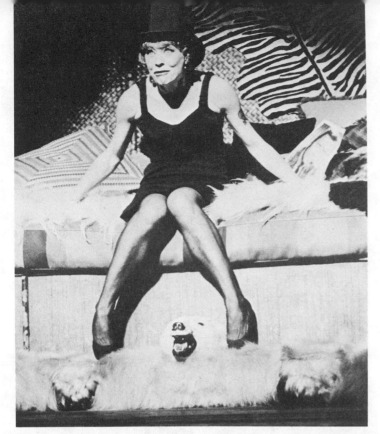

The star of *Sweet Charity*, Gwen Verdon, sings "If They Could See Me Now."

Gwen Verdon, Helen Gallagher, and Thelma Oliver singing "There's Gotta Be Something Better than This."

Coleman with Dorothy Fields, his collaborator and lyricist for *Sweet Charity* and *Seesaw*.

Coleman (*right*) embraces Tony Bennett and Chita Rivera.

Spender," and they were all spangled. The lights hit them, and you couldn't hear a lyric or see a face. Bob Fosse was absolutely furious. She kept insisting they were in the sketches, and he was telling her the spangles were *never* in the sketches. It was a battle royal, and I think Irene's classic line, in response to Bob's remark, 'The number will never work this way,' was 'Cut the number!' "

Coleman and Fosse wanted to strangle the designer at that moment. "It doesn't take anything away from Irene Sharaff's talent; it's just that tempers were pitched high, and Bob was prepared to throw out all the costumes. When he threatened that, she sprayed the spangles, and the spangles did not glow in the dark anymore."

There has to be a captain of the ship in every show—the "muscle," as William Goldman calls it in his book *The Season*. We mentioned to Coleman that Richard Rodgers once said, "If a show succeeds or fails, it's the producer's fault. He has to make those decisions and be the captain."

"I think he was unduly hard on himself," says Coleman. "I think the success or failure of a show relates to many elements. It's difficult sometimes because the producer can't get rid of certain people. For example, I had a great show with Dorothy Fields, and we couldn't get it produced. Everybody disliked the book, and the show contained one of our best scores. But the book writer didn't want anybody coming in and changing anything."

When asked what property it was, he hesitates briefly, then says, "Oh, what the hell, it doesn't bother me, it was about Eleanor Roosevelt. We spawned all those TV things. Jane Alexander, who later did "Eleanor and Franklin" was somebody I was working with for that role."

The score didn't completely die, however. "I raided it. We used 'It's Not Where You Start" and put it into *Seesaw*. I put a song called 'Scream' into *Seesaw*. In *Barnum*, the music to 'Out There' is the Teddy Roosevelt song. There's a lot more. I hated doing it, but I just figured it was good, and I wanted to do something with it."

Coleman admits that finding a good book writer is difficult. "But so is everything. Good lyricists are difficult. Good set designers, good everything. *Good* is difficult.

"You can no longer just say, 'I'm a composer; I just sit down and write music.' You have to go out there and seek good people out. And you have to learn a dozen things. I have become an amateur *everything* in the theatre, or a professional as the case may be. I'm involved, and I think you have to be."

CHAPTER SIX

BETTY COMDEN
& ADOLPH GREEN

THE DEN IN BETTY COMDEN'S EAST SIDE TOWNHOUSE, located between Park and Lexington avenues, has a distinctly literary flavor. Framed playbills melt into the early American, antique flavor of the room, coming across as art objects rather than mere announcements of past accomplishment.

Nonetheless, impressive credits are there to remind any observer that Betty Comden and Adolph Green have been performing and writing partners since their college days in the mid-1930s.

In the best, most enduring partnerships, collaborators generally begin to listen and respond as one voice. They retain their individuality, but in the course of conversation, one will finish the sentence of the other or prompt the other with a good story.

Comden and Green are perfect examples of this powerfully subtle teamwork. They've written librettos and lyrics (*On the Town*) and librettos alone (*Applause*). They're responsible for the witty, eternally fresh screenplay of that MGM masterpiece, *Singin' in the Rain* (which was adapted for Broadway in 1985). They also wrote film scripts for *Good News*, *The Band Wagon*, and *The Barkleys of Broadway*. Most remarkably, they've been successful on Broadway from 1944 to the present—they were nominated for a Tony in 1983, for *A Doll's Life*—and show no signs of slowing down.

Betty Comden was born in Brooklyn on May 3, 1915; Green was born on December 2 of that year in the Bronx. When asked how they met, Comden laughs, "Oh, we don't need to go back that far, do we?" Then she continues, "We met when I was at NYU, through a mutual friend. We rarely saw each other then. We became close doing work in the theatre."

Their initial theatre work in 1937 revolved around a quintet of singers and comics, the Revuers, which featured them both as performers, along with Judy Holliday.

"There were Adolph and two other boys, Judy, and me," says Comden. "We looked for outside material and then found out that you had to pay royalties for it. We couldn't afford that, so we all chipped in and bought a pencil and started to write material for ourselves—lyrics, sketches, music, everything."

Green doesn't play an instrument, however, and as for Comden, "I play four miraculous chords." The chords eventually proved too limiting, and Comden stopped writing music.

In the meantime, the Revuers did satirical shows on the social mores of the times. "We stayed together almost five years. Leonard Bernstein was an old friend of Adolph's who came to the Village Vanguard to see us, and we all got to know each other and become close. Leonard and Jerome Robbins decided to do *On the Town*, which came out of an idea for Leonard's ballet, *Fancy Free*. He got us the job of doing the lyrics. They didn't know much about us, but Leonard knew us and our material, and he knew we could write."

How did they learn to structure a show?

"We learned just by doing it," says Comden. "We were theatre addicts. We *loved* going to the theatre. We absorbed all we could from Noel Coward, Gilbert and Sullivan, Rodgers and Hammerstein. We admired all these people and learned a lot from them."

The craft was evident in their work from the beginning, and Comden and Green worked industriously. "Sometimes when you're on a project, you go all day and into the evening," Green says. "Sometimes you just work only a short time. It depends on what stage the project is in. But we work together every day, like going to the office, whether we have an idea or we don't have an idea."

They didn't have an idea how the 1944 *On the Town* was going to turn out— they felt their way, meeting what Green calls "the challenge of doing something vital and original. It was a challenge to do something fresh, based on a pattern already familiar in movies—of sailors on leave. We decided to take a chance and plunge in."

Plunging in meant selecting a whole list of locales. Then Comden and Green drew up a character for each of the three sailors and their girl friends, nailing down individual traits.

"We've always written not just *songs*, but songs for the show, songs that reveal character. And there was an additional plus—the play was set in wartime, which gave it a built-in poignancy," Comden explains.

Comden and Green are proud of their 1944 musical *On The Town*. The songs aren't just songs, says Comden, "but songs for the show; songs that reveal character."

Leslie Uggams records a song from Comden and Green's musical *Hallelujah, Baby!*

There was built-in structure too. "What we find most effective is structuring the book as much as we can before writing any songs," says Green. "The more structure you have, the better off you are, and the more tightly the songs and the plot will mesh."

That doesn't mean," adds Comden, "that you don't start working on the score before the book is written."

Structure doesn't mean rigidity, because, as Comden points out, "people like Leonard Bernstein, Jule Styne, Cy Coleman are *dramatists*, and they always write for the theatre, for situation and character. It's collaborative, flexible."

Comden and Green remain proud of *On the Town* today. Adolph feels that it is "the only gay, lighthearted young people's show that has ever been written in that idiom—there is no other—a full dance musical, with a texture that is symphonic. It had serious symphonic music."

Comden and Green remember that the creative route to *On the Town* was ever-changing. "Sometimes Leonard had some melody that he decided should be used, and we put words to it. Other times we came with a full lyric, and he'd work on it. Still other times we'd have an idea and start working on it together. And we'd use patterns of other songs and start putting a few lines of lyric to them, just to get a start."

They recall how thrilling it was to work with George Abbott.

"He was the director, and we were all kids. He was this venerable patriarch," says Comden. "He's ninety-six now, so he was in his middle fifties in 1944. It was exciting."

It was also a time that tested their flexibility. "We were having trouble with the book," says Green, "and George wanted some changes. He was ready to do the show immediately based on the idea by Leonard and Jerry Robbins. Then we had our backs against the wall. We came up with a whole new book, which fell into place."

"We gave it to Mr. Abbott at his house over the weekend," Comden says. "And he was so excited he said he wanted to jump off a train, it was so marvelous. We felt as though we'd won the Nobel Prize." She smiles, the memory obviously still vivid. "We never found George intimidating. He was always willing to listen. He certainly had his own ideas, but he'd ask, 'What do you want to do instead?' He was terrific."

Comden and Green remember their experience with *Bells Are Ringing* (1956) as a pleasurable one too. For one thing, it reunited them with their old performing partner, Judy Holliday.

Holliday scored a triumph as Ella, the switchboard operator who falls in love with one of her faceless clients, playwright Jeff Moss. The score brought out the diversity of her talent—comedy as well as pathos.

"The score was written in a week," says Green. "The actual working out of the book was more spread over a period of time, because we wrote a movie in between. But yes, the completion of the music was very fast. We dug in at Jerry Robbins's apartment, and we never left."

Bells Are Ringing contains some of Comden and Green's most popular, best-known hit songs, such as "Just in Time."

"We began 'Just in Time' but didn't finish it right away," Comden says. "But we knew it was a song that was going to be in the show. Julie Styne had this melody, this simple melody. It remained 'Da-Da-Da'—those were the only words—for many months. We always knew it worked; we played 'Da-Da-Da' at parties with great success. When we found the situation in the book that gave us the title, we wrote 'Just in Time.' "

The idea for *Bells Are Ringing* was an outstanding one. How did they conceive it?

"We were in Adolph's apartment, looking in the phone book," says Comden, "and suddenly we saw this ad for an answering service. We called up Julie and said, 'This is an idea for a show.' His answer was, 'They have got to *fall down*.' So we knew we had a show. After we'd done some writing, we took it to Julie."

Once it was written, they also took it to Judy Holliday.

"Judy was very professional about everything, but she did make changes," says Comden. "There was a thing in 'The Party's Over' that she wanted—she didn't want to sing, 'Burst her pretty balloon, they're taking the moon away.' She said it didn't sound to her like Ella Peterson. We changed it, and it worked."

"We wanted larger-than-life lyricism," Green adds, "but Judy wanted to stay in character. We also had scenes that explained the character, which we liked a lot. But Judy felt, 'You don't need these ramifications in the script. I bring them on stage with me.' "

The show went smoothly, which is not always the case. Often there is that famous second-act trouble.

"That's probably because the story isn't spreading itself out in inevitable fashion, which is what you strive for," says Green. "Very often the problems are in the first act. The second act has to pay off whatever you've set up in the first."

Prior to either act, of course, is selecting the property. How do they decide on one?

"Agony," Green says. "Just read, think, kick around things, meet every day and stare at each other and say no to something for a year, then suddenly say, 'Let's try it.' Sometimes other people you're involved with get enthusiasm and pull you along, and suddenly you say, 'Well, this can work.' "

They admit that *On the Town* was a unique, totally satisfying project that worked immediately. "It was such a surprise," Betty recalls. "You can't match that first time as an experience. *Bells Are Ringing* and Judy—that was terrific—and *Wonderful Town*, because it was a show about grown-up people and life, and we'd matured. But we were very proud of that first show."

Working with Leonard Bernstein on *On the Town* and then Jule Styne on *Bells Are Ringing*, Betty and Adolph found a similarity between the two composers—a willingness to change things quickly, to try different alternatives. "With either one," Comden says, "if you say, 'This doesn't work,' they'll say, 'What about this?' "

"They're both totally different," says Green. "They're both mad, and they're both geniuses, and they're both theatre people, very creative and very generous."

They also love Jule Styne's enthusiasm, the enthusiasm that makes him say he's written the greatest tune, that it's absolutely marvelous and will sweep the nation.

"He's very prolific" says Comden, "and great, great fun to work with."

They find writing for the theatre "agony—like all writing is," laughs Green. "*Singin' in the Rain* was agony while working on it, but a joyous experience when we were finished."

Loneliness is another inevitability for writers in the midst of projects. "But there are two of us," says Green, "and we're lonely together."

Having a director you can work closely with can ease some of that pain. What was the difference between working with George Abbott and Hal Prince, with whom Comden and Green teamed up on *On the Twentieth Century*, more than twenty years after *Bells Are Ringing* hit Broadway?

"Hal inherited certain things from George," says Comden. "He's brisk, gets right to work, no nonsense, very organized. We worked closely with George—everything we brought to him and discussed on our three shows together. But with Hal, not from the very beginning on *Twentieth Century* but once we got involved with him, he was with us every minute. We went over every single thing, every step of the book, every character, every development, and worked out things very closely with him. His contribution was extraordinary. It was just tremendous. Brilliant staging on *Twentieth Century*."

On the Twentieth Century opened February 19, 1978, and ran for 449 performances. It focused on the squabbles between a temperamental producer-director and his actress wife aboard a speeding train. The whole tone was theatrical and extravagant, qualities heightened by Hal Prince's direction.

"Hal doesn't just direct—he gives you incredible input in every area," says Comden. "He's like a writer who doesn't write. He helps you find out what you want to do."

Another way of finding out what they want to do is to listen to the audience. "You listen to what they're saying, not necessarily to the critics," Comden says. "We like the idea of going out of town. You have to listen to the audience, *plus* keeping in mind what your own intention was."

Green concurs. "You can make changes in a show, but if you lose what your original intention was—what it's about, what you really meant, and what you meant to accomplish—you're in trouble. There are many changes you can make within that. If you listen to, say, the orange juice salesman at intermission, it pulls you away from your original intention, what you thought at first."

Sometimes writers flounder at the start, searching for a tone and style.

"We did that with *On the Twentieth Century*," says Comden. "It took place in the thirties, and none of us wanted to do a thirties pastiche, thirties songs. What happened was, Cy Coleman, our collaborator on the show, sat down one day and improvised things, like Rossini. We knew then that it should have this comic opera flavor, and we knew where to go with it. If we had ever decided to change the style, or maybe put in different kinds of things, we'd have worked against that, lost what the show had."

Green agrees. "You can't fall into thinking, 'Let's make it entertaining'; you have to think, 'Let's make it *work*.' Naturally, it should be an entertainment, but when you surrender to 'Let's get something up there for applause,' you're liable to lose track of what you're after. There has to be a certain amount of integrity, or you don't like yourself much, and the audience doesn't like you either."

Audiences did like songs such as "Our Private World" from *On the Twentieth Century*. The lyrics displayed Comden and Green's stylish wit:

> Our private world
> Is like a play
> About a pair of lovers—
> The plot says only we may enter,
> And only we may share the light of love . . . stage
> Center

The public also loved "The Party's Over," from *Bells Are Ringing*. Were they aware that it would become such a hit song?

"We were amazed," says Comden. "It's funny. Whenever I say in Jule's presence that all the songs and words come out of a situation and character, Jule says, 'But we want to look for a hit song, too.' And he's right, and that's honest. He's got such a sure sense of this kind of thing that maybe he intuitively knew that 'Just in Time' was a big hit song. We couldn't be sure."

"Jule knows something," says Green. "He had six songs on the 'Hit Parade' in one week! We don't know how we get along with Jule. We seem to be in two different worlds, and yet it all matched. We laughed a lot, which we do quite often. We overcame all the barriers very quickly. We shared a sense of the absurd."

 Edmund Lyndeck, George Hearn,
Norman Large, and David Vosburgh
sing a number from *A Doll's Life*.

Lauren Bacall won a Best
Actress Tony for her
charismatic portrait of aging
actress Margo Channing in the
1970 musical *Applause*.

Pop hit or not, a show's opening song often requires special attention from the writers, and Comden and Green's genius glows there too. They are particularly proud of "Christopher Street" in *Wonderful Town*, "although we had terrible troubles at first," says Comden. There was a song called 'Self-Expression' in that spot, then another called 'Life in the Village.' The opener was hard to come by."

Like Styne, Comden and Green recognize how crucial casting is. "It's always a big decision. We've probably made some mistakes, choosing a singer over an actor or vice versa. Or," chuckles Betty, "getting somebody who has a little of all qualities and isn't outstanding in any of them."

Critics and audiences alike found Lauren Bacall an outstanding choice for *Applause*, which Comden and Green helped bring to the stage in 1970. "Charles Strouse and Lee Adams wrote a lot of songs before we came in to do the book," Betty says. "They needed an editorial sense—what would work and what wouldn't."

Applause was a musical adaptation of the multi-Academy-Award-winning film *All About Eve*. Lauren Bacall won a Best Actress Tony for her charismatic portrait of aging actress Margo Channing, threatened by Eve, a younger rival. Comden and Green's libretto retained the original characters played by Bette Davis, Gary Merrill, Celeste Holm, and Hugh Marlowe in the 1950 hit, but eliminated Addison De Witt, the acid-tongued critic played to Oscar-winning perfection by George Sanders.

"We didn't have the movie rights, for one thing," Green points out, "so we had to make things up. We were rather glad to. We felt the critic was a wonderful concept in the picture, but he was a rather fanciful figure. We didn't know that his equivalent actually existed. And we knew Lauren Bacall very well, so one of the first things we tried to do was to make it all about *Margo*, to try to make the character and Bacall's character merge."

Applause was a star vehicle. Sometimes, though, even in a star vehicle, a secondary player shines strongly.

"It happened to us in *On the Twentieth Century*, with Kevin Kline. He was so brilliant," says Green.

They didn't change the basic slant of the plot for Kline. "We couldn't. The necessities of the story were such that we couldn't build him up," says Comden. "I think Hal, knowing Kevin's acrobatic flair, used it, and put it wherever he could. Kevin had a wonderful sense of acrobatic nonsense, and when Hal recognized how valuable it could be to the show, he utilized it, built it up."

As a result of Prince's inventiveness, and the lyric genius of Comden and Green, Kline won a Tony as Best Featured Actor in a musical.

When they reflect on their favorite shows, both agree that *Guys and Dolls* is brilliant. "Cole Porter was marvelous; Steve Sondheim is today. Actually," Comden says, recalling an important vignette from her past, "I wish we had written *My Fair Lady*. Leonard Bernstein, Adolph, and I were offered it. We went to see *Pygmalion*, and it was such a superb film—definitive—that we left the theatre drenched in tears. We didn't want to go near the property."

In the case of *My Fair Lady*, Comden and Green were brought in to consider an existing project. "We usually create our own," says Green. "Rarely has a producer come to us and said, 'Here's a project; do it.' *Applause* was something Larry Kasha brought us into. *Peter Pan* we were called in on, and we worked on that with Julie. Most of the other things started with us."

They've considered creating a record album first—with Cy Coleman—the way Webber and Rice did on *Jesus Christ Superstar* and *Evita*. Their minds are open to new approaches, as evidenced by Comden's response when asked if there should be a certain ratio of production numbers to ballads in a production.

"Isn't that kind of an outdated concept for shows today—that you have to lay out the story the way it should be told and then, if there are moments when you all sing and dance and explode, you'll have what's known as a 'production number'? The numbers come out of plot need, whatever kind they are. It is true, though, when you lay it out, that you don't want to have a solo followed by another solo. You do have to think in those terms somewhat, that there's variety and pacing and different combinations of characters doing things."

This type of knowledge and skill accounts for the two Oscar nominations, eight Tony nominations, and six Grammy nominations Comden and Green have earned. More significantly, it accounts for the respect accorded them by their peers and public. Their artistic aim also illustrates why the body of their work is so enduring and enjoyable.

"We write with humor about basically serious things," summarizes Comden. "We like to think we're expressing something of ourselves, something of what we feel is important in the world today. At the same time, we try to help audiences feel the way they should when they leave the theatre— that is, glad to be alive. That windows have been opened, fresh air has been let in, and they're leaving as happy people."

CHAPTER SEVEN

GRETCHEN CRYER

I DON'T MIND BEING CALLED A FEMINIST," says Gretchen Cryer, lyricist and librettist for the much-admired Off-Broadway musical, *I'm Getting My Act Together and Taking It on the Road*. "I am a feminist, but I'm also a humanist, and I consider feminism as part of a general humanistic thing. As soon as you get pigeonholed as a feminist you can sort of be dismissed. And it's not the type of thing people want to go and see, a 'feminist' musical. So, in a way, being called a feminist *can* limit you. That's what I think women writers are up against."

Talking to Cryer in her spacious West End Avenue apartment in Manhattan, it's easy to see that her concerns are for all people, for their ability to maintain fulfilling relationships. A speech in *I'm Getting My Act Together* eloquently states her questions about male-female conflict:

> I'm standing here on my thirty-ninth birthday, wondering if it is at all possible for men and women to have decent constructive relationships with each other when our culture and our past so conspire against it—when we can hardly pick our way through the myths and distortions of what we are. Our very definitions of love depend upon the extent to which we "feel like a man," or "feel like a woman" and the extent to which we feel like a man or woman depends upon our culture's stereotypes of what it is to be a man or woman.

Cryer's feelings are understandable, given a Broadway environment in which commentators consistently (and in wide-eyed fashion) refer to her partnership with Nancy Ford as "the *only* female lyricist-composer team that has ever written for the Broadway stage." More importantly, Cryer and Ford have brought a vital, fresh, and innovative voice to musicals, at a time when the musical theatre desperately needs it.

Gretchen Cryer was born on October 17, 1935, "forty miles east of Indianapolis in a little town called Dunreith. It's got a population of two hundred people, and I lived outside the town. I was really brought up in the country, and we are talking about rawboned, rednecked country."

The theatre bug hit Cryer when she was a child in Indiana. "When I was very young, five years old, we lived so far out in the country that there were no other kids around. During the long winters I'd write plays for my brother and me to do. I hadn't seen any plays. I didn't really know what plays were, but I would rig up a curtain in our house, and we would perform."

When Cryer was eighteen, she met Nancy Ford at DePauw University.

"She was a music major from Kalamazoo, Michigan. I was majoring in English literature, and I took a few music courses."

The combination of Cryer's literature background and Ford's music background proved to be a good one. The pair decided to write a musical.

"Nancy and I sat down and made a list of what qualities a good musical should have. We thought it should have color and some exotic appeal. We made a checklist, and then we concocted a story that would encompass all these qualities. Our first show, *For Reasons of Royalty*, was about a princess from a Far Eastern country that had gone under economically. This girl had been sent as an emissary to the United States to learn secretly about technology. She found herself in the Northwest, masquerading as a male lumberjack. And she falls in love with another lumberjack. It was the most absurd thing. It had nothing to do with anything that I particularly felt anything about."

Her second musical was written about the slums of New York. "This is back in Indiana, when we were nineteen! Neither of us had ever been to a slum or to a city larger than Indianapolis at the time.

"Then I went to graduate school at Harvard, and Nancy and I wrote another show. This show was a very romantic story about love between a college professor and a student, so we were dealing more with what we knew at that point. That show was put on at Boston University."

Cryer married the director of the play, David Cryer, soon afterward.

"David and I married in Indiana, the day he graduated from college. We walked straight from the graduation ceremonies into the church and got married. Then he went to divinity school, and Nancy married a man who was also going to Yale's Berkeley Divinity School. So we all went to Yale together. We lived in the same married dormitory. Nancy and I kept writing at night.

We had secretarial jobs during the day at the same chemical corporation and worked right down the hall from each other. As a matter of fact, Nancy got me the job because she was a crack secretary."

The road from secretary to Broadway composer was a rough one, especially since Cryer has never had any formal training. "I studied English literature, but I have never had any courses in playwriting. I never had any courses in the theatre. My husband went to drama school, but I never did. I felt a little intimidated when I came to New York at age twenty-six because of this lack of training. But I had performed as a chorus girl in summer stock since I was eighteen, and that was really the best training of all. We did every musical that was great from the thirties, forties, and fifties. It was the best background I could have had—I got to know intimately the structure of every musical play. Every summer I did stock, so by the end of five or six years I had covered just about every musical of importance and had done several of them a lot of times. They were in my bones."

She was fortunate that her family remained supportive. "They encouraged me. They had never had anything to do with the theatre, though. I think I was a distant cousin of Cornelia Otis Skinner. I was told that when I was a child, and I know I'm somehow related to David Niven—distantly. He's a cousin of my grandfather. But that's the only connection I was ever told of as a child. Now, maybe having been told that—that I was a distant relative of these people—I got stars in my eyes."

Cryer and Ford decided they had to come to New York if they intended taking the theatre seriously.

After arriving in New York, the team tackled a serious musical entitled *Now Is the Time for All Good Men* in 1967. Cryer's husband David and a man named Albert Poland produced it, because "we had taken it around to about fifty people, and nobody wanted to do it. Doing it ourselves was a last resort."

Now Is the Time for All Good Men, which opened off Broadway September 26, 1967, dealt with Cryer's brother and the struggles he faced as a conscientious objector. "The show is about a conscientious objector—my brother, actually—who returns to teach in his small hometown in Indiana. It's very close to the bone, because when my brother was a pacifist in the early sixties, he was completely ostracized in our little hometown, even though he had been a star student in high school. First he was a draft resister; then he joined the war resisters' league here in New York. He was one of the first people to go swimming out and lay his body across the bow of nuclear submarines. You know, direct action—direct passive resistance."

What sort of music did Ford write for *Now Is the Time for All Good Men*?

"I would say it was very much in the Rodgers and Hammerstein vein, as were the musicals we wrote in college. Even though the show had a very gritty story, it had a very romantic score."

"The show ran for four months Off Broadway. It had a following, I suppose you could say a cult following, among pacifists. That big pacifist audience kept it running for that length of time. We had not gotten good reviews. That's when I first became immunized against the New York press. I still thought the production was good. I was in it; my husband was in it also. We had to go out there and show our faces nightly; but even after the bad notices, people continued to come anyway."

Their next show, *The Last Sweet Days of Isaac*, opened Off Broadway in 1970 and had a happier run.

"It was a big critical success," says Cryer. "Across-the-board raves, the kind we will never get again in our lifetimes. It was just amazing. And yet it only ran a year and a half, which is strange. It won every award possible Off Broadway—the Obie and Drama Desk awards and Outer Circle. But in spite of the incredible critical acclaim, it encountered bad times because there was an actor's strike and a newspaper strike. It started out with the newspaper strike, so we couldn't advertise the show."

What was the story about?

"It's about a character called Isaac who considers himself a life poet. He feels he must capture every moment of life and record it, because his life is his art. In the play, he's stuck in an elevator with his secretary, and during the course of the hour that they're together he tries to teach her the meaning of life and how to live most fully. A child of technology, he's constantly trying to record himself with his tape machine and camera equipment. His problem is that, once he starts recording his life, he stops living it. That's the dilemma that the show talks about in the age of technology—that we lose the direct, one-to-one relationship because we're so engrossed in dealing with the images, the voice on the answering machine, the image of the television. So it becomes a culture that relates to images rather than to the thing itself."

Nancy Ford wrote baroque rock for *Isaac*, leaving her Rodgers and Hammerstein tradition behind. "Not that she wouldn't use Rodgers and Hammerstein if it was fitting. For example, the show we've currently written about Eleanor Roosevelt uses all the music from the twenties, thirties, and forties, so it sounds much more in that old bag again. Nancy can use that when she wants to, but the style we wrote in 1970 for *Isaac* had a strongly contemporary feel."

Whatever the approach, they are in complete agreement. When Cryer and Ford work together, Cryer always does the book and lyrics first and decides where the songs will be constructed within the play.

"I write the piece. I may talk to Nancy about what it's going to be about, but often I don't even tell her too much about it."

Ford does agree up front about the subject matter, however.

"After that initial decision, I usually write a whole chunk. With *The Last Sweet Days of Isaac*, I handed her the whole first act, including lyrics—everything. Now this is not to say that what I come up with is engraved in stone. It's not. This is the starting point. Then she takes it and quite separately gets the feel of what she's doing, decides on how she wants to treat the thing as a whole, and starts working on it piece by piece.

"When Nancy finishes a song, we get together and discuss whether I need to alter the lyrics, which I do if it has to go in a slightly different direction. It's interesting. I know a lot of people who sit in the same room and write together. Kander and Ebb, for example; Comden and Green. Nancy and I never sit and write together—it's quite separate. But the amazing thing is that we're *always* on the same wavelength. Well, we've known each other since we were eighteen years old, and we've been writing together since that time."

In describing their ability to operate on one wavelength, Cryer says, "To facilitate my own writing of the lyrics, I do have rhythms, a meter, a musical idea in mind, which I may not necessarily tell Nancy about at all. And incredibly enough, often Nancy comes up with exactly what I was thinking in my mind, as to feel and meter, but it's always much better than I could have done myself."

Unfortunately, inspired teamwork doesn't always pay off. People didn't flock to Cryer and Ford's first Broadway venture, *Shelter*.

"That was in 1973. I think it should have been Off Broadway, because it was a small chamber musical, four characters and a computer. It's about a man who lives in a television studio. He writes commercials and lives on the set where they film the commercials—that is, the living room they use for the commercials, the bathroom, the kitchen, and so forth. It's about self-delusion. He has created an entire life for himself, manufactured his own life along with his best friend, a computer named Arthur.

"This was in 1973, before people had personal computers that could talk back to them. Actually, it was written in 1970, but we didn't get it on until three years later. But the main character's best friend was his computer, and he wrote commercials with the computer's help. He programmed Arthur to write jingles on any subject. The computer also provided the entire sound environment for this guy and could also control sunrise, sunset, the stars at night. In other words, *Shelter* was about a completely fabricated existence, which this man had come to live in as though it were real. It was also about his relationship with an actress who has come in to do a commercial after closing time at five o'clock. She stays there in his studio with him and gets pulled into the whole fabricated world, and she starts acting as if it's real too. When they open the doors of the set to go in, they start treating this as though it's a real house, and it becomes their reality, a separate reality, and they fall in love. So *Shelter* is, in a way, an extension of the idea we started on in *The Last Sweet Days of Isaac*, having to do with the image and the difficult line between the image and the thing itself."

"I was very disappointed with *Shelter*, because I think the show ended up getting far out of hand from what the original intentions had been. It got pleasant reviews, but what I ended up seeing on the stage of the Golden Theatre bore no relationship whatsoever to what I thought I had written.

"It's nobody's fault," she points out. "It slipped out of shape. All of us were at fault. *Shelter* should have been an Off-Broadway show. It shouldn't have been trying to fill a large theatre. We had to have a massive set to fill the theatre, and massive effects, and it got completely out of hand."

I'm Getting My Act Together and Taking It on the Road was Cryer's next production, and she considers it her most personal work.

"That didn't happen until 1978. These earlier shows all had very strong personal roots because I have very strong feelings about what technology and the contemporary human condition does to us as human beings, to our biological nature. But the most directly autobiographical stuff was in *I'm Getting My Act Together.*"

Especially because the show was a deeply personal undertaking, she loves the whole experience of having written and performed in *I'm Getting My Act Together.*

"Often writers don't get to savor the effects of their work, so I had the remarkable experience of being able, night after night, to feel the responses, get the feedback. In writing the thing, I felt I had put out something of myself, and I had the marvelous exhilaration of getting back, of having the circle completed night after night."

She elaborates on how the story came about. "For about five years, I wanted to write about the transition that women had gone through, having ideas about the relationships of men and women that were formed in the fifties, having gotten married in the late fifties, with certain expectations, and then having gone through the sixties and seventies. I felt that the role, all those things that women were supposed to be in relation to men, just weren't me at all."

Discovery began when Cryer read Simone De Beauvoir's *The Second Sex* in college. "The book truly gripped me because I thought it was absolutely true, what she was saying. I suppose the feminist leanings I have may have started at age nineteen, when I read it. Nevertheless, I was so powerfully a child of my culture at that time, the midwestern culture, that I thought the main thing I had to do in life was get attached to a man and become his helpmate and fit into his life. That is not an unworthy thought at all, but the ideal was to hook yourself up to a man who had a strong purpose, a strong goal in life. Well, I gravitated toward a man who was going to be a minister, you see. We were going to go on our godly mission together. I was going to be a schoolteacher, and I'd be supportive of him in his ministry. I really didn't think about what I wanted to do with my life, other than 'Well, I'll be a teacher,' because I thought being a teacher would fit in with being a minister's wife. I didn't think, 'What do I want to do in life? What kind of

Cryer's partnership with Nancy Ford has been referred to as "the *only* female lyricist-composer team that has ever written for the Broadway stage."

Lee Grayson (*left*) and Dean Swenson (*right*) join Cryer in another scene from *I'm Getting My Act Together*.

The idea for *I'm Getting My Act Together and Taking It on the Road* occurred to Cryer one night while she was performing. She wanted to write a show about "a woman who's getting her new act together, her new act being songs about the way she really is now, as opposed to what's expected of her." Here, in a scene from the show, Cryer sings her lyrics with help from fellow cast members Margot Rose *(left)* and Betty Aberlin *(right)*.

contribution do I want to make?' My contribution was going to be made through my husband. I'm not saying that this is a terrible thing or that women who do it are losing out. I just came to think differently about myself in later years.

"Also, that meant deferring to what the husband wanted to do. Not that my husband required that I defer to him at all. This was not something imposed on me; it's something I chose to do, having come out of the background I did. It was a kind of a cop-out. I didn't have to be responsible for my own life or my own destiny because I was hanging on to his coattails.

"Then I had two kids, and we were just starting out in New York. David was giving up his ministry and going into the theatre. I found the definition of myself was more and more one of being wife and mother. I was still writing, and I was still going out and working as a chorus girl in Broadway musicals at night and bringing in a salary. Still, I felt my main definition was as wife and mother. Basically, I was still deferring to David.

"Then my marriage came to an end. It just kind of played out its whole cycle, and I wasn't being truly myself during that whole marriage. I was still putting on a front of going out and working and doing all this stuff, but again not taking responsibility for my own existence. Therefore, I was not being real in the relationship, so the relationship could not survive. The break-up wasn't his fault. It was our lack of communication.

"That happened," recalls Cryer, "when I was thirty-three years old. After having left that relationship, I had to decide, 'Well, who am I now that I don't have a husband?' and that's a whole reevaluation and a whole rediscovery. I decided, on purpose, not to attach myself to anybody for a long time, at first out of fear that I'd do the same thing again. So, having gone through that personal odyssey, I wanted to write about what happens when the ground rules are knocked out from under you that way. That's what *I'm Getting My Act Together* is about.

"At first I was going to write a sort of conventional story about it. I didn't have any theatrical metaphor to put this story into, and then Nancy and I were writing cabaret songs for the two of us to sing, and we made a couple of albums for RCA. Right in the middle of performing one night, I suddenly thought, 'I'm getting my act together and taking it on the road.' It just came to me, because we had been getting our act together in the cabaret. But our act—all these songs we had been writing—were very personal songs about our personal loves. Suddenly, I thought that would be a wonderful metaphor for a show. I'd make it about a woman who's getting her new act together, her new act being songs about the way she really is now, as opposed to what's expected of her, her old act, which was a bunch of songs about the way people expected her to be."

Cryer mentions some specific examples from *I'm Getting My Act Together* to illustrate.

"One of the songs is called 'Smile,' and that's about the old. It says:

> I was Daddy's smiling girl
> I always tried to please
> I could make him happy
> And put him at his ease
> I would smile for Daddy
> And sing a little song
> And Daddy would take care of me
> That's how we got along

"That sets up how it used to be in her relationship with men. Then later in the song:

> Now I was Tommy's smiling girl
> I always tried to please
> I could make him happy
> And put him at his ease
> I would smile for Tommy
> And sing a little song
> And Tommy would take care of me
> That's how we got along

"So that song chronicled how she used to be, and it encompassed some sketches and stuff of her roots—of those feelings about what it was like to be a woman. One of the new songs, '(I've Been) Put in a Package and Sold,' was about a cabaret singer who had been packaged as a sex object. There's one called '(I Have Been A) Lonely Lady,' when the character realizes she has always been really alone and would have to decide things for herself. But that one starts on a more personal basis:

> I have been a lonely lady all my life
> And to tell the truth I'm scared of finding home
> I remember Mama crying in the night
> And making desperate calls on the phone

"So that is about having experienced an unhappy home life, which was not a good role model for a marriage."

Cryer's chronicle of a woman's emotional evolution is remarkable in a theatre scene where few, if any, musicals are written by women.

"That subject has come up for about ten years now at the Dramatists

Guild. We started a committee based on the obvious need. At that time, when we started this committee, the number of women getting produced in the theatre was *so* far behind men it was just absurd. I think it's for several reasons. First of all, there haven't been any role models in the past, until just recently. We're starting to get the Carol Halls, the Marsha Normans. Mary Rodgers was one of the few role models back fifteen, twenty years ago. So the image was that it was a man's world. When you think of songwriters, you think of men.

"Another problem, I think, is that if women write from the heart and write their true experiences, they may be writing about things that are not thought of as commercially appealing. I think we're still coming, basically, from a macho sensibility in our culture, as to what is valued. I mean, the action story, the adventure story about the guy who goes across the Himalayas and does a drug deal and smuggles it back across the line—most women do not have that experience. It's not grounded in their being. Their sense of themselves doesn't have to do with smuggling drugs or high adventure or being a test pilot. Now there are a few women who have been test pilots, but not many playwrights have as their personal vocabulary that kind of experience."

What about shows like *Mame* and *Hello, Dolly!*, which were built around women?

"I don't consider those women's shows at all. Those are shows written by men with a certain view of women. On a gut level, I didn't find any of them particularly having anything to do with my experience as a woman. They're about a lady; but they are seen from outside the experience, and they don't have authenticity. All right, let's take an obvious person who was a created image. Marilyn Monroe was a created figment of a man's imagination. Inside, there was an authentic person, but her image, the person we all saw and knew Marilyn Monroe to be on the screen, was created."

Cryer and Ford's next musical sets aside the traditional image of two historical characters.

"Now the Eleanor Roosevelt show, which is our next project, has a cast of twenty or twenty-five. It's going to have to be done on Broadway, and we're having a lot of trouble. First of all, it's not a conventional treatment of Eleanor Roosevelt. It's not putting Eleanor and Franklin up on pedestals and treating them as heroes. That's a problem.

"But it's true," insists Cryer. "It's true to who they really were. It's not tearing them down in any way. I think you ultimately come out with a greater understanding of them at the end. But the show is trying to get to the real people under there and what was actually going on.

"I love the frame the show is in, because I've taken it out of being just a linear historical show. It's about a hundredth birthday party thrown for Eleanor Roosevelt by her cousin Alice Roosevelt, long after they're all dead.

Alice, who loved to stir things up, has invited all the friends and enemies of Eleanor to this bash. Alice always had kind of a jaundiced view of Eleanor. She thought Eleanor was this goody-goody, too good to be true, a boring person; and Eleanor always thought Alice was frivolous. So we put them in a room together and let the chips fall where they may. It's as though they were all alive today—Franklin's at the party too—in a room at a party. What would happen? It's a settling of the scores. It deals with the history of these people, but in a contemporary fantasy."

Cryer's treatment sounds fascinating and innovative, one that might logically appeal to today's critics, who want original approaches to ideas. Does she feel that her offbeat treatment will intrigue reviewers?

"When you talk about reviewers, you're really only talking about Frank Rich of the *New York Times*, and we have to ask what Frank Rich is looking for today. In musicals, we know he likes *Sunday in the Park with George*. That is where he thinks the musical theatre ought to go. So anybody who's not writing that kind of musical has to be wary, of course. I don't know what to say. He has a rather narrow view of what musical theatre can and ought to be, and I think we all have to make contingency plans for our work if Frank Rich is going to give us a bad review."

What are some of those contingency plans?

"*I'm Getting My Act Together* became the success it was specifically because we were in a situation where we could beat the critics. It was produced by Joe Papp at the Public Theatre. He was going to run our show for six weeks after it opened to the critics, no matter what. The critics did come and slashed us across the board. We didn't get one major good review in New York. We got good reviews outlying, in Long Island papers, but not one in the city. Joe believed in the show and thought there was an audience for it, and the audience we had been getting had been incredible—people kept coming back time and time again. So, Joe thought, we'll make a run for it. By the end of the six weeks, we were starting to fill the house, so he extended us another six weeks. We were starting to sell out. Another six weeks. Finally he decided to move us to the Circle in the Square, where we ran for three years. Now that is only possible because Joe was a fighter and had the setup. He gave us a chance to find our audience. Most people don't have that luxury, and I've had it only that one time.

"This show we just opened, *Hang On to the Good Times*, was at the Manhattan Theatre Club. We were getting very good audience response toward the end, before we opened to the critics. Then they didn't like it, so we closed the following Sunday—just like that. But the point is, in a Broadway show it becomes difficult because there's such a big financial outlay there. Off Broadway, it's simpler to keep something running."

The theatre, as Cryer sees it, is in the middle of a boom-or-bust mentality. You have either a giant hit or a bomb—there's no room for a moderate success. *Cats* was sold out for six months before it ever opened here. It didn't get great reviews, so there are ways to do it, but you have to have the big money behind you."

Right now Cryer and Ford have the Old Globe Theatre in San Diego behind their version of Eleanor Roosevelt's life.

"Jack O'Brien produces the Old Globe, and he's also a director, and he loves the show. The Old Globe has a fantastic technical facility and a very good theatre, and it will cost only four hundred fifty thousand dollars to do it out there. It'll cost four-and-a-half million on Broadway. Before anyone will put that kind of money out, they have to see a production or a star director like Mike Nichols, or somebody in that league, to warrant the investment. So I think we'll go out of town and really work on the show before we bring it in."

Cryer is a perfectionist, and she feels several things should be present in a show that is constructed well enough for Broadway or anywhere else.

"I sometimes admire shows for their construction, for their technical facilities, because they touch me. Any number of things can touch me in a show. I can go to *42nd Street* and be touched by the incredible boldness of it, even though there's nothing to touch the heart particularly. But the bravado of it, the color and dash, are impressive. I'm not a person who necessarily goes for fluff, but I can be touched by something that is done very, very well. I must say I was enraged by *Cats* because I thought it was incredible sound and fury signifying nothing, based on the merest filament of an idea. I immediately thought, 'Well, we should go out and write a show about chandeliers called *Chandeliers*, and have it about old chandeliers and old warehouses and other chandeliers and everybody dressed up as a chandelier, and sing songs about lighting up.' *Cats*, to me, seems like just taking the mere slip of an idea and putting millions of dollars into the icing when there's no cake there at all. Now I must say it was done fantastically, the physical production, but that is one of the cases where I was not touched or moved by it because I was so enraged by how top-heavy it had gotten."

Cryer thinks the theatre offers something special that other media don't, when it's at its best.

"When it's real and true, when it hits you in the gut, theatre can be a transforming experience. And I think ultimately good theatre can transform people's lives because it can allow them real insight into the human condition. That's why I love live theatre.

"What I want to communicate," says Cryer with intensity, "is the power of the individual to transform himself or herself, so audiences feel it—that people can change and grow and are not necessarily tied into old patterns, bound by old behavior. It's what Eleanor Roosevelt was about—possessing the power to transform your own life."

CHAPTER EIGHT

HAL DAVID

WITHIN THE BROADWAY COMMUNITY, a general attitude prevails that pop writers are ill equipped to write for the theatre. There may have been some justification for this feeling in the past. Many pop writers tend to think in terms of hits, not stories, and don't conceive their material with an eye to character.

One of the first people from the modern pop world to contradict this premise successfully was Hal David, lyricist for *Promises, Promises*.

David, now president of ASCAP, is a soft-spoken but energetic man in his early sixties. Despite his conservative appearance, accentuated by black suit and tie, he radiates the enthusiasm of a teenage rocker making his first impact on the record market.

"My secret," says David, looking out his office window toward Manhattan's Lincoln Center, "is just that I love writing songs, any kind of song."

This love of songwriting was born, in part, from lifelong observation of another talented lyricist, his older brother. Mack David wrote "A Dream Is a Wish Your Heart Makes" and six other Oscar-nominated songs.

"During my New York boyhood—I was born in Manhattan, raised in Brooklyn—Mack was there to learn from. Not only Mack, but a composer named Arthur Altman, who wrote 'All or Nothing at All.' And Jack Lawrence, who wrote 'Tenderly' and 'Linda.' The Brownsville area in Brooklyn spawned a lot of talented writers."

David's lean, conversational style was developed through exposure to other important role models. "My favorite writers all through the years have been—and remain today—Johnny Mercer and Irving Berlin. "Mercer had an ability to write from roots different from mine. He was southern; I was Brooklyn. And he created the most wonderful images. He wrote lyrics I wished I could write, but I knew I couldn't because I came from a different base. He was the most original writer to me. Berlin had the ability to put a song together and make it look so damn *simple*."

David shakes his head for emphasis. "Simplicity. You know by writing how hard it is to be simple. It's so easy to be complex. Berlin took the most complex things and turned them into songs, and they just seemed to write themselves."

David became a songwriting superstar when he teamed up with Burt Bacharach and wrote for Dionne Warwick a series of legendary love songs, such as "Walk On By," "I Say a Little Prayer," and "Message to Michael." But he started writing long before the team broke through in 1964.

"I began writing lyrics prior to World War II," says Hal. "I *always* wrote, but before the war I worked as a copywriter for the *New York Post*, for an organization called Publisher's Service."

Copywriting offered great training for a budding lyricist, but "I was also writing songs at the same time, trying to get them placed. I wasn't having much success, but I knew I liked it. I was in the Army, finally, in special services in Hawaii. For close to three years I did entertainment shows.

"There was a composer there, a man named Roger Adams. We wrote sketches, whatever they wanted. The head of our outfit was Maurice Evans, the actor."

Although David did not get to Broadway until 1968, he was already polishing his theatrical craft while serving Uncle Sam. "RCA Victor recorded the score for one of my army shows, *Jumping Jupiter*."

David's next step, with army partner Roger Adams, was to create nightclub material in the mid-1940s.

"I covered it all," says David. "For records I did a thing called 'Horizontal,' which was cut by a man named Pat Flowers at RCA. And I wrote lyrics to foreign melodies. I really supported myself by being on the back side of some big hits. I was on the back of 'Ghost Riders in the Sky,' the Vaughn Monroe record."

What was his first big hit?

" 'The Four Winds and the Seven Seas,' in 1949. Don Rodney was the vocalist and guitar player for Guy Lombardo. I wrote it with him."

The David-Rodney combination continued, with so-so results. Other collaborators of the 1950s included Leon Carr, Sherman Edwards, and Lee Pockriss. Hits began coming: "American Beauty Rose" and "Bell Bottom Blues," a Number One smash internationally.

No steady partnership surfaced until the late 1950s, when David met Burt

Bacharach. Bacharach was working as a pianist and arranger but had never had a hit.

"I was pretty well established," says David. "And I worked a great deal in the Brill Building." He chuckles, recalling an improbable anecdote concerning his office there. "The Brill Building had these two bookies. I wasn't a horse player, but the building had these two bookies, and one of them used to use the piano in the piano room to hide his slips. So he'd walk in the room where I was writing and take his slips out."

The bookies didn't bother David or slow down his creativity. But the presence of Bacharach accelerated it.

"I was at Famous Music, and Burt also worked there. He was conducting and playing piano at that time for the Ames Brothers, Steve Lawrence, Vic Damone, and finally Marlene Dietrich. And he was writing songs."

No thought was given, at first, to establishing an exclusive partnership.

"Burt and I knew each other a little, and at that point everybody was writing with everybody else, trying to find a good song, a good combination, trying to get lucky. And one day we decided we ought to try a couple of songs together."

They did get lucky—as least mildly so—when their first song together was recorded by Alan Dale.

"Getting the record was somewhat of a victory, so we tried to do more, and included in the first four or five things we wrote was 'Magic Moments.' Perry Como recorded it for the other side of 'Catch a Falling Star'; that was a two-sided hit. A song called 'The Story of My Life' was cut by Marty Robbins and became a smash hit internationally too. All of a sudden we had two smashes at the same time, so we kept writing."

What was their method of working?

"Pretty much the way I work today with most people. On occasion I just think in lines, but most times the idea comes with a title. And often it occurs to me in two lines. I see things in hunks, rather than specific sentences. I'll think of an eight-bar phrase or a four-bar phrase—together.

"Whatever the song, though, and whatever the method I use to arrive at it, I like the material to have a sense of naturalness—to look as though it almost wrote itself. I like the feeling that a song happened spontaneously. It doesn't, of course—songwriting takes hard work—but I like it to feel that way."

Burt and I would meet every day at Famous Music. We now had one room; we didn't need two. We'd meet around eleven, twelve o'clock, and I was very hardworking, as he was. I was always writing lyrics; he was always writing melodies. The question asked repeatedly was 'What do you think of this? What do you think of that?' Either my lyric would set him off to write a melody or vice versa.

"One of the reasons we were so prolific," says David, "is that, even as we worked together on one song, he'd give me another melody or I'd give him another lyric, and very often we were writing three songs at a time—a song together, a song to his tune, a song to my lyric. So we had a number of things going. And we worked together every day, without fail!"

Their input was never hampered by rigid guidelines. "We both commented on each other's work. We were both willing to change things, and we had tremendous respect for each other's expertise. It was his melody, and if he really believed it was the better way, I'd defer to his judgment—or, in another case, he'd defer to mine. We were very helpful to each other."

The next stop, en route to Broadway, was Hollywood. They began to concentrate on movie songs in 1962.

"We were at Paramount—Famous Music is Paramount's music firm—so motion pictures surrounded us. Assignments came in, and there was very little money to be paid. They wanted a song for the movie *Wives and Lovers*, and I forget how much the pay was, but it was embarrassing. They couldn't get anybody of consequence to write it in California. The song wasn't meant to appear in the picture, only to come out as exploitation."

David and Bacharach didn't let the money stop them—they were astute enough to realize that getting in was the crucial thing.

"To us it was a step, a big deal," says David. "Same thing happened with *The Man Who Shot Liberty Valance*. 'Wives and Lovers' and 'Liberty Valance' became big hits because we took the assignments other people in California turned down."

An artist who had the talent to make David's lyrics sound spontaneous was Dionne Warwick, whom David and Bacharach discovered and nurtured in 1962.

"Originally, Dionne's family comprised a group called The Drinkard Singers. After they moved from gospel to R&B, they started working on sessions of the Drifters, Chuck Jackson, Ben E. King, The Coasters—all those great rhythm and blues groups. There was a Drifters session Dionne was working on, and we were there—we had a song on the date—and she came over and said, 'Could I do some demos for you?' We fell in love with her right away, and she started to do all our demos. Then she did one entitled 'Make It Easy on Yourself.' "

A confusion developed, however. Bacharach and David thought Dionne was doing demos, but she thought they were preparing to record her.

"When Jerry Butler cut 'Make It Easy on Yourself' and released it, Dionne was upset, and she protested, 'Hey, that's *my* song.' And we thought, 'OK, we'll try to get you a recording contract.' We took her to Scepter Records, made the deal, and her first record out was a hit in 1962, 'Don't Make Me Over.' "

David is quick to add that the road hasn't always been perfectly smooth. "Gene Pitney wasn't crazy about 'Liberty Valance.' Nor did he flip over 'Only Love Can Break a Heart' and 'True Love Never Runs Smooth.' "

David grins. "The story of my life. People turning down my songs. Fortunately, other people did them."

"Raindrops Keep Fallin' on My Head," which won a Best Song Oscar in 1969 after three previous Bacharach-David nominations, was rejected by a few artists, including Bob Dylan. B. J. Thomas was finally persuaded to do the record.

By the time "Raindrops" received Academy recognition, Bacharach and David had already been enjoying the Broadway success of *Promises, Promises* (which opened in December of 1968) for four months.

"We owe that to David Merrick. We were in demand, and he said, 'I want to do a show with you.' When he told us he had gotten the rights to Billy Wilder's Academy Award–winning movie, *The Apartment*—with Neil Simon prepared to do the adaptation—we were thrilled."

David was aware that prejudice against so-called pop writers existed in the theatre. "If anyone had a fear about it, though," he says, "no one expressed it to me."

Promises, Promises was, on the whole, a smooth experience. "Bob Fosse was the original director," David says, "and he did get to direct the song 'She Likes Basketball' and a few others. But he was offered a job directing *Sweet Charity* in Hollywood, and he didn't want to turn it down. So directorial hands changed."

Fosse's replacement was Robert Moore, who had directed *The Boys in the Band*.

"He was a book director," says David, "not a choreographer/director. He hired a young guy who we understood was very, very good, and we took him on. It was Michael Bennett. We hired him strictly on the strength of what people said. We didn't actually see anything he did, but our instinct told us to go ahead."

Their instincts, as later events proved, were correct. The show went into rehearsal, and the team began rewriting the score. "Some of the things that had seemed to work while we were writing at home in the living room didn't work choreographically," David explains.

He expresses unreserved admiration for Neil Simon's industry. "Neil—who *never* stops writing—wrote draft after draft after draft. We went to Boston and got marvelous reviews. We thought we had a successful show. We found a couple of areas that didn't work at all and revised all through Boston."

Promises, Promises opened on December 28, 1968, to critical raves. The Bacharach-David score drew applause for its innovative rhythms, modern sound, and witty lyrics. The show was cited Best Musical of the Year by *Life* magazine.

What about pop hits? Did the team consciously choose places for "step-out" songs, songs that had separate pop potential?

"Well, 'I'll Never Fall in Love Again' became a hit with Dionne, but it was

David became a songwriting superstar when he teamed up with Burt Bacharach and wrote for Dionne Warwick a series of legendary love songs, such as "Walk on By," "I Say a Little Prayer," and "Message to Michael."

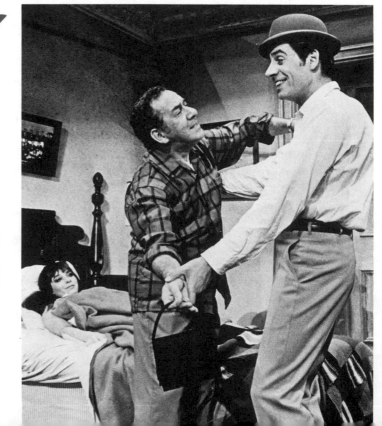

A scene from *Promises, Promises:* Jill O'Hara, A. Larry Haines, and Jerry Orbach perform "A Young Pretty Girl Like You."

written as a character song in the show. That was a song we put into a scene that was failing. It was a spot where four guys were performing, and it fell flat every time. Neil Simon suddenly realized that it wasn't just the song that didn't work; it was the *scene*. He saw that the scene should deal with the main character, who has been thrown over by her lover."

How was it finally staged?

"She's alone in her room, and we knew she played guitar, so it made sense to write something she could do with a guitar. A strange thing happened. Burt had pneumonia—he wasn't there—and I wrote lyric after lyric, three or four, and said finally, 'This is the one I like best.' And I used *pneumonia* and rhymed it with *phone ya*."

David Merrick emphasized the importance of writing a song called "Promises, Promises."

" 'Promises, Promises' was a very complicated song, but it was a hit, again with Dionne. I think a character song can also become a hit. Look at *The King and I* and all those marvelous Rodgers and Hammerstein shows. They had character songs dealing with the story, yet they became hits. Berlin wrote lots of hits for *Annie Get Your Gun*."

Having created the hit they had set out to write, David expected to pursue the theatre. But Bacharach felt otherwise.

"Burt lost his feeling for writing shows at that point. His experience was different from what he had expected it to be. He came out of a record background, and every time you play a record back it comes out the same. It doesn't change. But if you do a show, the tempo can be too fast, too slow; the singers or actors can change lines or notes. The audience doesn't know these things, but you do. And if you're a perfectionist, and of a mind to let it drive you crazy, you don't enjoy it. So Burt didn't want to do another one."

David, however, had been bitten by the Broadway bug, and he wrote a musical with Michel Legrand. The show, entitled *Brainchild*, opened March 25, 1974, in Philadelphia, and closed there April 6, without traveling to Broadway. Directed and written by Maxine Klein, it attempted to delineate the workings of a woman's psyche by having three different actresses play the various aspects of her personality—*Adrienne's Self Image*, *Adrienne's Emotional Self*, and *Adrienne's Mental Self*. Lena Horne recorded with composer Legrand some of the material from the production, including "Let Me Be Your Mirror," "Everything That Happens to You Happens to Me," and "I've Been Starting Tomorrow All of My Life."

"A show we both loved," says Hal, "but it fell apart in Philadelphia. I asked the producer to be kind enough not to bring it to New York, and she didn't.

"But," David adds, "*Brainchild* won't be my last musical. I have so much more to say, so much more writing to do. I intend to do another one—and soon. I can't wait to get started."

FRED EBB

"WHAT I LOVE MOST ABOUT SONG WRITING," says Fred Ebb, the talented lyric half of Broadway's much-admired Kander and Ebb team, "is when I overhear a truck driver humming a song of Johnny's and mine. I think there are a lot of guys writing for the theatre who write in an elitist way. They write to please a small group who come the first three months or the first three weeks. They're content to write that way, and I think everybody has to do his own thing. As for me, I always want to be popular, and I always want to be well liked. I love when people sing 'New York, New York,' " the song introduced by Liza Minnelli in the film of the same name and turned into a standard by Frank Sinatra.

The photographs on his piano of Fred with Liza Minnelli, Chita Rivera, Barbra Streisand, and Lauren Bacall show a few of the artists who have helped to make his work popular. The shows he has written with John Kander, his partner of twenty-one years include *Cabaret*, *Zorba*, *Woman of the Year*, *The Act*, *The Rink*, and *The Happy Time*.

"John and I have a very open sort of thing. We have enough confidence in the fact that I know he thinks I'm really good, and I think he's really good. We don't hurt each other's feelings and say, 'Ugh, that's awful; I really hate that.' We don't have that kind of problem. We've been working together for twenty-one years, you know."

It was a happy time for Ebb when he discovered and nurtured his passion for theatre as a child. New York, his birthplace, offered a perfect place to indulge this passion.

The ambition continued through four years at New York University. "Then I got my master's at Columbia University in English literature. I got out of college when I was only 18, because in those days they could accelerate you and I skipped grades a lot.

"Through it all, the theatre was exciting and fun and it was what I wanted to do with my money always. When I had fifty cents, or a dollar ten, it went to shows."

He preferred musicals to plays, although he remarks, with a twinkle in his eye, "I probably like plays more than musicals now. But anyway, I thought I'd like to be part of the theatre, and I had no idea how. My career grew in a very gradual way."

"I auditioned for an agent named David Hocker. And the way I auditioned was, I took well known properties like *Street Scene* and *Ah, Wilderness!* and wrote songs for those. David and his assistant Dick Seff called to say they'd represent me. And in the course of representing me, they suggested I write some material for Kay Ballard."

After that, Ebb wrote special material—specifically slanted comedy or satirical numbers to fit the images of the stars—for Carol Channing, Tommy Sands, and "literally anyone who asked me.

"In the early sixties, I wrote with a guy named Paul Klein," says Ebb. "Paul later opted for marriage and children and the waterproofing business. It was all too scary for him, the financial insecurity. I was ready to starve. But Paul and I did contribute sketches to a revue called *From A to Z*."

From A to Z opened April 10, 1960, and played for 21 performances. "Paul and I also did a book show, *Morning Sun*," Ebb recalls.

Morning Sun appeared October 6, 1963, at the Phoenix Theatre and was directed by Daniel Petrie.

"First I had Bob Fosse as director. I wrote the libretto and the lyrics, based on a 1960 story by a lady named Mary Deasy. The show led an enchanted life. Everyone we spoke to said yes, they'd do it. Fosse said yes. Our producer, Martin Tahse, said yes right away. Then Martin Tahse got into a fight with Fosse. I've never known the details. All I know is I lost Fosse at the end of it. Then Dan came in. I think Bobby might have given it the kind of flash it needed. Bobby wanted to do it like a ghost story, and he was right. It was eventually done Off Broadway, in a very tragic, very operetta-like style."

Ebb worked with another collaborator in the early sixties. "Phillip Springer," he says. "He composed 'How Little We Know,' 'Santa Baby,' and 'Moonlight Gambler.' "

Springer was impressed with Ebb, recognizing, as he puts it, "a beautiful lyric writing talent. I aggressively encouraged him." The team wrote a ballad entitled "Nevertheless I Never Lost the Blues," in the Cole Porter vein.

"Phil taught me everything I know: form, prosody—that is, putting the words to the music natually so the accent wouldn't be on the wrong syllable. AABA, as opposed to verse chorus. I never knew any of that. All I had was sort of an instinct, but no knowledge or technique. I did have an incredible memory for whatever people did—Larry Hart, Frank Loesser.

"Loesser! I wore the record of *Guys and Dolls* right down to the wire. It was the first time I'd ever done that. I just played it over and over. Not a day of my life went by when I didn't.

"Loesser had the best ideas for songs—the best titles, the best notions. 'On a Slow Boat to China'—great title. 'Baby, It's Cold Outside.' 'Measuring the Marigold.' Everything he chose to do he did superbly, I felt. I *loved The Most Happy Fella*. Larry Hart I enjoyed very much for his technique."

Ebb is a genuine admirer and fan of other people's work, a quality that keeps a writer fresh and growing.

"I dare say, I hardly ever go to a show where there's not a number I wish I had written," he admits. "I wish I wrote *Guys and Dolls*. I wish I wrote *The Most Happy Fella*, *The King and I*. I wish there was one moment in all of literature that was as perfect as the king putting his arm around Anna at the end of the show. I burst into tears. I think it's the most magnificent moment in musical theatre, because the audience clearly wants them to have a love affair that cannot be, and his mere touching her, his merely taking her arm, her waist, is the consummation of that romance, and it satisfies them. And they could have done that song eighty-five times.

"Tommy Valando put me together with John Kander in 1964," says Ebb. "John was writing with the Goldman Brothers at the time—Bill and Jim Goldman. John and the Goldmans did a show called *A Family Affair*."

A Family Affair opened January 27, 1962, and ran a modest 65 performances in New York, after out-of-town troubles in Philadelphia. But Kander and Ebb started off strongly with the hit song "My Coloring Book," recorded by Barbra Streisand.

Kander and Ebb's next step in 1964 was to write a musical called *Golden Gate*. "It was set right after the San Francisco earthquake in 1908 and was about this character who imagined himself to be the emperor of San Francisco. We wrote a complete score for it," Ebb says. "Then Hal Prince, who knew John socially, asked if he would audition for *Flora, the Red Menace*. There was no way for us to audition, given our meager output, so we played *Golden Gate*. It showed we could write for character and develop a story. Prince hired us. *Golden Gate* didn't get on, but it was invaluable because it helped us to get *Flora*."

Flora, the Red Menace, which opened on May 11, 1965, was a musical version of Lester Atwill's novel *Love Is Just Around the Corner*. The heroine, Flora, was a would-be fashion designer. In the story, she is persuaded by her boyfriend to join the Communist party, and conflict arises when she nearly loses him to a voluptuous comrade.

Liza Minnelli was not under consideration when Kander and Ebb signed to do the show.

"There was a girl in New York named Madge Cameron, who is now

Flora, The Red Menace (1965).
Pictured together around the piano
are producer Hal Prince, director
George Abbott, Liza Minnelli, her
co-star Bob Dishy, and lyricist Fred
Ebb.

Liza Minnelli,
in her first starring Broadway role,
sings in *Flora, The Red Menace.*

Carmen Zapata. She was performing with another girl, Liza Minnelli, out in Mineola at a carnival. Madge said, 'You've got to see Liza; she's wonderful,' and I had no interest in her, or a carnival, or anything about her. Madge was relentless. Liza had a contract to do an album, she said, and just on a professional basis, wouldn't it be a good idea for us to get a couple of songs on an album? I don't think we'd ever had that. Liza came over with Madge— *very* reluctantly—to meet us. We played her some songs, and she said, 'What are you writing now?' It was difficult and embarrassing for both of us. Neither of us wanted to be where we were.

"We told her we were writing this musical and played her some songs for *Flora, the Red Menace*. She suddenly became animated, jumped up, and said, 'Well, can I try singing that?' I felt more enthusiasm and joy with her. Then we asked her to come audition.

"We taught her a song from the show so she could audition and it would be clear she was our choice, 'A Quiet Thing.' And she came on.

"Mr. Abbott said loudly, as she walked across the stage, 'Well, *this* is a waste of time.' It carried that loudly in the theatre, and Liza heard it. She auditioned under those circumstances, and he did not take her. It was up to me to call her. Mr. Abbott wanted Eydie Gorme."

Eydie Gorme, it turned out, was "passionately disinterested. We couldn't get anybody else who was satisfactory, and Mr. Abbott went back to Florida. For a while it looked as if we weren't even going to have the play. Then we just kept at him. 'How about Liza? How about Liza?' We called Mr. Abbott with Hal Prince on the phone, and then Mr. Abbott relented and said, 'All right, take her. If you all like her, take her.' It was, in the end, as simple and as uncomplicated as that. He just took her on the telephone because Hal mentioned it again. It was extraordinary. I don't know what changed his mind. Desperation, maybe."

Fred recalls the backbreaking effort expended on creating *Flora*. "We wrote a lot for that show. Worked our asses off—twenty songs for one situation. I had no ego. It was 'Which do you like?' That sort of thing."

Despite the team's enthusiasm about Liza Minnelli, Kander and Ebb did not tailor songs in the show for her.

"We never changed a word. We added 'Sing Happy' in New Haven. The character just needed a statement at the end—she didn't have any.

"We were in Boston, and during the run of *Flora*—we were doing all right; we had gotten fairly decent reviews—Hal came over to the theatre and said, 'No matter what happens to this piece, would you guys like to do a musical version of *I Am a Camera*? I said, 'Fine.' The point was, who was going to give us a job? If he had asked us to musicalize *Command Decision*, whatever he said would have been terrific. The important thing was, someone believed in us, no matter what the outcome of this particular show was."

Liza scored a personal triumph in *Flora* both from Abbott, who grew to adore her, and from the Tony committee on Broadway, which voted her a Best Actress award.

Kander and Ebb turned their attentions to the musicalization of *I Am a Camera*, which became *Cabaret*.

Cabaret, which opened December 12, 1966, and ran 1,166 performances, centered on the Kit Kat Club in Berlin, and told the tale of singer Sally Bowles's romance with an English tutor. The production and score highlighted the decadent, immoral tone of pre-Nazi Germany, and the title tune, "Cabaret," became a popular favorite. The show won a Tony Award as Best Musical of 1967, and Kander and Ebb won for writing the best score of the season.

"We did the opening number first. We always do; it gives us a style. So 'Willkommen' came first. We don't work in order, though," says Ebb.

Everything turned out to be artistically satisfying about *Cabaret*, although Ebb laughs, when asked what his favorite song in the score was. "It was cut. In rehearsal Hal took it out. The trick is never to fall in love with what you write. I think if they had cut 'The Grass Is Always Greener' from *Woman of the Year*, I might have been hysterical. But other than that, I live with the cuts and rewrite."

Another song cut from *Cabaret* was "Roommates."

"It showed how Sally insinuated herself into Cliff's room. I thought it was OK. Hal never asked us to change it, but I thought, 'It's OK, but it should be peppier.' So we changed it to 'Perfectly Marvelous' and took 'Roommates' out."

Often a lyricist writes a song that transcends technique and has deep meaning to him.

" 'Maybe This Time' was very close to me," says Ebb. "There's a lot of writing that had to do with what other people told me, other people's experiences. That song, 'Maybe This Time,' told me a lot about Sally—how she always keeps trying. I related to that, and that's personal in a way. I can understand that deeply. But it was never about me.

"On the other hand, there's a song called 'See the Old Man' that I wrote on one of Liza's albums—it was about me when I turned 40, and it went:

> See the old man
> There in the distance
> See the old man
> Just look at him
> Now he's coming closer
> Now he's passing
> Did you see that he's smiling?
> Why would he smile at me?
> Oh, I won't ever get that way
> No, my love, I have you to keep me young as the years go by
> As the years go by

"That was—I felt that way," says Ebb.

Ebb feels that "What Would You Do?" is the most interesting song in *Cabaret*, thematically, "in terms of the dilemma and real emotion. But the song didn't land. I don't think I wrote it well enough. But I think I had a strong idea there. I wish I had it to do all over."

Reservations aside, *Cabaret* was a smash onstage with Jill Haworth, and it fared equally well on the screen. The 1972 screen version featured Kander and Ebb's protégé, Liza Minnelli. Minnelli won a Best Actress Oscar for her electrifying portrait of the divinely decadent Sally Bowles.

"I thought the movie was wonderful," Ebb says. "The choices by Bob Fosse were wonderful, very appropriate."

Ebb knew what was appropriate for *Cabaret*, onstage and on the screen, because he had carefully researched the subject matter.

"I listen to things of the period if I can find them. There was one time there that you might have thought I was a Nazi. I had all the gramophone records of the *Cabaret* period. I went and saw all movies and watched what was available to me.

"Some things are hard to research, though—French Canada, for example, which I needed for *The Happy Time*. I didn't know where to go for that. I suppose I could have gone to French Canada, but I didn't think that would do me much good."

The Happy Time, which opened January 18, 1968, and ran for 286 performances, followed the conflicts of a French Canadian family. It centered on a 14-year-old boy named Bibi, and his attempts to cope with adolescence, aided by an understanding grandfather and uncle. Robert Goulet was excellent as the uncle, and David Wayne had a show-stopping song called "Life of the Party."

In addition to problems associated with the research, *The Happy Time* encountered other tensions, notably those created by its producer, David Merrick.

"David came to see the show once, in California. He trusted his creative staff. He made a big thing about that. 'If I trust you,' he said, 'I don't have to come to see the show.' But when he did, he was real unhappy, and we had a lot of trouble. But he made the trouble with Gower Champion, not with us. He apparently had long running feuds with everyone. Gower even predicted, 'When we get to Los Angeles, at some point David will see it and threaten to close us at the Ahmanson unless we make certain changes. Don't worry about that. Just stay out of it. I'll take care of things.'

"About the third or fourth week at the Ahmanson, up comes David Merrick, and I get a call: 'I'm closing the show. Gower won't make the changes I want, and I'm closing the show unless you can influence him.' And I said, 'Gee, Mr. Merrick, I wouldn't know how to do that.' Of course, he didn't close the show. But Gower called it practically to the day."

Ebb wasn't nearly as happy with the 1981 revival of *Zorba*.

"It was more successful than the 1968 version," says Fred, "because of

The 1966 musical *Cabaret* revealed Ebb's innovative ability. Here he is pictured with Liza Minnelli, who starred in the film version.

Joel Grey and Fred Ebb backstage at *Cabaret*. The musical won a 1967 Tony for Best Musical.

Tony Quinn playing Zorba. But I preferred the earlier one."

The first *Zorba*, which musicalized Nikos Kazantzakis's novel, opened on November 17, 1968, and starred Herschel Bernardi. It ran 305 performances.

"The show was always too dark, too somber, too leaden. We got better reviews on the 1968 production than *Cabaret* did, strangely enough."

The 1981 revival benefited from the fact that Quinn had made *Zorba* his definitive characterization in the hit film *Zorba the Greek*. But Ebb was unhappy when pressured to change the song "Life Is" for the new version. "I compromised to keep the peace," he admits. "Joe Stein, the book writer, wanted me to change it. The director, Cacoyannis, wanted me to change it. Quinn didn't say anything, because he wasn't involved in the number."

Ebb does, however, have the courage to admit when a Kander and Ebb score falls below his expectations. This was the case with *70, Girls, 70*.

"Maybe a father loves his weakest child, but the show didn't work, I think because I didn't do it well enough. The score was pleasant, finally, clearly, audience-pleasing. But once I got started I had no idea how to beat the first twenty minutes—all that exposition. I did it very clumsily. I didn't have a director who could really help me. I had the best performers in the world, the best scenic designer. But to this day I don't know how to do those first twenty minutes. I wish I did, because I'm fond of the show. Beyond a certain point, I think, the show just rolls along and is really swell, but I don't know how to do that exposition."

Four years after the opening of *70, Girls, 70*, the 46th Street Theatre offered *Chicago*, the colorful tale of condemned murderess Roxie Hart who was rescued by legal manipulation. Gwen Verdon was Roxie, and Chita Rivera played another murderess, Velma. The satire was harshly entertaining, and *Chicago* ran 923 performances beyond its June 1, 1975, opening.

Ebb was stimulated by Bob Fosse's belief in his ability to co-write the libretto with Fosse for *Chicago*.

"He gave me the courage. When Bob Fosse says you can do it, you somehow feel you can. And it was my notion. The original play, *Chicago*, interested me. Then there was the screen adaptation, *Roxie Hart*, which was no good to anyone. It starred Ginger Rogers, but Bob never knew how to beat the material, how to make a musical out of it. And when we were working together, and we had *Cabaret* and an award-winning TV special *Liza with a Z*, we were close. Bob said, 'Can't you find any way to make this material musical? I think you could.' So I went home and made it vaudeville. I thought of all that stuff—that they were really performers. Everybody in the show was really somebody else: Roxie was Helen Morgan, Velma was Texas Guinan, Billy Flynn was Ted Lewis, Mama Morton was Sophie Tucker. You could draw those analogies, and that's how we made the musical. That's what I brought to Fosse, and that's what he liked, and that's what we did. And because he liked it so much, I thought, 'I can do this.' He gave me the courage."

Courage was a major theme in *The Act*, which opened on Broadway October 29, 1977, and ran for 233 performances. The musical concerned itself with a contemporary star seeking a comeback through nightclub performing. Out of town reviews made Kander and Ebb realize the dire necessity for rewrites.

"I couldn't begin to tell you all of them. That would be a book in itself. We made changes in desperation, to try to make it work. So you start the show with one idea, which was that one of the songs would relate to the plot. It would be literally a club act, going on at the time the heroine was reminiscing about her life. The audience kept looking for the connection. What was the link between her club act and these scenes? And that required, in fact, a whole different way of approaching the show. That's when you're in trouble, when you have to change ideas in midstream, or you really haven't been sure of what the concept is—good, bad, or indifferent.

"*The Act* was based loosely on the experiences of Shirley MacLaine, a lady with a strong screen career, who suddenly looks at her life and sees there's no work to be found.

"She says to herself, 'I'm going to get back into this arena. I'm going to get into a nightclub and go to Vegas,' and that's what Shirley did. That's how Shirley restarted her engine. *The Act* was really about success."

Success depends, to a large extent, on reviewers, but Fred remains baffled by them.

"I don't understand their attitudes. I've had shows they didn't like, and I really don't understand why. I've had shows that had critical approbation—*The Act* being one, which I thought was a rather sloppy exercise. *The Act* squeaked through on the basis of Liza's phenomenal energy. Some good numbers, but not until we got to New York. The reviews were terrible in California, worse in Chicago, hideous in San Francisco, and then, finally, good in New York. It was almost a reverse snobbery."

He continues on the subject of critics. "The theatre's in difficulty because it's all about reviews; it's about obscene amounts of money; it's about reviewers who say, 'Please take risks,' and yet the shows that do take risks don't have audiences. It's a catch twenty two. The critics are asking you to do something that doesn't seem possible, and they define what a risk is. I think it's unjust. I don't think your fate should be in the hands of one or two people, which is about what it is.

"The attitude seems to be, 'The public be damned.' The shows they're steering you to are boring. They're not popular, in that sense. Show music isn't being given any weight anymore. It's discouraging. You spend your whole life—the greater part of your adult life—learning how to do these things from masters before you, and now there are no rules."

One rule, to ensure box office, used to be the presence of a star. Ebb doesn't think a star is crucial these days.

"Look at the evidence you have against that: *Dreamgirls, La Cage aux Folles, Cats*. We don't have stars, so who is it going to be? There are some—Liza, Lauren Bacall—but very few. That sort of star vehicle is rare, because stars hardly exist."

Ebb's next show, *The Rink*, again featured Liza Minnelli, along with the dynamic Chita Rivera. It was a touching, powerful story of a mother who has sold the roller rink she owned, and must cope with the objections of her daughter who returns after fifteen years. Their conflicts were beautifully realized through such numbers as "The Apple Doesn't Fall," "Chief Cook and Bottle Washer," and the memorable "All the Children in a Row," in which Minnelli sings of her trip to the West Coast and her sad experiences during the sixties.

"*The Rink* was disappointing," Ebb says, "because the two stars were my best friends—Liza and Chita Rivera—and I'd worked longest on it of any show we'd ever written. We were on that show before *Woman of the Year*. Then we did *Woman* and came back to it. I did it for Chita because I love Chita—and then Liza came along and asked to be part of it. It suddenly became a terrific responsibility to come through for all these people."

Although Ebb defines *The Rink* as his greatest disappointment, he thinks partner Kander disagrees. "He really loved *The Rink*. I'm more susceptible than John to criticism and bad notices, and I can be talked out of my pride in a show by bad notices. I mean, I'm very vulnerable that way.

"I wouldn't know how to do *The Rink* better than I did. I can think of ways I might experiment, but then I'd be trying to please four men, not audiences that are standing up and cheering."

As for the workshop concept, which *The Rink* utilized, Ebb doesn't necessarily feel it's something to cheer about. "I don't like it. I'd rather travel with a show—go out of town and get reviews. I can't see that it helps a writer very much, because the audience you're inviting are friends. You're going to fill fifty, sixty seats with cast member friends, your friends, and I think they're apt to be quite tolerant."

"I think *Woman of the Year* was a mistake. We did it because it was Lauren Bacall and it was a good title. I didn't have any real conviction about it, which I should have had. I didn't have the fire, the passion. I don't want to work anymore without passion. Passion is the most important thing. You should love what you're doing."

Ebb does love his work, though Broadway is currently suffering from growing pains.

"A lot of my life is like the American dream," he says. "It's remarkable: you think where you come from and how few succeed. I'm blessed. I think I've had an extraordinary amount of luck too. To be in the right place at the right time is very important.

"I believe everything's going to be all right, and the main thing is survival.

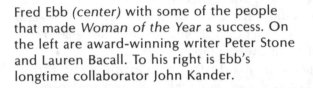

Fred Ebb (center) with some of the people
that made Woman of the Year a success. On
the left are award-winning writer Peter Stone
and Lauren Bacall. To his right is Ebb's
longtime collaborator John Kander.

Anthony Quinn in a scene from the
Kander and Ebb musical *Zorba!*

John Kander *(at piano)*
and Fred Ebb.

Ebb with legendary Broadway
director George Abbott.

Come to the Cabaret and make the most of it. If you look at my shows, there's a statement in all of them like that. You've got to survive. The grass is always greener. You've got to keep going. Things are funny; things are tough; but you survive. You get through with a sense of humor. I believe that."

Despite his conviction, Ebb doesn't think any of the so-called trends on Broadway have really changed musical theatre.

"I remember when *Hair* came out, and they said it was the musical against which all other musicals would be measured. That didn't happen. *Hair* was one show. It did very well, it had a wonderful score, but it was just one show. It didn't change anything."

Whatever happens on Broadway, Ebb plans to be a part of it. He describes his next show.

"The tentative title is *Who Killed David Merrick?* It's a murder mystery, an original by Peter Stone. It takes place in Boston and centers around a musical comedy about the foreign legion—a terrible flop. Mr. Merrick goes to New York to raise more money to keep it open, and he gets murdered. It's a whodunit. Then the leading lady gets murdered.

"It's about obsession," Ebb continues, "But it's closest to farce. It has a trick ending. You'd have to see it, but it's fun. A wonderful fun thing—the audience will have a hell of a good time."

He grins boyishly, searching for exactly the right words to summarize his attitude: "I want people to say, when they see a Kander and Ebb show, 'We've gotta go because it's fun.' I want them to look forward to our shows, saying, 'My God, I bet it's fun.' "

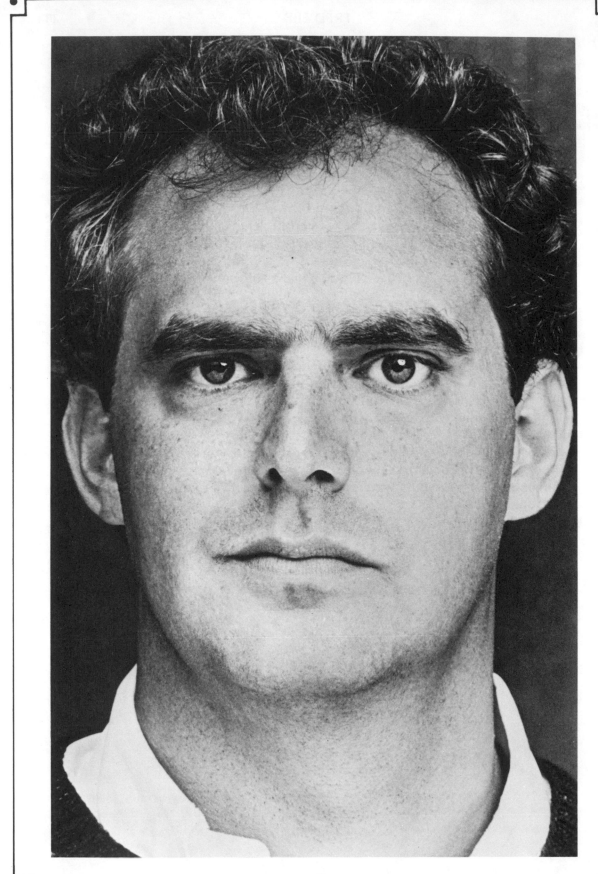

CHAPTER TEN

WILLIAM FINN

O N APRIL 10, 1981, Frank Rich of the *New York Times* expressed his view of William Finn, composer-lyricist of an Off-Broadway show entitled *March of the Falsettos*:

"I can't even remember the last time I attended a musical—on Broadway or off—that introduced a new composer or lyricist of serious promise. And that's why I had trouble believing my ears at a new show with the unlikely title *March of the Falsettos*."

Finn's talent and originality is unlikely in today's theatre. The circumstances of our meeting were equally strange. We had originally intended to talk with Finn in a small West 75th Street theatre where his production of *In Trousers* was being presented, but an unexpected rehearsal made it impossible. We wound up at a neighborhood coffee house, the American Restaurant.

"I've never been interviewed in a coffee house before," screams Bill Finn, the thirty-three-year-old object of Rich's praise.

His scream is necessary, an effort to be heard above deafening construction in the rear of the American Restaurant. He's good-natured about the pounding noise, only occasionally jamming his hands into his ears to shut out the racket.

"We could leave, I guess," says Finn, "but, oh hell, I've already ordered my English muffin."

Finn has an engaging grin and a self-deprecating sense of humor, but appearances are deceptive. Underneath the floppy orange sweater and baggy pants are obvious self-belief and an iron will. Bill Finn defines himself with one reference to the director of *In Trousers*.

"I was telling him, he can't tell me what to write, because it's hard enough for *me* to agree, to get things by *myself* in the first place. When I say something's finished, he's got to say, 'Fine.' I can only write for me." Then the self-deprecation returns, accompanied by a hearty laugh. "But listen, I'm crazy."

Crazy, in Finn's case, means idiosyncratic. Everything he writes is off-center, as exemplified by the opening number of *March of the Falsettos*, entitled "Four Jews in a Room Bitching."

Even Finn's explanation of the way *Falsettos* developed is comedic: "I had a 105-degree temperature, and I didn't think I was going to make my mark on the world. I was really desperate, and when you're really desperate and have no money for a doctor, you begin to hallucinate. And while I was hallucinating, the story came to me. I never would have written it if I didn't have a 105-degree temperature."

Finn's musical fever mounted without the aid of formal training. "I wish I had more. I used to flunk music courses all the time because they were in the morning and I could never get up for them. There was no musical training in my household either. It's like I was dropped from outer space."

He remained on the outer fringes throughout high school and college. "My music was of a different sort even then. A friend of mine thought we should start a band. We did one day, and it was pathetic. We were playing Broadway show tunes—or rock tunes with Broadway show tune arrangements. We quickly gave it up."

When we mention how much patience, perseverance, and dedication the theatre requires, Finn says, "It takes me a long time, a *very* long time to come up with things. I'm not a very patient person, as you can tell. I'm going to die very young."

But there's an inner vibrancy in Finn's face as he talks, particularly when he discusses his development as a lyricist. "I was an English major at Williams College, and I guess I thought being a novelist was the greatest, the highest art form. Since I didn't have the patience to be a novelist—I don't know how they do it—I used to read poetry and write lyrics. In the ninth grade this teacher told me Dylan Thomas was the greatest poet—his favorite poet. I tried to emulate Dylan Thomas, and my poems either put people to sleep or were terribly embarrassing. But *then*," and his voice rises, as though reliving the exciting moment of discovery that came years later, "I suddenly discovered I had a *voice*. A voice of my own, a colloquial, slangy voice that hadn't been explored in the theatre. And because it was college, nobody said, 'you can't do that.' They said, 'fine, just do anything, finish it.' "

He finished three shows while at Williams, all of which bucked the commercial tide. The first, *Sizzle*, with collaborator Charles Rubin, was a musical version of the Rosenberg case, through their final execution. Finn explains with a chuckle, "I always thought that musicals could be anything, and I still do. Their scope can be limitless."

Acting on that theory, Finn next conceived two shows for which he wrote the books, in addition to lyrics and music. *Rape* was a musical characterization of Aubrey Beardsley. Then came *Scrambled Eggs*, about a whorehouse.

"I was tipping my hat to Kurt Weill. There was a song called 'Out of the Question Blues,' the first showstopper I ever wrote."

Unfortunately, life outside the theatre has been a greater struggle for Finn.

"I was writing history plays for seventh graders to tenth graders. I was doing temp work too—ugh."

He found a creative soul-mate in director James Lapine, who in 1983 directed Stephen Sondheim's Pulitzer prize-winning *Sunday in the Park with George*.

"I saw a show he did, *Table Settings*, and liked it a lot. He was at Playwrights Horizons, on 42nd Street, where I did *In Trousers*, the first part of *March of the Falsettos*. When nobody else gave me the time of day, Playwrights Horizons did *In Trousers* twice."

Finn has nothing but raves for Lapine—artistically and personally. "Lapine is so calm, working with him is like taking a vacation. You feel no pressure, only a sense of 'Of course you're going to finish, of course you're going to do good work.' He stages things; you never have to watch a thing he does. He comes to you every day and says, 'If you don't like it, I'll change it.' And there's *nothing* to change, nothing you don't like."

On March 3, 1981, a production of *In Trousers*, done at the Second Stage on West 73rd Street, received less than rave reviews. Critic John Corry in the *New York Times* entitled his review WATCHING A NEBBISH, in reference to Marvin, the play's bisexual hero, but conceded that some of Finn's songs were "smashing."

Five weeks later, on April 9, Finn's *March of the Falsettos* opened at Playwrights Horizons, with Lapine directing. *Falsettos*, a sequel to *In Trousers*, explores a three-way triangle among the hero, Marvin, his ex-wife, and his male lover. The show retained all the wit of *In Trousers*, along with an added poignancy. Its most touching aspect was a subplot between Marvin and his adolescent son, who fears becoming gay like his father.

We asked Finn if there was anything autobiographical about *Falsettos*.

"Not overtly autobiographical, no, but yes, it's autobiographical in a sense. You use everything. I have a terrible memory. That's why everything in my work seems so internalized."

March of the Falsettos is filled with zany humor, but there's a beauty and sensitivity to the sentimental songs, such as "Father to Son," the show's closing number, in which Marvin reassures his son that he'll be a man, "if nothing goes wrong."

We mention the impact this number had on us, and Finn responds, with unexpected seriousness, "I find love the hardest thing to write about. It touches a nerve. I like 'Love Is Blind' in *Falsettos*. You know, where he breaks down? It's the closest thing to *me*, personally."

As personal and autobiographical as some of Finn's creations are, they also reflect his expert and very conscious craftsmanship. "I conceive all my songs as character songs. And even if directors don't use my staging, I at least know the numbers *can* be staged."

He's bold and experimental with tempos, but claims, "I'm not aware of what I do specifically. I'm only aware that something has to vary at certain times. Then I'm aware, after I do it. But I don't say, 'I'm going into a triple meter now.' I just do it and it seems . . . right."

What feels right to a songwriter isn't always commercially successful. When asked his definition of a commercial property, Finn replies, "I don't have a clue. My stuff isn't that sunny; it's more on the dark side. I always respond to the darker side of things. I thought *Falsettos* would get killed. I didn't want it reviewed at all, and it got a wonderful reaction. So I can't tell."

Falsettos turned out to be *artistically* right in all respects, but Finn's approach was unorthodox. "I went into the show with five songs, and then I wrote the rest in rehearsals. Now I think the writing should be done before rehearsal."

Finn is an emotional composer, so it's not surprising that he adores Beethoven. "He just takes your breath away. That's because he doesn't pull any punches."

Neither does Finn. One song title in *March of the Falsettos* reflects his daring, unconventional spirit: "My Father's a Homo, My Mother's Not Thrilled at All."

"That song was one of the only times I've written the lyrics first and then the music. Usually I get a title, which suggests the music. When the music's finished, I go back and write the full lyric out."

March of the Falsettos and *In Trousers* were small, Off-Broadway-style shows. The next vehicle Finn hopes to get produced, *America Kicks Up Its Heels*, is considerably larger in size and scope.

"This is not a little piece. It's about a soup kitchen over a fifty-year period, starting with the Depression. The show keeps being put off because the book's taking longer than we planned. But if we can get it together," he concludes confidently, "it'll be great."

Perhaps this new project will provide an entree into the pop market. "God, I'd love a hit," Finn says. "But the pop market doesn't seem to miss me very much. I think there are a lot of my songs that, if you play them, they're real catchy. I don't know why someone hasn't picked up on something."

He does concede, however, that "Billy Joel's structures are more—much more—together than mine. Mine veer all over the place—when they're working well, that is. My structure really *is* structured, very strict, but if you catch on to it, I'm doing something grievously wrong."

When we mention that many theatre aficionados feel there's something wrong with the medium today, Finn states emphatically, "Broadway's dead right now; theatre's dead. We're here to give it new life. It's a sick animal, and the unions have done it, and because theatre tickets cost so much, the

A scene from *March of the Falsettos*.

producers have done it. Cheaper tickets are a must; otherwise it's a dead end. Because, let's face it, a show can't become a hit without New York. If it's not a hit in New York, forget it."

Finn is open and adventurous about charting new territory in his words and music—an attitude that may help to bring new life to Broadway—but he doesn't see the new technology that has hit the stage as the answer.

"I don't deal very well with machines, even though I like synthesizers. What I care about is projecting my own voice. And I care about comedy. I like things to be funny."

"I want people to notice the way I bend the language, to see I have not only a personal voice but a smart, neurotic voice. That I don't follow a line."

And the contribution he would like to make at the moment?

"If I had to have a philosophy, I'd want to give songs a kick in the ass. And theatre too, give theatre a kick in the ass."

CHAPTER ELEVEN

MICKI GRANT

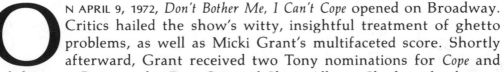

ON APRIL 9, 1972, *Don't Bother Me, I Can't Cope* opened on Broadway. Critics hailed the show's witty, insightful treatment of ghetto problems, as well as Micki Grant's multifaceted score. Shortly afterward, Grant received two Tony nominations for *Cope* and took home a Grammy for Best Original Show Album. She has also been a Grammy nominee for contributions to *Working* and *Your Arms Too Short to Box with God*.

The day we saw her, Grant looked petite, almost childlike, in jeans and sneakers. Her spacious West Side apartment in Manhattan, lined with posters of her shows, seemed to overwhelm her. But when she spoke, her eyes sparkled and her strength of personality shone beyond the schoolgirl demeanor.

"My style is rather eclectic," says Grant. "Growing up in Chicago, I played Tchaikovsky and Rimsky-Korsakov while listening to rhythm and blues on the radio. I grew up attending a Baptist church, so I was affected by gospel. You'll find gospel elements in what I write, like 'We're Gonna Have a Good Time' in *Your Arms Too Short to Box with God*, and West Indian elements too."

Grant's style was influenced by a musical childhood. "My father played piano by ear. He couldn't read music and never studied, but he played for parties. My sister studied piano, and I took violin. From there I went to double bass." She indicates the double bass in the corner, next to her piano and guitar.

"I came to the theatre as an actress, but I wrote all the time. I started writing poetry when I was about eight. I fooled around with guitar and wrote tunes. I guess I got into lyrics through doing poetry. In fact, in my high school yearbook, I said I was going to be a popular novelist."

Her writing evolved without joining workshops or studying. "I learned by *doing*," she stresses.

Don't Bother Me, I Can't Cope began as an Off-Off-Broadway showcase. "That's the kind of situation where you can experiment and try things—Off Off Broadway. Unfortunately, the minute people discover a new wine that's modestly priced, the price shoots up, so now everybody wants to drink that wine of Off Off Broadway, and you're looking for another closet to experiment in."

The experiment paid off, however. "We got a really marvelous review in the *Times*, and everybody was interested—producers and everybody else were coming down to the Urban Arts Corporation to see it."

The interest was generated by Grant's lively, foot-stomping score. Its examination of ghetto problems was timely and Grant musically dramatized the need for peace. She also focused on black achievement by referring to such contemporary heroes as Flip Wilson and Godfrey Cambridge.

Cope began its run on Broadway, April 19, 1972, and drew crowds till October 17, 1974, when it completed its run of 1,065 performances.

Vinnette Carroll, founder of the Urban Arts Corporation, conceived and directed *Cope*.

"Vinnette and I also worked on *Your Arms Too Short to Box with God*, but I wasn't on at the beginning. That's why the billing reads Music and Lyrics, Alex Bradford; Additional Music and Lyrics, Micki Grant."

Grant's welcome additions to the show made this musical rendering of the Book of St. Matthew a vivid entertainment. Crowds were caught up when the gospel singers and dancers on stage praised the Lord, responding fully to such joyous numbers as Grant's "We're Gonna Have a Good Time":

> Don't be afraid to raise your voice
> Let's have a good time
> The Lord said make a joyful noise
> Let's have a good time

Audiences had a good time in 1976. The show was Tony-nominated as Best Musical and Delores Hall won Best Actress in a Featured Role.

"When they decided to take it to Broadway, they asked me to come in and do some things. I worked closely with the book writer. I suppose because I do both—words and book—I work alone a good deal of the time."

Since Grant writes by herself, we wondered which came first, words or music.

"When you're working strictly from a book, the content sort of dictates what you have to say to move the story along. So you start thinking about the words up front."

Her method has contributed to a prolific theatrical career. In June of 1980, she became the only writer in history to have two shows open within the same week—a revival of *Your Arms Too Short* and *It's So Nice to Be Civilized.*

"*It's So Nice,* which started Off Off Broadway in 1979, didn't live up to my hopes," says Grant. "The show, you see, was about survival. Our central character in the Off-Off-Broadway version was a newspaperman who had been there for 25 years. He held the stage together as a protagonist. He knew everything about everyone on the street. When *It's So Nice* was taken to Broadway it became diffused. The newspaperman was removed, and a woman spokesman would come out and talk and tie it together. But with the newspaperman no longer on stage, we lost the center, the focus. Also, the show was over-produced when it came to Broadway."

Grant's writing and composing continues through the inevitable ups and downs of the theatre and she manages to maintain a steady acting career. "I just did a PBS movie as an actress. After *Cope,* I did very little except TV. I was on daytime soaps for a number of years. But I've performed very little on the stage except for *Cope* because fortunately, maybe, I keep getting work writing theatre pieces."

Grant discusses a couple of the current projects she finds exciting.

"I did a score for a show based on the character Hazel, the cartoon character. That was long-distance work, another kind of collaboration, because my partner on it, Ted Key, lives in Philadelphia. You'd be surprised how much can be accomplished long-distance if you maintain the continuity."

Her other project is entirely different, the story of an eighteenth-century poet, a black slave and the first woman to be published in the United States.

"The fun is that I'm writing about these vastly different women. The music for *Hazel* is music I'm culling from my classical background."

Grant laughs merrily, echoing the thought of all composers in her enviable position. "It's nice to turn down things, to be in demand, to pick and choose. I like that."

Sometimes, however, a writer of Grant's stature turns down a property that becomes a hit. "*A My Name Is Alice* for instance," Grant says. "It was a revue and they asked me to add songs. I couldn't get to it. The director was Julianne Boyd, who directed *Eubie.*" She shrugs philosophically.

Being that busy can be demanding in terms of time and energy. How does she handle such a full schedule?

"I'm terrible, *so* undisciplined. From a former violinist, no less. That's why I gave up the instrument. In fact, when I was studying double bass, my teacher told me, 'Micki, your trouble is, you simply want to pick up and *play.* You don't do it that way. You have to practice!' "

Grant admires people who maintain a regular routine. "I read about these

Right: Grant examined ghetto problems and musically dramatized the need for peace in *Don't Bother Me, I Can't Cope.*

Salome Bey sings the role of Mary while Mabel Robinson dances it in the original Broadway production of *Your Arms Too Short to Box with God.*

Your Arms Too Short to Box with God, a musical rendering of the Book of St. Matthew, received a Tony nomination for Best Musical in 1976.

people all the time. People who have offices. I do come to my studio and spend an awful lot of time there. I read magazines." She laughs again, putting her hand to her mouth, like a child who's done something naughty. "I've never been able to say specifically, 'I will do this from ten to two.' I've worked all hours of the night. I work when I feel like it. I know when I must have something done, and that's the idea."

Sometimes the impetus of a collaborator's energy urges on the creative process. "I suppose I've been most disciplined when working with Vinnette, because she is so disciplined. She'll call a rehearsal and have twenty people sitting there waiting, and suddenly I know I have to have something for these people to rehearse. That automatically makes me do something, get myself moving."

Once she does have something finished, does she mind making changes?

"I don't if you can convince me. I'm not one of these prima donnas that, if you take out something, I'm going to have fits about it. Sometimes I've begged people to take something out if it doesn't work. I don't think I'm difficult to work with in that sense. I want a piece to function well.

"Where I *am* difficult is when people change things without my knowledge. I don't want to walk into a theatre and hear my lyrics or my music altered."

Grant is right, of course. A writer has an overall vision, and inappropriate changes—often the whim of an actor, a musician, or a director—can damage the line of thought. Fortunately, writers are protected by the Dramatists Guild. Legally, no one in the company can change their work without permission.

Changes are the lifeblood of creative development, however, and Grant approves of musical workshops. "It's like discovering *another* new wine. I think it's wonderful if you can continue the workshops until the show is in good shape. Michael Bennett has just gone through two, and he's about to mount another on the same show. Most people can't do those kinds of workshops, and I certainly understand the benefit of it. The way things are, it's practically the only way you can work with something that takes as much time as a musical. You can't give a show six weeks and think you're going to have it in shape."

But even when armed with such a realistic attitude, songwriters can be hard-pressed to deal with the tension-charged atmosphere during the early development of a show. How does Grant handle the ups and downs?

"I love it, see. I love the theatre. I'm doing exactly what I've wanted to do since I was eight years old. I have a *passion* for it."

Grant's passion results in an impressive blend of emotional drive and literacy. For instance, in "Something Is Wrong in Jerusalem" from *Your Arms Too Short to Box with God*, she has Mary sing:

Oh, my son, dearest one
Who's dining with you tonight, I wonder
I can't dispel this premonition
That all is not well in Jerusalem

Passion pushes Grant along and keeps her stimulated, though she admits, "I don't like dissension. I'd rather things be fun."

One aspect of the theatre that few songwriters actually enjoy is getting financing. We asked Grant if she feels financing might account for the paucity of women in the theatre.

"I think the small number of women in the theatre basically stems from a pattern that's outmoded and outdated, but even so, it takes time to change it. I think changes are happening, though. It's going to build in regional theatre and then the shows will come to New York. People are becoming more aware, because women are taking the reins and *making* them more aware. Also, because women now have more money, they can come into the producing end more."

She admits that financing for black writers and black shows is still a problem.

"There's a built-in suspicion on the part of producers that it's going to be harder to recoup and harder to sell. My contention is that, by affixing a label to a show—in other words, if you call a show a *black* show, as opposed to a show where the theme happens to deal with a black family, a black subject, or a black situation, or that happens to have been written by a black or has black performers on the stage—producers guarantee that it will run into trouble."

She cites *Fiddler on the Roof*. "Nobody called *Fiddler* a *Jewish* show. It's about certain people who live in a certain place and a certain time. Nobody calls *The Octette Bridge Club* an Irish show, even though it's about Irish sisters."

Grant brings up another difficulty, as exemplified by one of her own close friends. "She recently told me—she was embarrassed about it—that when she first started going to the theatre she didn't see *Cope*. I was stunned. And she said, 'Well, it was a black show.' She really thought at the time that a black show was meant for only black people to go in and see. Her level of sophistication has, of course, done a complete turn at this point, but people are still afraid that, if they go to a black show, they'll get lacerated from the stage."

Grant expects the situation to improve. "It's obvious there's an audience for shows with black themes, and it's obvious that you create a larger audience by bringing in those blacks you didn't know were there, who started coming to Broadway in the 1970s."

Grant collaborated with Stephen Schwartz, Mary Rodgers, James Taylor, and others to fashion a musical based on Studs Terkel's best-selling book *Working*. The show received a Tony nomination for Best Score.

In the end, all that matters, according to Grant, is to stop "categorizing in terms of where we're going to put financing, based on that single issue alone. It's just got to be a *good* show, and I think audiences will attend a good show."

What is her definition of a good show?

"A good show has a subject that can in some way involve me, that I care about. It doesn't have to be a subject of major import. I'm not averse to simply being entertained. I find nothing wrong with that. At the same time, I'm a great believer in using the musical theatre to say serious things and address serious questions."

Grant also favors a show with an inventive emphasis on dance. "I love choreography, and at the same time, I recognize you can do a musical with a minimum of it. I think today's audiences expect a musical to have choreography. A show has to be *very* special not to have it."

Despite the growing influence of rock in theatre, an influence represented strongly by the Andrew Lloyd Webber–Tim Rice shows (*Evita; Jesus Christ, Superstar*) and the Krieger-Eyen score of *Dreamgirls*, Grant feels a healthy Broadway requires all types of music.

"I feel that the great thing we can look forward to in theatre is having all influences. They should be able to coexist. The revival should coexist with what I call standard theatre music. The *Superstars* and the *Godspells*—they should all be in there, and I think that would be a cornucopia."

Grant has a similar philosophy about the electronic innovations that are becoming part of modern theatre: "I hope it doesn't become *too* electronic. I think music is becoming overly electronic for my taste. If it's used well, fine—but it has to be used *so* well, so it blends in with what's going on. Otherwise it can become a distraction. This whole generation has been raised on sights and sounds—electronic music."

A longing for the past creeps into Grant's tone. "I was telling a friend the other day that there are young people who don't know the sound of an acoustical bass: they can't identify with it. Clarinets—they don't hear on this level. I've begged conductors—and I haven't gotten my way in the past, but maybe I will in my new show—I want some acoustical sounds, *please!* I want some acoustical sounds.' "

Electronic or acoustical, Grant wants *her* music to represent optimism and survival.

"I guess the song that most people remember about me, which says it all, is 'It Takes a Whole Lot of Human Feeling.' And there's another song, 'So Little Time'—you shouldn't use up that precious time with hate and name calling."

A specific verse in "So Little Time" sums up Grant's attitude:

> Loving comes easy once you start
> Cause hating just takes too much heart
> And the river's rolling
> And there's so little time.

CAROL HALL

"I HATE THE BLUES," says Carol Hall, composer-lyricist of *The Best Little Whorehouse in Texas*. "I only like to write songs about survival and going on."

Hall quotes from a song in *Whorehouse* entitled "Girl, You're a Woman"

Girl, get a hold now
Straighten up
Look alive
Girl you're a woman
You'll survive
Remembering one good thing
When you're moving on
Is wonderin' what you'll find
And one good thing about a past that's gone
Is leaving it behind

Carol Hall is a perennial optimist. "I'm one of those people that, no matter how grim the situation, I always search for the one good thing. It's a dreadful Pollyanna strain."

It's also the secret of Hall's gracious, upbeat charm. She speaks softly, with a lilting southern accent, and her captivating smile draws us into the world of Abilene, Texas, where she was reared.

"My family had the only music store in Abilene," Hall explains. "Not the best, the *only* music store there. Hall's Music Store.

"My mother was a very well-schooled classical musician, and she played in the local symphony. If she could have written a musical of my life, she would have wanted it to be *Gypsy*—only instead of being about a fan dancer, it would have been about a concert pianist. So I was well taught and took classical music all my life. In fact, I was writing songs as I studied classical, because I already knew my passion was theatre songs.

"I always wanted to write musicals," Hall points out. "I remember being quite young and raised up in Dallas after my mother left Abilene. At that time the theatre that was very lively was the Margo Jones Theatre, one of the first regional theatres in this country. That's where Tennessee Williams used to try out his plays.

"Though I was from a small Texas town, and later Dallas, I had this sort of mother who longed for the big time. She thought nothing of letting me go to the theatre as much as possible. On school nights we saw everything. When the Met came to Dallas, for example—for five nights—we were at all five nights, which is five times more than I've seen it since I came to New York," she chuckles.

"There was this real rich cultural background. On the one hand, what we got were road shows, so that I specifically remember *Oklahoma!* as the first production I ever saw and how it thrilled me. Many years later, *Oklahoma!* was the first show my children ever saw."

Movie musicals, such as *Singin' in the Rain* and *Snow White and the Seven Dwarfs*, also had great impact on Hall's development.

"*The Wizard of Oz* was probably the strongest. And also at that time, Sheldon Harnick, who was a young whippersnapper—before he got together with Bock—did a musical in Dallas called *Horatio*. That influenced me enormously, because I'd never seen a musical done with just two pianos and a chorus of six people. That, I remember, was a tremendous groundbreaker.

"I had this strange juxtaposition of standard cultural things. By the time I got to New York, there probably wasn't a concert artist I hadn't heard many times over in Texas. Most people think you don't get culture until you come to New York, but I had a rich, rich background.

"Also, because Mom was a musician, we knew people. There were always classical musicians in our house.

"I can recall going to Margo Jones herself when I was about fourteen years old and saying, 'I want to write music for the theatre. What can I do, and how can I educate myself?' Margo discouraged me at first, but then we sort of decided together that there was nothing to do but *work* in the theatre—as an actress or a techy or whatever—so that's how I proceeded as a young person going to college. Working summer theatre. Actually, summer theatre was so small in Virginia, so small and so unimportant, that they—in the midst of their Shaw and so forth—actually let me write a musical, produced at this tacky little theatre in Virginia. That was the first thing I ever had. It must have been some time in the fifties—'56, something like that."

Hall continued writing songs throughout college.

"I went to two colleges, actually. One was the college my family picked for me, because they thought it was highly respectable and far enough east for them—that was Sweet Briar College, in Virginia. And I wrote a lot of shows for the boys' schools around—that was in the days of boys' schools and girls' schools."

Hall laughs, recalling an amusing, if discouraging, encounter with one of her teachers. "He gave me an F in music, and said, 'You think you're going to New York to write a Broadway show. Well, I'm going to show you you didn't do your work in counterpoint.' Well, I went to New York and had a Broadway show, and I guess I didn't do my work in counterpoint.

"Then I got to Sarah Lawrence, where I studied with the well-known American avant-garde composer Meyer Kupferman. As I was finishing my work at Sarah Lawrence, about 1959, 1960, there was a man named Mervyn Nelson who did a wonderful thing, before the Broadway composer Lehman Engel set up the BMI workshop—before anyone. He organized a little school for people who wanted to be singers, and he thought they should have a place to find original material. The Beatles hadn't really hit then. This was Lesley Gore time on the pop scene—not a gargantuan group of people with guitars going to San Francisco with flowers in their hair. Everyone was kind of depending on doing songs they heard on hit records, and Mervyn's idea was that singers ought to be in touch with writers. So he advertised in *Show Business* magazine, saying WANTED: SONGWRITERS, figuring he could gather together a group of talented writers to meet the needs of singers.

"I remember going to his audition—there must have been *seven hundred people* in that room, and only two of us were women—me and Treva Silverman, who later came to fame and glory as one of the creators of the Mary Tyler Moore show. Both Treva and I were picked. They picked five writers."

Hall worked on a regular basis, for one year, at the Mervyn Nelson school, creating material for singers, including Leslie Uggams, who later conquered Broadway in *Hallelujah, Baby!*

"When I joined the BMI workshop in New York in 1966, which trained theatre writers and was run by Lehman Engel, the kind of assignments Lehman gave us weren't new to me. You know, write a musical to *A Streetcar Named Desire*. Well, Meyer had done it before, and Mervyn too. It's just that nobody knows about those people, and Lehman, because he was a successful Broadway conductor, had a way of bringing his Broadway power to the forefront."

Armed with useful creative guidance from her three mentors, in 1963 Hall did a score for *Room at the Top*, the 1959 film drama that had won an Oscar for Simone Signoret as Best Actress.

"It didn't get off the ground," says Hall. "And neither did *Harvey*." A theatrical lawyer and friend, Seth Schapiro, had introduced her to *Harvey*'s author, Mary Chase, "and Mary and I met on many, many afternoons. We went to dinner and had a table for four, and she insisted on a table for five—I presume for the memory of *Harvey*. I was sure I was going to get it then."

It was in the mid-1960s when Hall pursued *Harvey* as a project. But she began to realize that music had changed and that the tale of an invisible rabbit might be out of step.

"The music of the period was so much more interesting than it had been. Also, by this time I was married and had a baby. I had to move out of New York. I'd come into New York, though, to see shows, and frankly, they weren't one iota as interesting as what I was hearing on the radio. I lost my heart to Jimi Hendrix and the Beatles and Janis Ian and people who were writing about things that struck my soul very deeply. And then I came to Manhattan to see *Man of La Mancha*. It was a skillful and melodic production, and I'd probably like it better now than I did in the mid-sixties. It's not that the shows of the period weren't good; it's just that new ground had been broken.

"I particularly remember Janis Ian's 'Society's Child'—so innovative. I decided then—I made a deliberate choice—that if I wrote a musical, it would need to be something that hadn't been done yet. That's what set me off to write *Room at the Top*, as a matter of fact, because I thought to write a musical that was dark, not operatic—a musical with some real substance—would be fulfilling.

"I'd do these musicals—this was 1966 by now. I had an agent, and I'd come to New York and audition, and they wouldn't get on. I never had the rights either. I was totally ignorant. I mean, I'd just do musicals I had no rights to, if they struck my fancy."

Hall says she was shameless in those days.

"I remember Johnny Mathis coming to town, and I just phoned him and said, 'Hello, I write songs.' The poor man was fast asleep when I called, but he was polite. I'm sure he didn't know what I was saying. By this time I really did write songs because Barbra Streisand had done 'Jenny Rebecca' on her *My Name Is Barbra* album. I had some recordings by decent artists. Mabel Mercer had begun doing my songs, only because I called her and said, 'May I show you my material?' So once Mabel Mercer does your songs, you can easily get to an upstart like Barbra Streisand. Barbra later recorded 'Jenny,' and I think she heard it from Mabel Mercer. I'm pretty sure of that."

By 1970, Hall was divorced, with two small children. However, she also had an agent at the William Morris Agency.

"At first they sort of switched me from the twenty-second floor to the thirty-second floor. I was kind of shunted from the musical theatre department, where it turned out that I hadn't really, in their minds, done very much, down to the little man who handled women that played piano and wrote songs. To my astonishment, Scott Shukat, an agent there, got this record deal for me with Elektra Records.

"The album I eventually recorded, with me singing my own songs, got me in contact with brilliant writers such as Kris Kristofferson and Don McLean.

"I was a young mother, working odd hours with Kris Kristofferson at the Bitter End. Kris was just starting out on his songwriting career. And now I see this as one of the most fruitful periods of my career. I was about thirty or thirty-one. But, without the record contract, I'd never have known Don McLean. I would have been playing the homecoming weekend at Rutgers normally, feeding my kids instant oatmeal, and racing out of the house to do this. And the record deal put me in touch with a kind of music that didn't really happen until '70 or '75—I found it very instructive."

In addition to McLean and Kristofferson's country influences in her writing, later utilized for *The Best Little Whorehouse in Texas*, Hall began to write for children.

"Things like 'Sesame Street,' " she says, "and the thing I'm proudest of, more than anything I've ever done—the book, record, and television show of *Free to Be You and Me*. It was a children's album of songs, stories, and poems, produced by Marlo Thomas, which broke down the stereotypes of what boys and girls had to be like.

"It's the only project I expect to be involved with in show business where there were simply no egos. Everyone wanted to make a revolutionary record, which would change the way people thought, and to make it highly entertaining, which we did.

"The other thing—when you're writing out of the heads, hearts, and minds of children, you're writing theatre songs. So when you write a song for Big Bird, you know he has a very specific character, and he's the child on 'Sesame Street.' He's the kid who isn't quite certain he can cross the street alone. Gordon and Susan on the show are parents and teachers. All of those people have very specific jobs. So when you do that kind of writing, it's simplifying and getting to the essence of the character.

"Somewhere in here, I got a little show on at La Mama on the Lower East Side, and I also did something at Playwrights Horizons—little bits and pieces that no one remembers. The funny thing is, when you start out, and somebody says to you, 'You may be thirty-five, and no one will have heard of you,' you're such a little whippersnapper that you say, 'Impossible. Everyone will have heard of me by thirty-five.' In fact, when I got to be thirty-five, I was sort of keeping my head above water. I was supporting my kids by myself. I was doing jingles, getting little plays done at Playwrights Horizon and the Lion Theatre Company—all of which are quite wonderful little theatres."

Hall wrote all these projects alone. "Recently, though, Lesley Gore and I have been writing together. David Shire, who wrote *Baby* for Broadway, and I have been writing together too. David's great."

For *Whorehouse*, though, Hall wrote both words and music.

"I had these friends from Texas," she recalls, when asked how the project took shape. "I had a dear friend named Peter Masterson. I took him and his wife Carlin to see *Vanities* because it was all about Texans and we're all from Texas. Jack Hefner, a friend of mine who's also from Texas, wrote the play. We'd known each other forever, and our kids have always been friends. In fact, we were sharing a house together in the winter, which involved wonderful convivial weekends with five children and three grown-ups. I had not remarried yet. I took them to *Vanities* and said, at the dinner afterward, 'I've always wanted to write a show about home, and if I was ever to write another Broadway production, I'd want to do *The Last Picture Show*.

"That property involved all the things I've talked about: people that I loved—a depth in seeing people. I'm interested in secrets, and that's a whole movie about everyone's secrets. What Pete said then was 'Hell, you can't get the rights to *The Last Picture Show*. But I know something you might be able to get the rights to.' He showed me this article that Larry King wrote, 'The Best Little Whorehouse in Texas.'

"Now Larry and I were very close friends, and I had been intending to introduce him to Pete—had tried several times, in fact. You know, Texans are sort of like White Russians; they stick together. We hold each other together with barbecue and memories.

"Pete arrived the next morning with Larry's article. I thought it was really funny, and I thought it would work. I called up Larry and said, 'I have this friend. He's an actor, mostly. That's right. He's out of work. Sometimes he directs. No, nothing you've heard of, but we'd like to do a musical of your piece.' Larry said, and I believe he quotes himself in his book, 'Hell, I *hate* musicals. A bunch of candy-assed tippy-toed tap-dancers stomping all over the dialogue.'

"But he came to meet us, and we outlined how we hoped to do *Whorehouse*. Larry hit upon a truth when he said, 'You know, this is a show about hypocrisy. That's.the secret.'

"We began fashioning it in an odd way. We invited Larry to write down the rules of Miss Edna's whorehouse as he remembered them—she was the madam—because it was true that she ran an extremely tight ship. Larry went off to write them, and Pete outlined the scenes and left me by myself. The first song I wrote was 'Twenty Fans,' which opens the show. That was basically a visual. I simply wrote out of Larry's initial opening lines;

> It was the nicest little whorehouse
> You ever saw
> Lay about a mile down the road.

Edna Milton, the real madam of the chicken ranch,
lassos Delores Hall, Henderson Forsythe,
Carlin Glynn, Tommy Tune, Peter Masterson,
Larry King, and Carol Hall on the first day of
rehearsal for *The Best Little Whorehouse in Texas*.

The winning football team dances in preparation for a night
at the chicken ranch, compliments of the madam.

 At first Larry King didn't want his article on a Texas whorehouse
to be a musical. "Hell, I *hate* musicals. A bunch of candy-assed
tippy-toed tap dancers stomping all over the dialogue."

"It describes the house and the trees and how simple the house looked, how there were air conditioners in every window. I thought, well, this is interesting. Why don't I use gospel chords because this is a show about hypocrisy? Why don't I use gospel chords to describe a whorehouse? And why don't I describe the simplicity of the house, which was in fact a white clapboard shuttered house with porch and swing. And why don't I change the air conditioners—that's not so pretty—to fans? And use the juxtaposition of cooling off, because they had to have a way to cool down. That was my creative process for that song.

"What happened was that Larry so enjoyed writing down the rules that, in fact, he wrote a very long, very funny opening scene that involved Miss Mona—as we'd now named her, instead of Miss Edna—interviewing one girl for the job. In the scene, she related the rules. When Larry saw how funny his scene was, he said, 'Hell, is that all there is to writin' a musical? It sure beats writin' books.'

Hall feels that the flavor of the characters was caught accurately because all creative hands involved knew each character intimately.

"They were all from Texas," Hall says. "And we really understood these people inside and out."

Pete Masterson was a member of the Actor's Studio, and by the time four songs and four scenes were written, he suggested they be presented to the studio for initial reaction.

"Of course, they're kind of serious at the studio, and Pete's brilliance was that he did not take it to the playwriting unit. We'd still be there, discussing its flaws, if he had, I'm quite sure. He took it to the acting unit.

"Well, you know, the last funny thing anybody brought to the acting unit was *The Three Sisters*. The actors were just hysterical, they were so happy. People jumped up and down, saying, 'Can I be in your show? Can I be in your show?'

"What's fascinating about all this," says Hall, "is that *A Chorus Line* was on its way under Joe Papp's umbrella, and *Ain't Misbehavin'* was under the umbrella of the Manhattan Theatre Club. But we were sort of by ourselves at the Actor's Studio, and I think to this day we're the only ones who ever kind of found a room to say—it's like an old Judy Garland musical—'let's do our own show, let's get a barn.' Our barn was the studio. We did the four scenes and the four songs for everybody. All famous people."

By the time *Whorehouse* was completed, word was out on the streets that a potential hit had been written.

"For two reasons. One, it was the Actor's Studio, which had never done anything like that before—coming in with a musical. I was playing piano in my limited way, and we were hiring only people who could sing in the keys I could play in. And the other thing was, Larry King did not start life doing press for Lyndon Johnson for nothing. He'd go to Elaine's, and he'd say, 'I was just over working on my musical,' and next thing you knew, it would be in the *New York Daily News* in the Liz Smith column 'cause she's from Texas.

"Liz would say things about the Larry King musical. And one of the funniest moments of my life was at a dinner party, where I sat all evening long discussing my new project. When I finished, someone said to me, 'I just *hate* to tell you this, but that's being done.' I said, '*No*, it can't be!' You know how it is; no matter what you're doing, it's always being done. She said, 'Oh, yes, it's in production. This is the Larry King musical.' Like *hell* it's the Larry King musical,' I said.

"It was wonderful for us, though—the attention. Because by the time the limos were pulling up, letting out Tennessee Williams and Elaine and Kurt Vonnegut and Norman Mailer and Robert Redford—it helped put that kind of heat on that you can't pay for."

The Best Little Whorehouse in Texas had no dancing in it at first. "You know, Tommy Tune's also from Texas, and Tommy had gone to high school with Carlin Masterson, Pete's wife. They'd worked at the Alley Theatre together, but Tommy was a *real* person—we'd have had to *pay* Tommy. He hadn't done a Broadway show yet, but he was brilliant. He had done *The Club*, and he was working on a show called *Sunset*. We talked to Tommy about it. Since we were working for free, though, we couldn't afford him."

Eventually, producer Stevie Phillips was brought in by Hall's close friends, novelist William Goldman and his wife Ilene. "Bill and Ilene are the godparents of the project, because they came to see it and brought Stevie. At intermission Stevie made a deal.

"It was an interesting deal and rather historic," Hall explains. "None of us were members of the Dramatists Guild—I didn't know what the Dramatists Guild was. I'd never gotten anything on Broadway. How could I know? Pete was an out-of-work actor, and Larry King didn't even know how to do a musical. We made a deal with Stevie where we would sell her the movie up front. Basically, it's what I would call the Rumpelstiltskin theory. She spun our straw into gold, and what happened was, she came and saw a basically completed musical.

"Stevie said, 'I'll put on your show,' and everyone wanted it. Everyone wanted it, but they all wanted stars. Stevie wanted it with Pete's wife Carlin. She also said, 'I want it just as it is, but I want to get Tommy Tune to do the dancing.'"

Carlin Masterson was delighted with Stevie's attitude.

"Carlin never did anything before then," says Hall. "She was thirty-eight years old; she had raised three kids. She was a member of the Actor's Studio, but there was no way in the world someone was going to come to Carlin and say, 'Would you like to have the lead in this Broadway show?'

"So Stevie wanted to go with it as it was, and she said to us very clearly, 'I will give you the most expensive Off-Broadway production that there has

ever been, and you will give us your movie'—*us* being Universal Studios—
'and if it works, we'll take it to Broadway. And if it works, we'll also make it
a movie.' "

Everyone was pleased. " 'You people are gonna pull this off'—that's what
Bill Goldman said after seeing *Whorehouse* grow," Hall says. "We had this kind
of Chekhovian musical that was *very* well balanced and had no stars, and if
we'd had stars, as was proven later in the movie, we'd have had to make it fit
the stars, and we'd have lost the whole thing.

"Tommy was wonderful. Tommy was thinking these glorious things, like
the fake girl, and Bill said, 'It's Tuesday and it's raining and look at this
audience. They are really on their feet.' "

Universal moved *Whorehouse* to Broadway in the summer, which is rarely
done, since Broadway box office sags during the summer months.

"We didn't have terribly good reviews when it opened Off Broadway, so
we didn't invite the reviewers to see it again. Luckily, Richard Eder of the
Times had completely lost his power by the time we came in, so we became a
hit."

Whorehouse became a smash show and then a financial (if not artistic)
success on film with Burt Reynolds and Dolly Parton. Since then, Hall has
concentrated on other projects, notably a story about the world of athletics,
called *Good Sports*. Her collaborator was librettist Susan Rice.

To Whom It May Concern followed, opening to rave reviews at the
Williamstown Theatre Festival in Massachusetts on July 17, 1985. Her
friend, lyricist-librettist Gretchen Cryer, starred—a nice irony, since Hall
appeared in Cryer's show, *I'm Getting My Act Together and Taking It on
the Road* for a six-month period.

"I did everything for *To Whom It May Concern*—book, words, and
music. It's based on a communion service in the Book of Common Prayer.
So I used the service, but my people spoke and interrupted. I wanted to
show what went on in people's minds in the church."

The subject matter of Carol Hall's shows—ranging from a whorehouse to
a church—sums up her ability to handle a variety of subjects with charm
and humor. The southern belle from Abilene, Texas, has just begun to hit
her stride.

CHAPTER THIRTEEN

MARVIN HAMLISCH

"MY BASIC DISAPPOINTMENT is that I'm not taken seriously," says composer Marvin Hamlisch.

Hamlisch's disappointment is surprising, given his legendary achievements: three Oscars in one night (two for the film *The Way We Were*, one for *The Sting*), making him the only composer in Hollywood history to accomplish this feat; the longest-running Broadway musical to date, *A Chorus Line*; a smash success with book by Neil Simon, *They're Playing Our Song*; and a Pulitzer Prize.

"It's not that I haven't received recognition," Hamlisch continues, pacing quickly across the living room floor of his Malibu beach house. "But people think of this as the Sondheim era, the Andrew Lloyd Webber era. That's because the shows I've done so far have been other people's babies. *A Chorus Line* is Michael Bennett's *A Chorus Line*—he did the direction and choreography. *They're Playing Our Song* is Neil Simon's thing. I still have to do my 'Rhapsody in Blue.'"

What motivates Hamlisch is a compulsive desire for perfection. His perfectionist tendencies surfaced at age five, when he fell in love with Broadway theatre and vowed to dedicate his life to it.

"Other kids in my class saved their money to go to a ball game or saved their allowance for a stamp collection. I saved my money to *stand*—to get a standing-room-only seat—at shows, particularly matinees."

He was encouraged by a father who played accordion, among six musical instruments. "My sister was taking piano lessons," Hamlisch recalls. "I had perfect pitch and could play in any key. So I'd walk over to the piano and do what they were paying money for her to learn. The household started to revolve around my music very early."

Did he ever plan a classical music career?

"No way. At Juilliard they were grooming me for a classical career, but I realized early I wasn't going to be this great concert pianist because my nerves couldn't take it. I could not go out and play something and know that, if I was playing Bach, they were comparing me to, seeing if I was as good as Gould!"

In other words, he dreaded rejection?

"Exactly. I realized that rejection—all kinds of rejection—was terrible for me. When I tried to write a rock and roll song and came to the office of a publisher, they'd say, 'Wait.' After two hours they'd finally say, 'No, it's no good' and I'd be crushed. In school I kept writing shows, and it was something I loved. Most of all, it seemed to me I could battle better in that world than I could in the rock world. Plus show music was what I wrote best."

His focus never wavered. "I went to a professional children's school and hung out with a lot of kids who were in shows, like Liza Minnelli. But fate took a hand. I was supposed to do *Fade Out—Fade In* with Carol Burnett, as a rehearsal pianist, and Carol got pregnant." He pauses, reliving the incident. "Pregnant! I was convinced she did it just to spite me. But anyway, I went into *Funny Girl* instead. To start off with that kind of show and Barbra Streisand was like *wow!*"

Hamlisch found *Funny Girl* both educational and exciting and relished the lack of pressure. "That was the best time of my life, just being a rehearsal pianist, the period when you're not under the gun. You don't get reviewed; you don't hear anybody say, 'The dance arrangements were mediocre.'

"Actually," he says, "I was also the assistant vocal arranger, which meant I also got the sandwiches for everybody."

He wasn't serving sandwiches for long. After *Funny Girl*, Hamlisch did dance arrangements for *Henry, Sweet Henry*. A musicalization of the 1964 film *The World of Henry Orient*, it starred Don Ameche as a man about town, relentlessly pursued by two infatuated teenage girls. The show, which opened October 23, 1967, ran for 80 performances.

After *Henry, Sweet Henry*, Hamlisch furnished dance music for TV's *The Bell Telephone Hour.*

"You couldn't have picked a better show to prepare me for *A Chorus Line*. I was around dancers all the time. Maybe that's the reason I'm perverted whenever I see a leotard."

Where did *A Chorus Line* begin?

"Off Broadway. It opened April of 1975, and played 101 performances at the Public Theatre. It was always planned as a show that would move to Broadway eventually. Because we were a show made up of unknowns, the feeling was, let's go off Broadway, where it can't cost that much, where we don't have any stars. Just let us grow. Obviously we grew fast." On July 25, 1975, a little more than three months after its Off-Broadway opening, *A Chorus Line* arrived on Broadway.

The growth came from dedication and sustained intimate relationships with the show's dancers. "I *knew* what dancers felt like by being around them so much. If you're a dance music arranger—someone they don't fear—you're one of the boys, one of the girls, so to speak. I talked to them all the time."

Did he have any idea he was creating a landmark musical?

"None. I knew we weren't just writing about dancers, that we were using them as a kind of metaphor about life. But it took a while to grasp that we were doing something very important."

Yet this now-classic property was developed in a totally atypical way.

"Till then, for most shows you wrote the book, wrote the lyrics, wrote the music, and when it was all ready, you went into rehearsal. That was the normal way. *This* show—well, we had no songs. We finally went into rehearsal with one song and tons of dialogue—four and a half hours worth. Then it turned into four songs and four and a half hours of dialogue. But we were tailor-making the songs with the people, and that launched the whole workshop process. It was literally written as we went along."

Improvising—feeling your way creatively—can sometimes result in a shapeless, unfocused final result. Hamlisch credits director Michael Bennett with a keen eye and firm overall vision. "Michael is brilliant. And he didn't want to be stuck with anything from the old school. Also, I think he knew that we—my lyricist Eddie Kleban and I—would give him carte blanche because he was the leader, and he likes working that way."

Why did Michael Bennett choose him to write the score?

"Michael and I have known each other for years, going way back to our work together on *Henry, Sweet Henry.* I think he wanted a new young team, new people with new ideas. Plus, I won the Academy Awards in April, and he called me in June. I think the exposure gave me an added boost in his eyes."

The success of *A Chorus Line* boosted Hamlisch in the eyes of audiences and critics as well, although he's quick to point out, "*A Chorus Line* did not get across-the-board good reviews for the music. The score got killed a few times. And it hurt; it really did. I had hoped that *this* would be my 'Rhapsody in Blue.' "

Continuing on the subject of critics, Hamlisch says, "I just keep in mind that Leonard Bernstein lived a *tough* life when it came to critics. And let's face it: he's got more talent than anyone. He wrote one of the greatest movie scores of all time, *On the Waterfront,* and the definitive Broadway score for *West Side Story.* What you finally learn, I guess, is that critics don't know the first

A scene from *A Chorus Line* (1975). One of the most successful musicals ever, *A Chorus Line* was Hamlisch's first Broadway score.

time around. You're asking a critic to watch an entire show, write a review in two hours or so, and, without listening to an album, tell you musically what it was all about."

There are parallels in the way Hamlisch and Bernstein approach things. "Bernstein starts with rhythm. I do that too. I always think, before melody, how do I want this to flow?"

The flow comes first, but even more vital, in Hamlisch's view, is the reason a composer writes a score at all. "The most important thing about a show is there's got to be a reason for it to *sing*. *Pygmalion* sang when it became *My Fair Lady*, but we all know hundreds of shows that didn't. A pet peeve of mine is singing the dialogue, without even trying to rhyme it. Yes, a line from the script could be, 'Hey, baby, what's for lunch?' That line doesn't offer a real reason to sing, in my opinion, yet new shows use this sing-the-dialogue device all the time."

Why did the trend begin?

"Because the other type of show—the *My Fair Lady* type—is very difficult

to write. There's an art to that. This is an easy way to go. And if you give audiences enough dancing, enough singing, enough energy, and a lot of visuals, people are still full."

Hamlisch shakes his head. "There are two types of meals. You can go and get yourself a gourmet meal and feel satisfied. Or you can gobble down fast food and feel satiated. I hope we can come up with something that is as fulfilling as the old-fashioned show yet is not old-fashioned itself.

"Still, the essence of a show's success, to me, is what the stomach feels like and the heart. It's a goosepimple feeling. I still remember when Eliza Doolittle in *My Fair Lady* looks at the Ascot Gavotte and yells, 'Move your bloomin' arse!' Or Tevye in *Fiddler* saying, 'You know why I do all this? Tradition!' Your whole body reacts. What finally gives you that feeling in your stomach is when something resolves in a book, resolves in a song— something *happens* up there. When Carol Channing came down with those waiters, that was it, in *Hello, Dolly!* Empathy."

What did *A Chorus Line* have that made it a classic?

"What I've just mentioned. Empathy. People cared. They saw themselves in it. The feeling that we're all on the line; we're all auditioning, the way we all do, in one way or another, every day of our lives."

Theatre, Hamlisch agrees, is auditioning for its very life in this era of skyrocketing ticket prices. "It's disgusting. Everybody should be charging less. Think of it! A fourteen- or fifteen-year-old kid, taking his girl to a show. It's going to cost seventy, eighty dollars. You always hear, theatre grosses are up this season from last season, but not because of more people. It's because prices went up."

Don't people come to the hits anyway?

"That's just it. They come to see *only* hits. The same with movies. The attitude is, 'Let's see a name picture,' like *Beverly Hills Cop*. Or stay home and roast marshmallows. Same with shows, only worse, because shows cost so much more."

As bleak as the picture seems, Hamlisch is fundamentally optimistic. "In the end, though, if something's good, you'll get an audience. I've been lucky. I've worked with great people. Eddie Kleban was terrific on *A Chorus Line*. I've just written *Smile* with Howard Ashman—he did *Little Shop of Horrors*, and he's brilliant. And of course, Carole Bayer Sager on *They're Playing Our Song*."

They're Playing Our Song, which opened in February 1979, is the tale of two songwriters who become romantically involved, a situation suggested by Hamlisch's real-life love affair with collaborator Sager.

"Yes, the character bears some resemblance to me," he admits. "But it's a loose, a very loose resemblance. So I didn't feel intimidated about writing it. The world thinks I'm cool, but I'm much more neurotic than that character is.

"The way we found the title was somewhat personal. Neil Simon, who wrote the libretto, didn't have a title for the show. He came over one day to figure out the song for the discotheque scene. He wanted the characters to dance, and I said, 'Well, *I* don't really dance, if the character is me'—and then I said, 'I would get crazy if they played my song.' He jumped up, we called in Carole, and the thing was off and running. Because that *is* what songwriting's about, that excitement when you hear your work in a restaurant or in a car. That's the thrill."

Even so, Hamlisch insists, he did not intend to bare his inner soul. "At first Neil wanted to collaborate on a musical of his play *The Gingerbread Lady*. But *Gingerbread Lady* didn't *feel* like a musical. Later he called and sent me a script about two songwriters, based on my life with Carole. And the reason I liked it was I felt it was a novel idea to have basically two people in a musical. To tell the truth, I like breaking rules. *A Chorus Line* broke rules. Even conservative Rodgers and Hammerstein did, when they started *South Pacific* with a slow song called 'Dites-Moi.' "

The idea of a show like *They're Playing Our Song*, without production numbers and flashy choreography, was quietly revolutionary in its own way, and there was enthusiastic public reaction. "I wish, though," Hamlisch says regretfully, "that the show had lasted longer. I wish we had been able to replace Robert Klein and Lucie Arnaz and gotten a superb follow-up cast."

Hamlisch elaborates on the problems of casting. "A composer has input into the casting of a show, but he's the guy who has to make major concessions. For instance, in *A Chorus Line*, the dancing is of paramount importance. A girl comes in, and I'm crazy about her voice, and Michael says she can't dance. Who's gonna win?"

There are other problems a composer faces. "Choreographers," Hamlisch explains, "can make or break a number. I've seen it happen. They try too hard and blow it. And when you have an argument with a choreographer, you don't run to the producer. You hope the choreographer will see the light, or you're stuck. That happens a lot!

"Another major problem," he emphasizes, warming up, "is the lack of great directors. When we write a show today, we all have the same three or four people we think of to direct—and after that, it's as if we now reached the 'B' list! I mean, how can Broadway zoom along if there are only four great directors?"

He leaps ahead, answering the obvious question before we can ask it. "Why Broadway instead of movies, then? I'll tell you. It's an ego thing. Nobody goes to see a movie because they hear it's got a good Michel Legrand score. You go because Robert Redford's in it. One's background music; one's foreground. People know the names of those who write shows; they know those people. Broadway is a *composer's* medium. The ego gratification is tremendous."

Ego gratification is the icing, though, and Hamlisch loves the whole theatrical process. "I consider myself basically a melodist. I care about a melody madly. And I don't think about the end result when I begin. I think about what's correct for the *show*. For instance, there's no big, flashy ballad in my show, *Smile*. No 'Memory.' Because the characters are seventeen-year-old girls, and a tough, belting ballad would be inappropriate for where they are in life. In *A Chorus Line*, I didn't try to write hummable ditties. I wrote for what the *show* needed. I think it's amazing that a song like 'One' has had its own life. It is catchy, but at the time no one thought it was catchy. And I love 'At the Ballet' in *A Chorus Line*. Certainly not a Top Five record, but it fits the show."

Then Hamlisch remembers "What I Did for Love."

"OK, that song was a real cheat. I said, 'Listen, guys, we have nothing to play on variety shows. You can't put "Tits and Ass" on television.' So I wrote 'What I Did for Love' as a song you could literally pull out and do on Mike Douglas. Toward the end, Joe Papp said he wanted to cut it, because it felt stuck in. And I said, 'You're absolutely right, *absolutely* right. But if you cut it, you'll lose something that could be valuable later on.' He was right, and I was

Hamlisch poses with Lucie Arnaz
backstage at *They're Playing Our Song*.

right. But it's true, with that song you felt a bump in the show. No matter what we did, you felt the bump."

Despite the commercial compromise of "What I Did for Love," Hamlisch insists, "I want any show I write to be great. You give me a six-year run with no hit songs and I'll be a perfectly happy person. Give me four weeks and two Number One hits and I won't be happy. Because it means I haven't done my job."

Doing his job means adhering to a daily schedule. Writers who wait for "the mood" never get anywhere, and Hamlisch writes every afternoon. "Two or three hours and that's it," he says. "My brain goes off. You're not under the gun when you do a show; you make your own schedule. You're much more under the gun when you're rehearsing or in previews, and then you have to write a song quick."

During his work period he follows a strict pattern—writing songs in order. "Lots of writers do their opening song at the end, when they find out what the show is about. My way, I can figure how many ballads I need, how many up-tempo songs. I get a sense of balance, a clear perspective. I know how to pace everything, and *that's* the real secret of successful scores—pacing.

"Look," he says, "there's no foolproof method, of course. Even when you write in order, it can be wrong. I wrote an opening song for *A Chorus Line* called 'Resumes,' and we had to tear it up later, after I realized the show wasn't about resumes at all."

Hamlisch also believes in thorough research beforehand. "My father was the biggest believer in research. For *Smile* I went to a lot of beauty contests just to get the feel of what was going on there, and I'd tape them. When I did the film *The Sting*, I researched Scott Joplin thoroughly, got all the music together before I chose anything."

Hamlisch's painstaking research is always coupled with an abundance of healthy self-confidence.

"There are two songs in *A Chorus Line*. One is 'I Can Do That,' the other is "I Hope I Get It.' Both of them fit me, but 'I Can Do That' is my philosophy. I'll say yes to *anything*, and then I'll study it—take a quick night course or something. You need *chutzpah* in this business. I remember being asked if I did dance arrangements. I never did one in my life but I said, 'Of course I do dance arrangements.' You must seize the opportunity and know that it's a break. Recognize that a given situation is important, seize on it, and then deliver."

Hamlisch delivers by thinking visually. "When I write a show, I always conceive of what it's going to look like on a stage. Staging is top priority. And if a song doesn't mentally come to me as a picture, I discard it."

Sometimes, however, all the creative labor, all the integrity, results in disappointment. This was the case with Hamlisch's show *Jean*, which chronicled the life of Jean Seberg, a smalltown girl destroyed by drugs, misguided

Hamlisch receiving award from
former president of ASCAP,
Stanley Adams, and mayor of
New York City, Edward Koch.

Over the years, Hamlisch has
emerged as one of the most
versatile show business composers.
He has penned music for Broadway
musicals, feature films, Las Vegas
shows, and popular recording
artists.

political activism, and stardom. Jean was based on a fine biography by David Richards, but fared poorly in its London debut.

"That was my best score, no doubt about it," Hamlisch says. "But *Jean* hasn't had its day in court. The British didn't like the fact that we Americans would *dare* to sit in their national theatre. That really drove them crazy.

"The thing that tempered it for me was that it happened in London. When and if I have my first disaster in New York, it's going to be hard. You can go directly to New York Hospital. Send all cards and flowers there."

The kind of prejudice Hamlisch encountered in Britain also hits California show writers, because New Yorkers tend to look down on Hollywood composers. Hamlisch, with his numerous Oscars and Golden Globe awards, is viewed by the Big Apple as a West Coast creator.

"All I can do is go on TV and remind them I'm a New York boy. I feel very strongly about that. My father used to say, 'New York is a disease, and if you're stung with the disease, there's no getting away from it.' "

Hamlisch also believes there's no getting away from the theatre once it's in your blood. "Look, I love manipulating an audience. Seeing them go nuts. Seeing a song not work, then making it work the next night. The applause. And to be crass, there's a lot of money to be made if you have a hit show. In terms of a composer, tons more than a hit film. You get a percentage of the gross each and every week, in every town and country. You rarely, if ever, get percentages from movies."

To make sure he isn't misunderstood or thought purely mercenary, he adds, "But you have to love the show you're working on, love the idea, the music, the overall project. Carole Sager once told me the story of her show *Georgy*. She said that everyone loved the idea, and then it slowly was taken over by the director, then the actors, and everyone changed the original concept. She never felt it was her show anymore.

"So she didn't really like it. Wasn't that a criminal waste of time—to be reviewed on a show you didn't even like? So you'd better love what you're doing."

CHAPTER FOURTEEN

SHELDON HARNICK

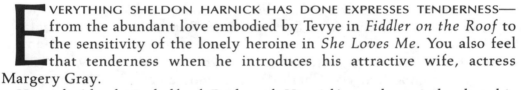

EVERYTHING SHELDON HARNICK HAS DONE EXPRESSES TENDERNESS—from the abundant love embodied by Tevye in *Fiddler on the Roof* to the sensitivity of the lonely heroine in *She Loves Me.* You also feel that tenderness when he introduces his attractive wife, actress Margery Gray.

Harnick (the lyric half of Bock and Harnick) speaks quietly, but his listeners are still aware of his passion. He places his hands on his chin frequently, as though drawing out facts like a method actor. He takes his glasses on and off, his mind obviously racing.

"Like so many young Jewish boys, I went for the violin," he says. Lessons began in Chicago, when Harnick was eight years old. "I had a terrible teacher—wonderful man, but *terrible* teacher. I just wasted the eight years with him. But that was one side of my creative development, the violin. The other side was that my mother, for some reason, celebrated every family occasion by writing a poem, and that became the thing to do for both my sister, Gloria, and me. Gloria wrote good poetry, actually. She won an all-Chicago high schools contest. I didn't write serious poetry. I concentrated on what was meant to be comic verse. I didn't know if it was or not, but that was what I was trying to do. Also, I had an uncle who was crazy about the theatre—he was a singer. I saw him in Gilbert and Sullivan shows, which is where I learned about Gilbert and Sullivan. I was terribly impressed with the patter songs. So I was exposed to a number of influences from different directions."

Harnick wrote parodies in high school and contributed "supposedly comic poems" to the school newspaper.

"When I was a junior in high school," he continues, "I met a young man who wanted to be in the theatre. His sister was a member of some semiprofessional Chicago little theatre group. He got involved in a production they did, and I was in one of the plays. We wrote together."

In Harnick's senior year, he and his partner met a comic in Chicago who was desperate for material. "He had to be desperate to like what we were writing," Sheldon says. "We gave him twenty minutes worth of stuff for twenty-five dollars. As I remember, they were mostly puns, but he bought them. That was the only professional writing I did. I was drafted in 1943 and spent three years in the army."

When Harnick's army hitch ended, he went to Northwestern University. "I thought I was going to be a violinist, but I also knew that Northwestern had a reputation for having the biggest student revue in the Midwest, and I was writing more and more at that point. I wanted to contribute songs to the revue, and by the time I left I had gotten involved with it. I knew by then what I wanted my career to be."

Harnick came to New York after college, encouraged by his brother Jay, who had arrived in Manhattan first.

"Jay was a very handsome young man with a lovely voice, a good musician. He got into the chorus of a show, *Alive and Kicking*, and stayed on. When I came, he was in the chorus of *Gentlemen Prefer Blondes*. He was one contact. Another was a man named Sol Lerner, whom I had met in the army. He was an agent. He'd seen me performing my own material at USO and camp shows. Most important was Charlotte Rae, who had been at Northwestern and had sung one of my songs. Charlotte was doing well as an actress. She wrote and said she was surprised that there wasn't as much first-rate songwriting talent as she had expected and felt that, if I came, I'd have a good career. She urged me to come."

The timing was perfect. Harnick was ready to abandon the violin. "I had developed anxiety about the instrument, a combination of nerve exhaustion and muscle fatigue in my right arm—in both arms, actually. The doctor advised me to lay off for a year. So I thought, 'What the hell? Writing's really the answer.' My uncle from the theatre helped a lot too, setting up an appointment for me with Jay Gorney, who had written 'Brother, Can You Spare a Dime?' with Yip Harburg. Jay was tremendously encouraging."

So was lyricist Yip Harburg, when Harnick met him at the Village Vanguard. Charlotte Rae was performing that night and made the introductions.

"Charlotte was my guardian angel," says Harnick. "Next thing she did was to connect me to Leonard Sillman, the producer of *New Faces of 1952*. Charlotte asked me to write a piece of material for her—she was in *New Faces*—and I wasn't sure. I didn't see myself as that kind of writer. I still don't.

But I felt obligated to Charlotte. She had introduced me to Yip. She had been instrumental in my coming to New York. I thought I ought to try, and I got lucky. I use that term deliberately. I *dreamed* the song. I woke up out of a dream with the song still going through my head. I jotted down the lyrics and went back to sleep.

"Next morning I woke up and thought the song must be awful, something you write down at four o'clock in the morning and have no perspective about. But I looked at it and thought, 'Oh my God, it's wonderful.' It needed a fourth verse, but the fourth chorus was inherent in the first three. So I finished it, showed it to Charlotte, and she began to use it. Someone said, 'Let's use it in *New Faces*.' Unfortunately, the producer of *New Faces* was having difficulty raising money; and after a year Charlotte had an offer to do another show, called *Three Wishes for Jamie*, by Ralph Blane. She left the show and took the song with her. At the time, she owned it; I later bought it back. But, meanwhile, someone said, 'Do you have anything else?' And I started on a new song, 'The Boston Beguine.' It got great reaction—Alice Ghostley performed it." However, money was still scarce at that point.

"Yes, money was tight, and I was married. When I came to New York I had a lot of money—not a lot in terms of living costs today, but a few thousand dollars I had saved up both as a working musician in Chicago and from war bonds. I got married to a girl I had met at Northwestern. She appeared in the show *Top Banana*, and was the breadwinner for a while. When we needed extra money, it came from my savings. *New Faces* was a hit for the first six or seven months. My take-home pay was about $60 a week. With *Two's Company*, starring Bette Davis, I got up to $110 a week, which was nice money in those days."

Harnick also tried to crack the pop market.

"I didn't have the feel for it, though," he says. "I met with a talented writer, Phil Springer, who had had a couple of hits. I told him I wanted to write commercial stuff, and he said, 'I don't think you could write anything commercial if your life depended on it.' I figured he was probably right, because most of the stuff I wrote was strange. But I did try, and I did take things to publishers. They all turned me down. The only thing that worked for me was theatrically oriented material."

Harnick continued to write comedy songs, a crucial staple of theatrical writing. How did he write comedy songs?

"Jay Gorney gave me good advice. He said, 'If you're writing for the theatre and you're going to audition for producers, don't worry about the love songs or ballads. *Anybody* can write those. Write the special material, the comedy stuff, because that's what's hard to come by.' I took this seriously. Years later I found at auditions that everybody wanted to hear your pop song or your love song or your big hit. But I started conscientiously to search for offbeat ideas, strange ideas. Some came out of dreams. 'The Boston Beguine' came out of anger. A number of my songs came out of anger."

"The Boston Beguine" started as a comic idea. "My first wife was in *Top Banana*, and I went to Boston to visit her. To get to the theatre, I took shortcuts through Boston Common. At that time Boston was very sleazy, not like today, and the Common was dangerous. My wife said she was insulted by the suggestive comments and odd-looking people. She stopped cutting through the Common because it didn't seem safe.

"On the bus back from Boston one day I was sitting next to a man listening to Tony Martin on the radio, a song about Johannesburg and what an exotic place it was. I started this song making fun of it. While I was writing, not knowing where the song would go, I saw an article in the paper about an attempt to suppress a book or some books by the church in Boston and by some other bluestockings, and that upset me. So the song took a turn toward that kind of point, satirizing the book ban. That was anger, the anger that made the song come to life."

The combination of a romantic beguine tempo with satirical lyrics made 'The Boston Beguine' a special-material classic, and Harnick continued to search for offbeat ideas. "I'd try to develop anything that struck me as offbeat. And this approach got me a job writing a theme with music for the DuMont 'Cavalcade of Stars,' which featured Jackie Gleason."

A series of events led Harnick to Jerry Bock, the composer with whom Harnick would eventually write his biggest hits.

"My first steady collaborator was a composer named David Baker. At the beginning, I had no collaborator. I was writing words and music myself; but one of the things Yip Harburg said was, 'There are more capable composers than there are lyricists, so you might advance your career by writing with other people. They're always looking.' It turned out to be true. Anyway, the pianist in Bette Davis's *Two's Company* was David Baker. He wanted to compose, and I found him very gifted. We had songs in some Off-Broadway shows, but we never got to Broadway. After the relationship came to a close, I was called in secretly to rewrite lyrics to a show called *Shangri-La*. Jerome Lawrence and Robert E. Lee, who had done the book and lyrics for that, had a problem because they were already committed to the stage play of *Auntie Mame*—the straight play, not the musical. That was 1956. The schedule conflict put them in a hole, and they needed someone to do repair work on *Shangri-La*. I came in and met actor Jack Cassidy—Jack was in that production. Jack introduced me to Jerry Bock, and we got along. Shortly after, we teamed up. Jerry had just split with Larry Holofcener, with whom he'd written *Mr. Wonderful*. Shortly after, we worked on *The Body Beautiful* together."

The Body Beautiful, which opened in 1958, was centered on prizefighters. "I wasn't particularly selective about choosing the property, though," says Harnick. "I wanted to do a book show. I was desperate to do a book show. I was nearing thirty, and it didn't look like it would happen. But it did; my show, *Horatio*, was produced in Dallas around my thirtieth birthday, and I thought, 'I've just gotten in under the wire.' The strange thing is, I'm not interested in boxing as a sport. I did some research on *The Body Beautiful*, but that wasn't what motivated me at that time."

Discouraged by poor reviews, the public was not motivated to see *The Body Beautiful*, a fanciful tale about a Dartmouth graduate who becomes a successful prizefighter. Steve Forrest played the rich, cultured hero who entered the boxing world, and Jack Warden was his manager. The show left Broadway on March 15, 1958, after 60 performances.

Fortunately, producer Hal Prince and his partner, Robert Griffith, liked the work they saw by Bock and Harnick.

"They liked my work, but they weren't sure if I was the right lyricist for a show they wanted to do, *Fiorello!* They were sure about Jerry; they hired him right away. Both Bobby and Hal knew my revue stuff, and Jerry told me they felt my work was too sophisticated, too satiric—they wanted warmth from a lyricist. They finally got down to Jerome Weidman, who wanted to do the lyrics. He was the book writer, along with George Abbott. Weidman wrote lyrics on spec, and they wanted him for the book but not, as it turned out, the lyrics. They also wanted Yip Harburg; but Yip, regrettably, had a reputation of being stubborn. They went to Steve Sondheim, Hal's old friend, and Steve, thank God, had reached a point in his own career where he said, 'No, I really want to do words and music now, not just words. So I have to turn this down.' Finally, it narrowed down to Marshall Barer, lyricist for *Once upon a Mattress*, and me. Hal called and said, 'I'll be honest. I don't think you're the right person for this, but if you're willing to write four songs on speculation—without pay—and prove us wrong, you have the opportunity.' I said, 'I'd love to.' I worked with Jerry, and he was so cooperative. They wanted a song that sounded like an Irving Berlin tune from 1917, a waltz for a big going-away party. Jerry went off and wrote four waltzes. He came back and played them and asked me, 'Which one do you like best?' I picked one, and he said, 'Oh, good, I like that one too.' So I had the music, and I auditioned for the producers. They liked two out of my four things, and that was enough. I got hired."

What was it like working with the legendary director-librettist, George Abbott?

"He was very discerning and a good taskmaster. He rarely suggested places for songs, although he did on one or two occasions. I would go through the book and think, 'Here's a good place for a song.' Weidman didn't know any more about writing a musical than I did, so George would say what was in the right place and what wasn't. I'd suggest where I thought a song ought to be, or Jerry would, and we'd write it. We'd audition it for Hal or Bobby or George, and George was the deciding voice. He had a wonderful way of stimulating and encouraging you.

"For instance, I brought him a lyric that I thought was pretty good, and he listened to it. Then he put his arm around me and asked, 'Would Larry Hart have been satisfied with that?' Implying that I could do as well as Larry Hart or better if I put my mind to it."

Fiorello! benefited from the Abbott perfectionism and the guidance he gave to his youthful composers. It opened on November 23, 1959, and ran for 795 performances. The use of a politician as a central figure had been tried before—with *I'd Rather Be Right* (portraying Franklin Roosevelt) and *Of Thee I Sing* (satirizing fictitious government officials). *Fiorello!* had more bite and reality than either production.

The story followed Fiorello LaGuardia through his pre–World War I election, his fight to institute the draft, and his eventual race against Jimmy Walker for mayor of New York. One lyric, "Gentleman Jimmy," showed Harnick's skill at characterization:

> Who's that genial gentleman in the
> Silk hat
> Gray spats
> Striped pants
> Why, that's
> Gotta be him
> Gentleman Jimmy
> Who's that swell celebrity with the
> Glad hand
> Quick wit
> New York's fav'rite
> That'll be him
> Gentleman Jimmy

Another number, a lovely ballad called "Till Tomorrow," demonstrated Harnick's sensitive side:

> Twilight descends
> Everything ends
> Till tomorrow, tomorrow
> Since we must part
> Here is my heart
> Till tomorrow, tomorrow

"My favorite is 'The Name's LaGuardia,' " says Harnick. "That actually was the idea of the original director, Arthur Penn. Arthur, in fact, still participates in the royalty. He was doing a TV piece at the time on LaGuardia, and he brought it to Prince and Griffith to mount the material on Broadway. But Arthur couldn't solve the construction problem—at least that's what I've been told—and they brought in Abbott to help construct the story and write it and direct it. Arthur left, but he did come up with some lovely ideas, including LaGuardia's production number."

Euphoric after the success of *Fiorello!*, Harnick and Bock plunged into *Tenderloin*, which opened on Broadway October 7, 1960.

"Too quickly," says Harnick today, "and without investigating the problems carefully enough. I wasn't investigating the book; I was just doing my usual thing of saying, 'A song goes here; a song goes there.' When we opened in New Haven, it went badly, and at a meeting immediately afterward, George Abbott assembled us. Being the absolutely candid man he is, he said, 'Well, I had an idea for a show, and it doesn't work. Does anybody have any help?' When his eyes searched around and in my direction, I thought, 'Don't look at me. I don't know anything about book writing.' So it was panic from then until we opened in 1960. We almost made the show work. We did a lot of good things, but problems that were there from the beginning remained. It was a very flawed show. There are a lot of good things in it, though."

One of the good things, in Harnick's view, "is a song, 'My Gentle Young Johnny,' and another is a production number, 'The Picture of Happiness.' The opening number, 'Little Old New York,' which I'm told is in a new album, worked well."

What *didn't* work?

"I think the storyline got confused. In the original novel, the main character is this young boy from New York's corrupt Tenderloin district, who's trying to get ahead and has this terrible conflict. There's a part of him that wants to be a decent young man. And there's a part of him that will stop at nothing to carve a career for himself. The catalyst is the minister he meets, who wants to clean up the Tenderloin. The boy develops a relationship with the minister—he looks on him as a father, and yet at the same time he knows he has to destroy the minister to achieve his own goals. It's a good plot. We made the mistake of making them equal roles, and in the book they're not. The minister really is the catalyst; it's the story of the boy. The minister is, unfortunately, a do-gooder, and do-gooders on stage are rather boring. So half the show was given to the problems of the minister, and audiences didn't care. The fun of the show was the boy and in the Tenderloin, so it was just out of balance. That was a problem we never solved."

The musical was a turning point for Harnick.

"I thought, 'If I'm lucky enough to be invited to do another show, by God, I'm going to get involved in the book and start to learn something at this point in my career.' The next offer was *She Loves Me*, so I did get involved in the book—not writing it, not collaborating on it, trying to *understand* it, trying to anticipate problems, offering suggestions."

The 1963 show *She Loves Me*, produced by Hal Prince with Lawrence Kasha and Philip McKenna and directed by Prince, was a delicate tale of two clerks in a perfumery who hate each other but unwittingly correspond as pen pals. In the end, they discover—with relief and joy—each other's true identity. The romance is developed through appealing songs such as "Dear Friend":

> Charming, romantic,
> The perfect cafe.
> Then, as if it isn't bad enough
> The violin starts to play.
> Candles and wine, tables for two
> But where are you,
> Dear friend?

"In that particular show, Joe Masteroff, the librettist, said, 'How do I write a musical comedy book?' Jerry Bock and I simply told him, 'Why don't you absorb the source material? There's a play and a film, *The Shop Around the Corner*. Why don't you absorb that material and write your own version of it? But only let it run for an hour and fifteen minutes, not a full-length evening, and the rest of it will be music—we'll find our music. This is a piece that's not going to be hard to find music for.' In fact, we found too much. Everything wanted to be sung. Our initial mistake, which I think we rectified, was that we decided we were going to have musical bits. We were going to have songs and developed pieces, but we were also going to have a lot of musical fragments. What we discovered was that it's hard enough on first hearing to absorb all that music. Then, if you deluge audiences with additional bits, ultimately the mind will stop hearing. The audience just gives up."

After *She Loves Me* came *Fiddler on the Roof*. In the classic tale, a dairyman in czarist Russia reluctantly accepts the suitors two of his daughters choose but can't accept the gentile his third daughter wants to marry. The beautiful "Sunrise, Sunset" and "Do You Love Me?" (a duet sung by the hero, Tevye, and his wife) were very personal songs for Harnick. But he had difficulty with "Now I Have Everything."

"It's about a man who is a revolutionary by temperament," says Harnick. "And it was very hard for me to write that song. I read books and biographies on revolutionaries, but the song still came out different from what I had planned. The most difficult songs in any musical, for me, are the ones that are remote from my own feelings. Those are the songs that call on craft.

"In *She Loves Me*, we needed a big song for Jack Cassidy in the second act at the moment when he's fired. We needed a number to get him offstage, and I had no feeling about that, so again I called on whatever craft and imagination and revue-writing techniques I could think of. What could he sing there that would be offbeat? We came up with a thing called 'My North Avenue Drugstore,' in which Jack had a fantasy about a store selling drugs and toys, one that even had a string quartet. Jack made it a showstopper, but

Tom Bosley won a Tony for his portrayal of Fiorello LaGuardia, the legendary New York City mayor.

Jerry Bock, Barbara Cook, Harold Prince, and Harnick prepare for the 1963 musical *She Loves Me*.

I was never happy with it. I got to know Jack and realized he needed to be bitchy and terribly funny—but there was an innocence to the bitchiness. It was witty rather than mean, and I thought, 'This is the kind of song we'll try.' We came up with 'Grand Knowing You.' Jack was very reluctant at that point to do a new song, because 'North American Drugstore' was stopping the show. You couldn't argue with that, but we showed it to him and said, 'Jack, this is a better song. It's a *character* song.' Jack listened and said, 'OK, I'll try it,' because it was reasonably short. He didn't believe it was better than the other one, but he did try it, and it was wonderful. It was a combination of his character, his personality, and the character of the show. It was, in fact, one of the high spots of *She Loves Me*."

Harnick believes in writing for the character, the situation, and the book, paying little attention to the actor who might play it.

"But an actor does occasionally influence you," he admits. "When we knew Zero Mostel was going to play Tevye in *Fiddler*, we went and watched him in *A Funny Thing Happened on the Way to the Forum*. When his opening song for *Fiddler* was written, we put in animal noises, crossed eyes, things like that, and it worked very well. The irony is that, when we were in rehearsal for *Fiddler*, I got scared of the fact that the song 'If I Were a Rich Man' suddenly became serious at the end. I wanted to cut the ending and keep the song comic. Zero fought it. He said we were crazy. 'That is the man, not the comic stuff,' he protested, and he was absolutely right."

Fiddler gave Harnick a chance to reacquaint himself with his Jewish roots. "The major sources," he says, "were the Sholom Aleichem stories themselves and a book entitled *Life Is with People*. I read a pictorial book of the Jews. I also read some Russian history, some world history. I was trying to familiarize myself with the history of the people. Jerry Bock, on the other hand, was afraid to do research. He was afraid some of the music might work its way into what he was doing, so he just called on his own emotions and his own memories of when he was growing up."

The team followed the same procedure in developing *Fiddler on the Roof* as they had in developing *She Loves Me* and all their other projects.

"Jerry would go off and write music. When he had the piece developed as far as he thought he wanted to develop it, he put it on tape. I'd be off somewhere studying the book, thinking of places for songs. Before I actually started a lyric, he'd give me the tape, which had somewhere from ten to two dozen musical moments—bits of tunes, themes. I'd go through the material, seeing which melodies sounded like they would fit the ideas I was mulling over. There were always a couple, and then there were always things on the tape that were just so exciting to me that they would suggest ideas I hadn't had before. I'd think, 'Oh, what a marvelous piece of music. I can't wait to do a lyric to that.' "

The results were gratifying, and *Fiddler* went on to become the longest-

Fiddler on the Roof does not open with a traditional razzmatazz production number. Director Jerome Robbins told the composers, "If this is a show about the breaking of traditions, we need to *show* the audience some of the traditions we're going to see dissolved. There has to be an opening song about tradition; it's a must."

Actor Hisaya Morishige as Tevye in a Japanese production of *Fiddler*.

running musical of its time (3,242 performances), until overtaken by *Grease*. The reviews, though, were only mildly favorable. In New York they were, as Harnick puts it, "terribly qualified. Walter Kerr said, 'Too bad, near miss.' The *Times* critic said, 'Oh, what a show this could have been if they had gotten Ernst Bloch to write the music, or maybe Leonard Bernstein, instead of Jerry Bock.' The *Journal American* was also mixed. The reviews were certainly not what we had expected. But it didn't matter. As in Washington, where we'd played before, there were long lines at the box office."

Fiddler broke with tradition, ironically, when Bock and Harnick came up with "Tradition" as an opening. "It wasn't a razzmatazz opening. I guess 'til then there had been the tradition of the two-four and the cut-time opening. But we believed and trusted Jerome Robbins's instinct. Robbins said, 'If this show is about the breaking of traditions, we need to *show* the audience some of the traditions we're going to see dissolved. There has to be an opening song about tradition; it's a must.' We put it together in bits and pieces. But we brought all the pieces to Robbins. He told us that the first image he had in rehearsal was one of the oldest folk forms, the circle, the folk circle; and it was his image of beginning with a folk circle and carrying that through to the end of the evening, when people came out and touched hands and went their separate ways. During rehearsal, Joe Stein, the librettist, was writing some connective material lines for the various people as they introduced themselves; and the full-circle scene got put together. It was marvelous, watching Robbins, a master artist, weave something together out of various pieces of material, out of choreography, orchestration, lights, costumes, lyrics, and music—working with it all and creating something incredible. I wish I had the opportunity to see him work more, but as with every show I've done, most of the time I wasn't at rehearsal; I was off somewhere rewriting."

The rewriting was worth it. *Fiddler on the Roof*, initially regarded as uncommercial by most observers, gathered affection around the world. It served as a springboard for a host of effective Tevyes—Zero, Herschel Bernardi, Luther Adler, Harry Goz, and Jan Peerce, among others. "Matchmaker, Matchmaker," "Tradition," and "Sunrise, Sunset" all turned into enduring standards.

The next Bock-Harnick undertaking, *The Apple Tree*, proved less enduring, though it ran for a healthy 463 performances.

"It was a failure of resolve on my part," Harnick says. "It was a good idea to do three one-act musicals, and we had Robbins as director. But it was difficult to find three stories that seemed to link to one another. We read hundreds and hundreds of stories, and it took so long that Robbins eventually parted company with us. He claimed to have other commitments. But he left with one piece of advice: 'Keep this evening homogeneous. It must all add up to something.' Our original title was *Come Back, Go Away*,

I Love You, but we decided on *The Apple Tree*, since each story seemed to have a kind of devil figure. The source material included 'Diary of Adam and Eve,' from Mark Twain's short story; 'The Lady or the Tiger?' by Frank Stockton, and a Cinderella story about a chimney sweep, 'Passionella,' by Jules Feiffer.

"Robbins was right, though; we came out with less than the sum of our parts, not more. And that hurts.

"I said to Jerry Bock, and he agreed with me, 'Let's stop this thing now; we're going too fast. Let's think it through.' But Stuart Ostrow, the producer, said, 'We *can't* stop. We have Mike Nichols to direct if we want him, and he only has time to do the show if we start now.' The ambitious part of me wanted to keep working, and that part of me spoke loudest. So we went ahead, and, of course, the real problem of the show turned out to be that the pieces were not honestly tied together. The audience went away slightly hungry. They weren't satisfied. The show ran fourteen months because of Barbara Harris, Alan Alda, and Larry Blyden. The performances were wonderful, and Barbara won herself a Tony. But when she left, we realized it had become the Barbara Harris show; business fell off. What's interesting is, although the show does have stock productions, there are many more productions of the first piece alone, the Adam and Eve piece, which is the only one with genuine heart. It's produced a lot with other one-act musicals, and they go together much better than the ones we had."

The Apple Tree was surpassed, artistically and commercially, by the next Bock-Harnick piece, *The Rothschilds*.

The Rothschilds returned to the Jewish theme that had proven so fruitful in *Fiddler on the Roof*. It opened October 19, 1970, and dealt with a dynasty that took over the banking world. Hal Linden registered strongly as Mayer Rothschild, winning a Best Actor Tony for his efforts; Keene Curtis won a Best Supporting Actor Tony.

"It was a difficult decision to do *The Rothschilds*," Harnick says, "because of *Fiddler*. But finally we decided it was very different from the earlier show. Some of the meaner critics said we were trying to duplicate *Fiddler*, hoping lightning would strike twice, but that wasn't our reason at all."

Did he do *The Rothschilds* because it centered around a powerful male protagonist, such as Tevye and LaGuardia?

"There may be an unconscious element that drew me to those characters, but it wasn't deliberate. Unfortunately, *The Rothschilds* led to friction between Jerry Bock and me. It had to do with the original director of the show, Derek Goldby. He'd done only straight plays, and there's some mysterious, magical quality in a musical that a dramatic director just can't handle. He wasn't capable of handling a show of that size, I felt, but Jerry thought he was. Jerry felt—you would have to confirm this with him—that Derek had been given a raw deal. He was angry with the rest of us. He thought Derek was doing a good job, and when he was replaced by Michael Kidd, it caused friction. After that Jerry and I kind of drifted apart and never managed to drift back together, which is kind of awful. I called him a number of times, and the last time I called him he was agreeable to doing something. But he couldn't because he was involved with other things, and I had to go elsewhere."

Harnick's sense of loss is obviously as acute as it was when the initial separation occurred. "Steve Sondheim said that Jerry is one of the few composers with humor, honest humor, in his music. He's a wonderful man, one of the funniest and wittiest people I've ever met. I hope we write together again."

Harnick later had a chance to work with the legendary Richard Rodgers on *Rex*, but this treatment of Henry VIII and his attempts to find sexual happiness and to father a male heir never caught fire. Harnick's lyrics were as sparkling as ever. Rodgers, however, was past his prime when the show opened on April 25, 1976. *Rex* ran only 49 performances.

"The difficulty was," says Harnick, "that Rodgers had had various illnesses by then, including a mild stroke. He no longer seemed capable of writing music first. When we met, before we started working together, he said, 'How do you like to work?' and I said 'Either way.' He said 'Good, so do I,' but he never gave me any music first. I talked to a doctor about problems I was having with Rodgers, and the doctor asked if he had had a stroke. I said 'Yes, how do you know?' The doctor said, 'I didn't, but I've had patients who've had strokes, and they lose the ability to abstract. Music is abstract.' In one instance, Rodgers and I had a discussion about something that needed to be written, and he couldn't grasp what I was talking about until I wrote down a dummy lyric. Once he saw the dummy lyric and how everything was supposed to be laid out, he knew how to write the music. It was very strange and difficult because I wasn't used to writing every lyric first. I guess it was a good experience, though, because, left to myself, I tend to fall into A A B A, and it's comfortable."

Rex was a disappointment. It related the story of King Henry VIII and his adjustment after the execution of Anne Boleyn. "The subject matter had dramatic potential," says Harnick, "but there was something laborious about the whole enterprise that music didn't seem to alleviate. It wasn't one of my happier experiences."

Much happier was his experience with the film version of *Fiddler*. "When I saw it first I'd been so spoiled by Zero's performance, and Herschel Bernardi's performance, that I wasn't entirely happy with Topol. Although Topol *looked* like a Tevye, he wasn't totally comfortable in English, and some of the comedy was lost. But overall, I did like the film, and some years later, when it was rereleased, I went to see it. By this time the images of Zero and Herschel had faded enough, and I thought it was even better than the first time around. It was wonderful. Norman Jewison did a fine job."

Harnick collaborated with Richard Rodgers on *Rex*, a musical based on the life of King Henry VIII.

Harnick feels, in retrospect, that *Fiddler on the Roof* was as perfect as he had hoped it would be. "I wish I could redo parts of *Tenderloin* and *The Apple Tree*, though, and I think of going back to *The Rothschilds* and trying to fix things in the second act that should have been stronger. But I won't."

Aside from *Fiddler*, he's very satisfied with *She Loves Me* and *Fiorello!* "But I don't know what a surefire subject is anymore. At one time I thought I knew. I thought, if you told a good story and the songs were entertaining, lovely, and meaningful, you'd find an audience. It's hard to know where theatre is going today. The Broadway theatre seems headed toward spectacle, with substance secondary; or possibly toward intimacy, an intimate form of musical like *Sunday in the Park with George*—a far cry from what used to be a standard musical, with its large-size orchestra and lots of people in the cast. In *Fiorello!* we had forty people, and that was not unusual. So the musical is headed either toward spectacle or toward intimacy."

Does Broadway need stars now?

"Yes. To draw. Certainly a play that's less than extraordinary needs the draw of a name, and I don't even know who those names are. The Broadway theatre is in transition. I don't know where it's going. None of us do, and we're terribly concerned about it. The Off-Broadway theatre, on the other hand, appears to be flourishing. Joe Papp and the Circle Repertory Theatre and the Playwrights Horizons and the Ensemble Theatre—they do very well. But they're caught in the price squeeze, and they need additional support. I hope it's forthcoming."

He remains optimistic, though, and continues to work on productions such as *It's a Wonderful Life* with composer Joe Raposo, based on the 1946 Frank Capra classic. The subject matter—a man, trapped in a small town, who realizes how much his friends value him—is upbeat and hopeful.

Other projects include *Dragons*, a musical for which Harnick has done book, lyrics, and music.

"It's based on a Russian play by Yevgeny Schwarz, and so far I've revised it through two workshops and a production at Northwestern University. Next year it's being done at Colorado College."

His other recent projects include the score for a stage version of *A Christmas Carol*, which has had two regional productions thus far. He collaborated on *A Christmas Carol* with Michel Legrand, and his other recent partner is composer Jack Beeson, "with whom I've written two operas. We're currently finishing a third, *Cyrano*."

The tireless Harnick finds time to see current shows, no matter what his work load is. Those he admires from the past are *The King and I*, "which I adore. I love *A Funny Thing Happened on the Way to the Forum*. *Guys and Dolls*. *Carousel*. So many great ones, really."

Any particular composer?

"I've been asked that question a lot. I have favorites, but it's more individual lyrics, individual songs that I love, because there will be a song by someone who doesn't have a great body of work that I love as much as anything else. For instance, Martin and Blane; they haven't written that much, but some of their things, like 'The Trolley Song' from *Meet Me in St. Louis*, are among my favorites. I suppose at the head of the list of people I admire has to be Sondheim, because of his extraordinary talent, his extraordinary adventurousness, and his extraordinary integrity. He is just a constant yardstick to measure yourself by."

Maybe so, but Harnick also has Sondheim's gift for wit and cleverness, as well as for cutting to the core of human feelings. His lyric for "She Loves Me" demonstrates this quality:

> She loves me
> And to my amazement
> I love it
> Knowing that she loves me
> She loves me
> True she doesn't show it
> How could she
> When she doesn't know it

A whole range of emotions are expressed in that lyric—the hero's joy, his surprise, his trepidation that the woman he cares for isn't aware of his feeling. Above all, there's that tenderness Harnick values so highly.

"It was expressed best for me by Alan Alda in a conversation we were having. He said—and it hit exactly the core in me—he wanted to do things that brought people together, rather than separating them. What moves me terribly—is when one person does a kindness to another person. More and more, I hope my work will express that on the stage so that people watching—it's not that they'll learn anything—but they'll have their beliefs confirmed that loving kindness is important and can make a life richer. Maybe I can make their world richer."

CHAPTER FIFTEEN

JERRY HERMAN

JERRY HERMAN IS A GENUINE OPTIMIST. "When I wrote *Dear World*," he says, "I was attracted to the central character, and I gave her a lyric that went:

If Music is no longer lovely,
If laughter is no longer lilting,
If lovers are no longer loving,
Then I don't want to know.

That is how I honestly live my life."

There's contentment in Herman's manner, a warm, casual ease highlighted by his light green cashmere sweater, silk pants, and loafers. He has the fine features of a matinee idol, and his smile shines with wonder and the unclouded belief of a teenager.

His spacious home further underscores that optimism. Herman, once a student of the Parsons School of Design ("Designing was my plan for a life's work"), has turned his Manhattan brownstone into an ideal creative haven. His studio, which reaches twenty-five feet in height, features posters of his productions and a trapeze on which he exercises. The rooms, which reflect characteristics of London, France, and California, possess the same overall charm and variety that mark his music and lyrics.

"We've had a thousand songs about how wonderful tomorrow is going to be," Herman declares. "I think I summed up my feeling best in *La Cage aux Folles*, with the number 'The Best of Times (Is Now).'"

For Herman, the best of times began on 50th Street in Manhattan, at a clinic overlooking the Winter Garden Theatre. "My mother must must have known something," he says. "And she loved show business. She was a very talented lady who had a radio program called 'Ruth Sax Sings.' She was a wonderful pianist and singer, and she taught Hebrew music at the New Jersey Y. She also played accordion, and my dad played sax. Our idea of after-dinner entertainment was to play together—my dad on saxophone, my mother playing accordion, me on piano. We had a whole routine going."

Herman had no brothers and sisters, and admits, "I was spoiled rotten." That included being taken to Broadway musicals from an early age. He caught the Broadway fever after viewing *Annie Get Your Gun*, *Brigadoon*, and all the great classics of the forties and fifties.

In spite of Herman's instant obsession with show business, his father was skeptical about a full-time writing career.

"My parents both ran a very successful children's camp in upstate New York, where I spent all my summers. I had three hundred brothers and sisters for two months, and then I became dramatics counselor and put on shows there. My dad—and my mother too—wanted me to take over the camp."

Nevertheless, Herman continued to focus on writing. He was given formal training and revealed an ability to play by ear at age five, two years before actual lessons began.

"Working with my mother was marvelous fun—she made music a game. But when Miss Pessin, my first piano teacher, came into my life, and I had to practice every day between four and five, the whole thing became a chore. She brought 'The Happy Farmer' and said, 'In a few weeks you'll be able to do this piece.' I went over to the piano and played my version of what I'd just heard, with wild chords and arpeggios, and it blew her mind completely. She ran to my mother and said, 'I'm terribly sorry, but I really don't know what I can do with him.' She left my life altogether, and that ended my piano lessons for a long time. It wasn't until my professional days—when I was doing *Milk and Honey*—that I actually learned to read and write music."

During *Milk and Honey*, Herman worked with Hershy Kay, "one of the most brilliant arrangers of all time," and realized he couldn't explain specifically what he wanted.

"If for no other reason but to be able to have my wishes, my voice in the orchestrations, I learned how to notate and put names on everything. Now I have wonderful dialogues with my arrangers, like Philip Lang, who did six of my shows. And Don Pippin, who gives musical direction, as well as help and support."

As Herman's talent developed, he persuaded his parents to support his Broadway aspirations.

"My mother was thrilled, because she was the true musician in the family. My father was a little more practical. He asked me, 'How can you give up this

 A scene from *Milk and Honey.* The 1961 musical won critical acclaim for the way it captured the spirit of the young Israeli nation.

going business, where I can guarantee you X amount of money? Do you want to starve in some attic?' I said I had to try it!"

Playing piano in cocktail lounges protected Herman from tiny attics and the shadow of poverty.

"I got booked immediately into a whole series of East Side clubs—chic places where Mabel Mercer and Bobby Short sang. For four or five years, I'd play piano from ten o'clock at night till four in the morning, and I made enough money to sustain an apartment. My parents didn't have to support me, and I felt very good about what I was doing. I would write during the day, and in the afternoons I'd knock on doors with my briefcase and say, 'Hey, I want to write a Broadway show.' "

The first turning point came in 1958, when the owner of the Showplace on West 4th Street—where Herman played cocktail piano—listened to and liked his material. As a result, Jerry was granted an opportunity to put on a show at the club, budgeted at $15,000.

"I'm proud to say I discovered Charles Nelson Reilly. Phyllis Newman sent him to me. Phyllis was a great friend, and she agreed to do the choreography. So I put on this four-character revue and played the piano. It was called *Nightcap*. The audience reaction was terrific, but we couldn't get any press to come down. They had never heard of the Showplace. Finally, somebody got Richard Watts, the critic on the *New York Post*, to stop in. And he sat there with no expression on his face whatsoever. I thought, 'Oh, my God, this is the end of my career. Tomorrow morning I'm going to be a camp director.' "

The next day, still discouraged, Herman walked to the Showplace and saw a huge line. Public enthusiasm had been generated by a rave review from Watts.

"He called me the new Rodgers and Hart," Herman says. "Raved about the material, the performers, the whole flavor of the piece. And we ran for almost two years, which is unheard of in a cabaret thing. I kept it fresh by changing things. When Marie MacDonald was kidnapped, there was a big headline in the news. And I wrote a crazy song about it. The show was a satire not only of show business but of current events as well."

In the spring of 1959, Lawrence Kasha, stage manager of *Li'l Abner* (and later producer of *Applause* and *Woman of the Year*), saw *Nightcap* and thought it would make a popular Off-Broadway show if expanded. Herman was eager, and Kasha presented the altered show under the name *Parade*. Billed as "an intimate topical revue," it opened at the Player's Theatre in Greenwich Village and ran for six months with Charles Nelson Reilly, Dodie Goodman, and Richard Tone.

"Our budget was so low that I was stuck at the piano in the pit. We opened in 1960, and a gray-haired gentleman approached me after a performance and handed me a card. He wanted to do a musical, to be set in Israel, and would I be interested? I took the card and paid very little attention to it. But he was serious! His name was Gerard Ostreicher, and a month later he sent me to Israel to absorb the background and flavor of the country. A year later

I had my first Broadway show, and I owe it to Larry Kasha for giving me a shot with *Parade*.

"It's quite remarkable," Herman says. "Ostreicher simply trusted a kid who had had no experience writing a book musical. *Milk and Honey* was an operetta about middle-aged people in Israel. I certainly had no experience writing for middle-aged people. I'd written only the most traditional American show-biz stuff you can imagine."

The show, which opened on October 10, 1961, traced the adventures of seven women touring Israel, and contained a standout performance by Molly Picon as a widow who finds love on her journey. Its run of 543 performances was due to Herman's lively score, which contained such numbers as "Hymn to Hymie," and "Independence Day Hora." The Israeli theme appealed to New York's large Jewish population.

"I soaked in the Jewish flavor," says Herman. "I've drawn in all influences. I think a songwriter has to. He has to be prepared to immerse himself in all musical flavors and styles and write in any vein. It was no trouble to write in a Yiddish idiom.

"From the mid-forties on," Herman says, "I think I saw every important New York musical. I saw *Saratoga*. It probably ran only a few weeks, but I wanted to see a Harold Arlen musical. I wanted to know how it was constructed. But I have to say, and I believe this very strongly, *instinct* is the most crucial factor in knowing what to musicalize, where to put songs. Take any scene from any show of mine—there's more than one natural choice in that scene to sing about."

The songwriter's instincts which helped to make *Milk and Honey* a hit came through again with *Hello, Dolly!*. Every scene offered rich opportunities for music and Herman made the most of them, aided by star Carol Channing. Channing played Dolly Levi, a widow and matchmaker, who eventually solves her own romantic difficulties along with the love problems of her clients.

The show, based on Thornton Wilder's *The Matchmaker*, ran for 2,844 performances and became a classic, largely due to Channing's electrifying pivotal performance.

"I learned very early in my career to go for the actor," says Herman. For *Dolly*, he had a cast that included David Burns, old friend Charles Nelson Reilly, and David Hartman. But the crucial element was Channing.

"When Carol did those songs, they came to life and jumped off the stage. In fact, she *became* Dolly Levi. Her comedic acting made everything work. You can even cross out the word comedic. She made the beginning of *Hello, Dolly!* very moving as she made the speech about her dead husband."

Channing's power reminds Herman of a common thread in the properties he has chosen during his Broadway career.

"Almost every show—*The Grand Tour* was the exception—has had a larger-than-life lady on stage. The gimmick is wonderful."

It's inconceivable now, but producer David Merrick, after having seen *Milk*

This photograph of Herman and choreographer Onna White with the chorus of *Mame* provides a rare glimpse of the extensive work behind every Broadway musical.

Angela Lansbury, the original star of Herman's *Mame*, in a scene from a revival of the 1966 Broadway smash.

and Honey, was skeptical about Herman's ability to write *Hello, Dolly!* "He thought I was too *ethnic* for the piece," Herman chuckles. "Mike Stewart, the librettist, told me this, and I was hysterical. I laughed for twenty minutes. After all, *Milk and Honey* had been a stretch for me—my thing wasn't to write middle-aged operetta! But when I met with David, he said, 'I think you're very talented, but I don't really know if you can do Americana.' I asked him to let me try, to prove I could. I left his office and ran to my little apartment. I locked myself in with a copy of the first draft of *Hello Dolly!*, which I still own—on the cover it says *Matchmaker, Draft Number One*. I read it and read it and read it. In the next three days and nights I wrote four songs. At that time, by the way, I had an agent, a lady named Priscilla Morgan, and I didn't tell her I was doing this, because she never would have agreed—not while I had a successful Broadway show running. You don't audition when you're in that shape, but I didn't want anybody to tell me this was wrong. I wanted that property. I knew it was right for me. So I wrote these four songs."

Armed with a wealth of new material, Herman called Merrick's office and asked to see him for fifteen minutes.

"I said, 'I have some things,' and I played the four songs for Mike Stewart and David Merrick. I don't think to this day that that great showman has ever been as stunned by anybody. He couldn't believe I'd written those songs in three days. He obviously liked them, because he stood up at the end and said, 'Kid, the show is yours.' "

The writing for *Hello, Dolly!* proceeded smoothly, with one problem area— finding the right song for the spot that eventually featured "Before the Parade Passes By."

"We got to Detroit," Herman recalls, "and had a bad notice from the one critic there. He did us a great service, I realize today, because he made us work harder on a show that was only partially there. We had a first act finale number called 'Penny in My Pocket,' sung by David Burns, and it was all about Dolly's dream man, Horace Vandergelder. The number was brilliantly staged by Gower Champion. Audience response was terrific. Yet I was always dissatisfied, and I couldn't figure out why. The tune was melodic and catchy; the big company sang it gorgeously."

It didn't help that producer Merrick, in the midst of unsolved problems, yelled and screamed a great deal.

"One of those legendary out-of-town experiences," Herman shudders, "where everybody is a basket case. And I finally said, 'You're going to kill me, because I know how hard you've worked on 'Penny in My Pocket,' but the song is about the wrong person. The audience doesn't care about Vandergelder—they're in love with Dolly Levi.' "

The Matchmaker, Herman realized, had been an ensemble piece, but its musical offshoot, *Hello, Dolly!*, through the magnetism and charm of Carol Channing, had become a showpiece for a star.

Creating the new song that everyone agreed was sorely needed meant new scenery and new orchestrations, not to mention new and formidable expense.

"Gower totally agreed with me, though," says Herman. "I went to work writing 'Before the Parade Passes By' under terrible circumstances. Everyone was screaming to get those changes in—it was tension time. My experience with *Hello, Dolly!* in Detroit was a nightmare; it truly was. I closed myself away in my hotel room, and I remember very vividly having three candy bars on the piano, because I'm a chocoholic. I knew if I rewarded myself after a line or a melody, it would get me through, make things easier. I wrote 'Before the Parade Passes By' very quickly, out of tension. But, of course, I had been living with this character for a year or two of my life.

"There's a point I'd like to make. Everybody asks you, 'How long does it take to write a song?' The actual writing time at the piano, or walking on the streets of New York, may be a half hour or a day or a week, but the actual gestation time, the time that it has been percolating in my brain, might be a year and a half. So the answer is hard to be accurate about. I wrote the song 'Mame' in twenty minutes, or I wrote 'Mame' in a year and twenty minutes."

He agrees with the Oscar Hammerstein definition, that song writing is three-quarters thinking and one-quarter writing.

After "Before the Parade Passes By" was completed, Herman summoned Carol Channing, Gower Champion, and David Merrick to the piano in their bathrobes and won their hearty approval.

"It was the turning point for us. Now we had a through line, a sustained theme, a firm point of focus throughout. We had a woman who was locked away from the world because of the loss of her husband, spending her life fixing everybody else up, until the moment came when she clenched her own fist and said, 'Hey, it's time for *me*!' After that the show worked like a dream."

The Tony results in 1964 also were a dream for Herman. *Hello, Dolly!* captured ten Tony Awards, the most Tonys ever awarded a show in Broadway history. Carol Channing won Best Actress in a Musical against Barbra Streisand in *Funny Girl*—an irony, since Streisand later did the Dolly Levi role in the 20th Century–Fox film version. There were other upsets: Michael Stewart's triumph over Noel Coward (*High Spirits*) for libretto; Herman's win over Jule Styne, the man who had created Channing's first great vehicle, *Gentlemen Prefer Blondes*. Other *Dolly!* winners included director/choreographer Gower Champion, producer David Merrick, set designer Oliver Smith, and costume designer Freddie Wittop. *Hello, Dolly!* also became the biggest-selling cast album in the history of the theatre.

In the glow of receiving honors, a composer may forget emergencies such as "Before the Parade Passes By," but they recur in each new show. When they do, Herman has to go off by himself and dope things out. We wondered if the responsibility for composing words and music, without a collaborator, ever gets lonely.

"Yes," Herman says firmly. "It's very lonely. Sometimes I envy Fred Ebb

Carol Channing
wowed audiences with
her performance
in *Hello, Dolly!*

The tremendous success of *Hello, Dolly!* necessitated the use of a number of different stars to play the lead, including Ginger Rogers, Martha Raye, Dorothy Lamour, Betty Grable, Pearl Bailey, Phyllis Diller, and, shown here with Herman, Ethel Merman.

and John Kander, who are dear friends of mine. John can say, 'Hey, Fred, what do you think of this?' or vice versa. So I use the other part of me. I'll say, 'What do you think of this, Jer?' One part of me is Jer; the other is Jerry. I have these little dialogues with myself, and I try to listen with an objective ear."

Herman's objectivity has resulted in a series of hit shows that travel successfully throughout the world. His songs become hits too, such as Louis Armstrong's Number One version of "Hello, Dolly!" or the chart success of the Grammy-winning "If He Walked into My Life," from *Mame*.

The story of *Mame* was familiar to most theatre and filmgoers, a musical adaptation by Jerome Lawrence and Robert E. Lee of their own *Auntie Mame*. Angela Lansbury assumed the flamboyant part of Mame Dennis, a charismatic eccentric who adopts her ten-year-old nephew Patrick and exposes him to a bizarre, unconventional existence. *Mame* opened May 24, 1966, and ran until January of 1970, totaling 1,508 performances.

"I started that show with a hymn—highly unusual, nothing I had ever seen before. Where the idea came from I'll never be able to explain, any more than I can explain how I knew how to play 'The Marine's Hymn' at the age of five. There are certain things that come from our insides, from our genes, from our innate abilities."

It takes courage to act on instinct against established practices. It also takes courage to fight for unconventional casting, for actors who are not safe, obvious choices.

"I suggested Angela Lansbury for *Mame*, and the producers thought I was just demented. Their feeling was, 'This is a brilliant actress, there's no better actress in the world, but she's not a musical comedy performer.' But I had seen her in a Stephen Sondheim show, *Anyone Can Whistle*, and I remembered this lady belting out a song very, very well. So I said, 'She's a musical comedy performer, and all I want you to do is to get her a ticket to New York. I'll do the rest.' They were so pleased with the score I had just written that they gave me the three hundred dollars to bring her in."

Herman was more convinced than ever when Lansbury walked into his apartment, looking elegant and glamorous and not at all like Laurence Harvey's mother in *The Manchurian Candidate*.

"She was warm and funny, with a great figure, and she was everything I wanted Mame to be. We sat at the piano, and I fooled around with her voice. It was rough at that time because she had not been using it, but I knew it was there. I knew she was a really first-rate singer. So I said, 'I'm going to do with you something I've never done with any of the other ladies. It's no secret that a hundred ladies have auditioned. I'm going to teach you two songs from the score, and I'm going to sit in the pit, and they're not going to know it's me in the pit. And I want you to audition with two songs that they've never heard anybody but me sing, and I have a lousy voice. So no matter how you do it, it's going to sound like the Second Coming to them. Well, Angela worked for two days, day and night, on "If He Walked Into My Life" and "It's Today." We had decided between the two of us what she should wear, and she just threw a mink over some very glamorous outfit. She looked just perfect, not overdone. She has the greatest taste, you know, in clothes. She came in looking like a million dollars and walked to the middle of the stage and dropped the mink. They almost fell over. She had a contract about two hours later. In 1966, she also had a Tony Award for Best Actress in a Musical."

Despite his impressive achievements, however, Herman is occasionally referred to as too commercial.

"*Too* commercial? What is that? I think being accused of too much commerciality is like saying the bride is too pretty. To me, the ultimate compliment is being called commercial. It's my goal; and if you hit the goal you go after in life, you're successful. I love the word *commercial*. I believe the theatre is a business, and I think one of the reasons for the sad state of it right now is that we're not commercial anymore. Personally, I'm writing for all those people out there, and if I can't reach them by having them hum something on the way out of the theatre, I've failed. *Commercial* is what my middle name is."

Herman treasures a compliment from Alan Jay Lerner, in which Lerner refers to him as the Irving Berlin of this generation.

"I'm really touched by that, because Alan is an idol of mine. Irving Berlin is commercial, and his kind of commercialism is what I believe in. I hate seeing the old kind of Broadway song disappear. To me it's an endangered species. I want songs from Broadway shows to be able to be played at the Rainbow Room for dancing. I want songs from Broadway shows to be sung around a piano by a bunch of old drunks at two in the morning. I want to hear songs from Broadway shows in elevators. Talk about Broadway in the thirties and the forties—you and I could be here the rest of the day, and we'd never run out of song titles. I'd say "Some Enchanted Evening," you would say "You're the Top," and we could go on and on, and neither of us would lose this game. If we played the game about the past ten years, you'd say "Tomorrow," I'd say, "What I Did for Love," or "Cabaret," and one of us would lose in fifteen minutes."

Herman is quick to point out, however, that he doesn't want to restrict Broadway to one kind of traditional song.

"I've been accused—and very wrongly—of wanting only that kind of Broadway. Not so. I think an eclectic Broadway is a healthy Broadway. I love it when a really avant garde musical is playing next door. Maybe there's a revival of *Show Boat* around the corner from a rock musical like *Leader of the Pack*. That's a healthy Broadway to me. All I don't want to see happen is for us to lose the meat and potatoes of the Broadway show tune."

Despite Herman's realistic commercial instincts, his career went into decline after years of golden success. *Dear World*, *Mack and Mabel*, and *The Grand Tour* all opened to disappointing reaction.

With *Dear World*, Herman was reunited with *Mame* star Angela Lansbury. The 1969 musical was adapted from Jean Giraudoux's play *The Madwoman of Chaillot* and contrasted the ideals of dreamers with the materialism of the everyday world.

Herman poses with Joel Grey, star of the 1979 musical *The Grand Tour*. The show, about the adventures of a Jewish refugee fleeing the Nazis, earned Herman a Tony nomination for Best Score.

Herman poses with Bernadette Peters, the star of his 1974 musical, *Mack and Mabel*. The story about a romance between a pioneer of early moviemaking and his leading lady earned a nomination for Best Musical.

Mack and Mabel, which opened October 6, 1974, and had a run of 65 performances, had a promising subject. The central characters were Mack Sennett, legendary producer of two-reel comedy shorts, and Mabel Normand, the actress who loved him and turned to drugs when their romance ran into trouble. But colorful performances by Robert Preston and Bernadette Peters couldn't compensate for an overall heaviness in the book.

"*Mack and Mabel* suffered from dark lighting," says Herman. "The sets and ambiance didn't have the vibrancy of the score. The audience left dissatisfied, somber. They felt as though they'd gotten punched in the stomach. There are four or five legitimate mistakes that Michael Stewart and I are determined to correct. We intend to try with *Mack and Mabel* again. Even if it doesn't work the second time, we both feel it deserves another chance."

A novice becomes defensive when his works are criticized. Pros like Jerry Herman analyze, without overpersonalizing, so they can prevent errors in the future.

The Grand Tour, which opened January 11, 1979, and ran for 61 performances was "my mistake from the start," says Herman, though Richard Eder of the *New York Times* found it "a musical that is often amiable and sometimes more than that." *The Grand Tour* was adapted from a World War II play, *Jacobowsky and the Colonel*, which later became *Me and the Colonel* on film with Danny Kaye. The show followed the escape attempt of a Polish colonel and a Polish Jew, natural enemies who become friends.

"I really didn't want to do it. I thought it was a lovely play, but not my kind of material. Running from the Nazis just didn't seem to go with Jerry Herman. I wrote it for the wrong reason—because I hadn't found anything else I wanted to do. I *made* myself get excited about it. I have the capacity for making myself get excited about anything. I thought, 'I'll do it for Joel Grey.' I've always wanted to work with Joel Grey because he's such a terrific talent. It's not my best work by any stretch of the imagination. I don't think the show deserved to be a big hit. And it is a legitimate mistake. But it taught me *never* to write for the wrong reason."

"I wrote *La Cage aux Folles* for the right reason; I *had* to write it. I was absolutely chomping at the bit to write the score."

The film *La Cage aux Folles* was a natural vehicle for musicalization, the heartwarming and touching tale of a homosexual father who complies with his son's request to present a respectable image for the boy's fiancee—an image that involves hiding the father's long-time transvestite lover. The songs, such as "I Am What I Am" and "La Cage aux Folles" drew audiences into the world of the characters and made their joy and pain real and touching without resorting to caricature.

Herman knew audiences would respond to the universality of the basic emotions expressed, "but I wasn't hired immediately," he says. Rumors floated around Broadway that Marvin Hamlisch was set, the Maury Yeston.

One of the showstopping scenes from *La Cage aux Folles*.
The 1983 musical won six Tony Awards, including Best Musical.

It wasn't until Herman's old friends, producers Fritz Holt and Barry Brown, and Allan Carr, finally approached him with an invitation that his spirits soared.

"I didn't worry about comparisons with the movie, as good as it was," says Herman, "because I had already had a worse experience in that vein, which was *Auntie Mame*. Rosalind Russell had acted that part definitively. It was an exquisite film, one of my favorites. But Angela Lansbury came in and made *Mame* new, and it made her one of our great musical comedy stars."

He wasn't worried about the controversial nature of the *La Cage aux Folles* material either.

"I honestly think it's one of the most moral stories I've ever come across. It's about a family, and I think anybody who has ever been in a close family can take out a handkerchief at the end of the play. So why shouldn't it work the same way in a musical? In fact, in a musical you can enhance the emotional moments."

La Cage proved universal in its appeal. "The natural way to write it was to think of it as a true family situation, which I think it is, and for anyone who ever wanted to say, 'Hey, hey, look at me, I am an individual, don't put me in a group of people,' 'I Am What I Am' is the most important song in the score. It's not about a drag queen. Yes, it has the word *closet* in it, because I wanted it to be specific."

Herman visited a great many transvestite clubs around the country to capture the flavor.

•"They gave me absolutely nothing positive," he says. "I was depressed when I came out of them because they were all very sleazy, and I wanted to present a glamorous view of the situation. But even knowing what *not* to do is very helpful. Even that negative look at drag clubs was very helpful to me."

The end result was a touching, gloriously positive production. One of Herman's happiest experiences was visiting Tokyo and watching the ecstatic audience response. "The laughs came at the same places; the handkerchiefs came out at the same moments. The reaction was identical to what was happening at the Palace, yet it was in a foreign tongue. Another culture was accepting a story about two homosexuals, laughing, crying, coming out of the theatre as people do in this country. That's one of the most satisfying feelings a writer can have—reaching an entirely different culture, learning how similar all human beings really are through his work."

Despite the recent triumph of *La Cage*, Herman is concerned about the state of the theatre.

"I'm as worried as everyone else. The economics are a problem, the lack of songs, ticket prices. The apathy of the younger generation—they're just not interested in theatre. That's because we've been a television society. I often rent a film on Saturday night, and have a few friends in. We have a little dinner and watch, say, *Broadway Danny Rose*, which we all missed when it came out. It's a lovely evening without people talking behind us. All that composers can do is keep writing, keep giving producers new, entertaining products, trying to draw back some of the people we've lost."

The answer, logically, is *not* to do a *La Cage* because it costs so much—five million dollars. Wouldn't it seem a safer bet to mount a two-character musical?

"It doesn't work out that way," says Herman. "You just choose something you believe in and go with it."

Does he have a new project in mind?

"No, I don't. I'm reading scripts like crazy. I take one to bed with me every night. I don't want to do anything until I feel that surge of excitement that I felt with *La Cage*."

When Herman does find an exciting property, he intends to work with people who have talent, whether they have been known specifically as musical comedy specialists or not.

"We don't take enough chances," he says. "Arthur Laurents—another idol of mine—and I took a chance on having Harvey Fierstein write the book for *La Cage* because we saw one play of his—*Torch Song Trilogy*—that was brilliantly written. He obviously had a great talent. 'If he doesn't know the first thing about where to write a number, we can teach him,' Arthur said. It took two weeks, and Harvey is now as valid a bookwriter for the musical theatre as anyone else around. My point is, there are other Harvey Fiersteins out there. I saw *Isn't It Romantic*, and I'm absolutely positive that Wendy Wasserstein can write a musical book. She's wonderful. You can't be narrow-minded, put people in cliches. You have to experiment."

Jerry is pleased with the librettists who wrote his shows—Don Appell (*Milk and Honey*), Jerry Lawrence and Robert E. Lee (*Mame*), and Michael Stewart (*Hello, Dolly!*), He was less pleased with the film versions of *Mame* and *Hello, Dolly*.

"I wasn't happy about either one. Those are disappointments because, unfortunately, whole future generations will think of *Dolly* and *Mame* like that—and that's sad to me. I don't feel that Hollywood knows how to do a Broadway musical, with rare exceptions. *Cabaret* was brilliant on the screen, *Pajama Game* too. But 95 percent of the adaptations are not well done. My two were unpleasant."

La Cage aux Folles will eventually be a film musical, but Herman is optimistic. "I just sold the others outright," he says, "and I vowed never to do that again, without retaining some control."

The movies of *Hello, Dolly!* and *Mame* were all part of a period during which, as Jerry puts it, "nothing worked for me. The seventies were very sobering years. It brought me right back down to earth, and I realized you don't just write shows and they run seven years. I appreciated the *La Cage* experience even more than I would have had I not had those years. It also gave me a strength I didn't have in the beginning of my career."

There's a little sunshine even in the darkest period, and Herman considers

Herman is shown here with *(from left)* Jule Styne, Hal David, Ginger Rogers, Ethel Merman, and Lucille Ball.

Herman has worked with a number of different Broadway stars. He is seen here with *(from top, clockwise)* Gene Barry, Walter Charles, Leslie Uggams, Andrea McArdle, and Carol Channing.

Mack and Mabel his best score, despite the inadequate production.

"So, in the middle of that down period, I wrote what I still consider to be my best work. I had to learn from the bad times, and I think I did. If I have a period like that again, I'll be able to brush it off and say, 'This has to happen every once in a while." You can't expect them all to work. It's too sensitive and tenuous an art form, because we combine the talents of fifty people in one thing. Remember, anything can set a wrong tone. A tone can be hurt by a set or a score. One person can hurt the show badly. There are so many elements that have to mesh properly.

"One thing you must do when difficulties come is *stay with what you are*! I could have said, 'OK, I'm going to join the people who are writing rock musicals, because that seems to be the thing.' I can do that, but not as well as they can. I could have said, 'I'm going to write an operatic musical, and I can also do that,' but not as well as people like Steve Sondheim. Why would I try to be anything else than what I am? And self-acceptance takes learning too."

Herman is also looking forward to a future production of *Mack and Mabel*, with sets like technicolor. "They'll fly; they'll look like California sunshine. It's going to be a happy show—with a serious note and a bittersweet ending, but happy."

Happiness is not an emotion that fills the hearts of most theatre writers today. Jerry Herman is a refreshing contrast to so many other leading composers who pronounce Broadway dead.

"There's nothing more rewarding than a life in the theatre. You two know that firsthand; you've experienced it," he says, referring to our stage production of *Seven Brides for Seven Brothers*. "You both know what it feels like to step into a taxicab and hear your song on the radio, and the taxi driver doesn't know it's you in the back. Can you describe that feeling to anybody? I can tell you what it feels like for me to stand in the back of a theatre and for people to come out humming my songs.

"It's a blessing."

CHAPTER SIXTEEN

JOHN KANDER

THERE ARE MANY STRIKING FEATURES in John Kander's Manhattan brownstone: an imposing grand piano, bookcases filled with classical music, a staircase that winds narrowly, like an iron pretzel, for three flights. But most interesting—and most definitive—is an enormous blowup of a crossword puzzle. This framed puzzle says "Partner of Ebb" and then reveals the answer down below, "John Kander."

Partner of Ebb is a touchingly accurate description of John Kander; Kander and Ebb have been together for twenty-one years. During that time their words and music have captured contrasting worlds effectively—the depravity of *Cabaret*'s Kit Kat Klub, the high-style elegance of a talk show hostess's realm in *Woman of the Year*, the Greek atmosphere of *Zorba*. They discovered Liza Minnelli and got her the lead in *Flora, the Red Menace*, which resulted in a Tony for the stunningly gifted newcomer. They also fashioned *The Act* and *The Rink* for Liza.

Throughout, Kander and Ebb have remained best friends, mutually supportive, a solid, sparkling creative unit. John Kander is more than one half of a team, however. Standing before us in jeans and a blue sweater, he projects the warmth, easy charm, and graciousness that prompted composer Carol Hall (*The Best Little Whorehouse in Texas*) to call him "the nicest man on Broadway."

"Nice" seems inadequate. Kander is remarkable for one other trait: he makes those who write about him feel like the star, as though he's more interested in them than in himself.

"It's funny how I got started," he says, when we urge him back into the spotlight. "It's a bizarre story. I was out of town, seeing *West Side Story* in Philadelphia, seeing some friends. I was at the Variety Club, the old Variety Club, and there was a big bar. After the show was over, and it was about four deep in the bar, I couldn't get a drink. There was this little short man standing in front of me. He noticed my distress and said, 'What do you want? I'll order yours when I order mine.' He did. I told him what I wanted, and he ordered it.

"We sat and talked a little bit. His name was Joe Lewis, and he was the pianist for *West Side Story*. We struck up a conversation and kind of kept in touch. Some months later he took his holiday, and he called and asked me if I wanted to sub for him on the show. So I did. I played in the pit of *West Side Story* for two or three weeks, which meant playing rehearsals with Jerome Robbins and Ruth Mitchell, the producer, when they were putting new people into it.

"So Ruthie got used to me. When they were auditioning for *Gypsy*, she asked me if I could play the auditions and stick in the pit for people who came in. I said yes. We auditioned *Gypsy* hopefuls for months, then got ready to go into it. By that time I had been around so much that Robbins said, 'Hey, do you want to do this show with me?' Meaning the dance music. Literally, that was the conversation. So I did the dance music for *Gypsy*, which led to doing the dance music for *Irma la Douce*. By that time, if you've had enough professional experience, you can get a show to anybody you want to. I'm *convinced* till this day that, if I had been able to get my own drink at the Variety Club in Philadelphia that evening, I would have had no career whatsoever."

That's doubtful. Kander loved music from the start, and "there was music in my household. Nobody had ever done it professionally, but my grandmother played the piano, and my aunt played too. My father had a big, booming voice, a baritone voice. He loved to sing, and everybody loved to hear him, and my brother liked to sing also." He laughs. "My mother, though, is tone deaf."

Kander was born in Kansas City, Missouri, on March 18, 1927.

"I started playing the piano myself at about four," he says. "From then on, I was always into music. I'd always play, but I didn't know what was going to happen to me. I never had any great drive. I never said I was going to be anything."

Did the theatre attract him?

"I was always attracted to it. There was never a lot of pressure for me to work hard, to drive toward some great goal, but I loved music, and I loved opera. I really fell in love with broadcasts. When the old San Carlo Opera Company used to come through Kansas City, I'd go to it. I can remember seeing *Aida* when I was ten, sitting in the first row with my feet dangling.

"I listened to everyone—Strauss, Wagner, Mozart, Rodgers and Hart, Jerome Kern. I was busy listening and playing."

His piano teacher was a woman named Lucy Parrot. "I loved her name. That's why I remember it so well. I began with her when I was six years old. I had been playing for two years by then. She was a terrific woman. She was strict, and she *looked* like a parrot. I was a little afraid of her, but she was good for me. She was an eccentric, and if I had a particularly good lesson, she'd give me goat's milk and cookies and take out a recording of *Tristan and Isolde*. I'd sit there enthralled, listening to this music.

"Anyway, later on I went to study at the conservatory in Kansas City while I was in high school. I played at recitals, and I really hated it. It was just terrifying to me. I once had to make up the last two pages of the Rachmaninoff E-flat Major Prelude and decided I'd rather be dead than be there. Then, later on, the war came."

Kander entered the service when he was seventeen. When he was discharged three years later, he attended Oberlin College, then Columbia to get his master's degree.

"Douglas Moore was the head of the Columbia music program, and he became kind of a father. I was still sort of musically schizoid. I had written several shows in college and at the same time was writing some pretty dreadful chamber music. It was Douglas who made it legitimate for me to go into musical theatre. I remember him saying, if he had it to do over again, that is what he would do. Somewhere, in the early fifties, it's what I decided to do."

Kander had an assistantship at Columbia in the Opera Workshop and worked as an accompanist. He also coached singers and played auditions.

"Then, somehow or other, I found myself working up at summer stock outside of Providence, Rhode Island. I was assistant musical director and choral director, which meant I played piano in the pit and conducted the Saturday night shows. In those days, you did a different play each week, and it must have been horrible to handle that much. It was thrilling to me at the time, and it was a terrific school. I can remember the first time I ever raised my baton to conduct the matinee of *Finian's Rainbow* and looking down to see the score of *Wonderful Town*—because that's what we had done in rehearsal. Fortunately, the orchestra had the *Finian's Rainbow* score. This experience was good for me, though I still didn't have any particular vision of where I was going. I just sort of did every job that came along for itself. Then I met Don Pippin.

"Don was a conductor, but he was a pianist then too. He helped me, and I found in this business that everything sort of leads to everything else. It's like building blocks. If you do what you're doing as well as you can, somehow or another it seems as if somebody notices it. The point is, if anybody asks me to do something, I say yes and then go out and learn how to do it."

He learned show writing by doing, and his first project was entitled *A Family Affair*, a comedy about the tribulations surrounding a wedding. James and William Goldman wrote the book and lyrics. The show opened in January

1962 and played for 65 performances. Hal Prince was the director.

"Hal didn't want to do it, but he thought we were talented and had us get in touch with a big publisher, Tommy Valando. Tommy signed me, and the show was not a success, but it was noticeable. It wasn't a shame. Somewhere along the line Tommy said, literally, 'I'd like you to meet Fred Ebb. I think you two guys would like each other.' Fred was also signed to Tommy. He introduced us, and we started writing together soon after that. In fact, we wrote 'My Coloring Book' a few days after we met, and that wound up being recorded by Barbra Streisand. We've been partners ever since."

During these years. Kander developed his skill—and reputation—through dance music.

"It's a step that's extremely useful," he says. "I think the more skills you have, the better off you are. Also, regarding dance music, it's a good way to learn. It's a lot of work, but it's not a lot of attention. It takes some creativity—more hard work than creativity. But if you're good at it, people notice, and if you're not good, the show isn't going to fall apart.

"It's a wonderful education to watch a choreographer or director. In 'All I Need Is the Girl' from *Gypsy*—I don't know if Steve Sondheim remembers this or not, but it's true—when Tulsa says, 'Now we waltz, now the strings come in,' all that was stuff Jerome Robbins was saying while he was onstage trying to improvise this moment. It's an edited, refined version of it, but it really came from Jerry. In *Irma la Douce* the director, Peter Brook, said, 'Is there anything we can do with penguins?' and he turned to me and said, 'John, give us a little *penguin* music, please!' And that became the 'penguin ballet.' Somehow or other, all those things help you to learn a kind of theatrical looseness, a way of going with the immediate flow of your collaborators. It stretches you, but it also makes you not *think*. I mean, if Jerry Robbins is saying, 'Now I feel a waltz,' or the strings are going to come in, you just go with it. There are wonderful guys today who just let the ideas flow, and they're not afraid to make fools of themselves. You have to be willing to write *anything* and go back later and say, 'That's terrible,' but if you have the censor inside you all the time, you can't get anything done."

A person who helped Kander to get things done, by offering encouragement, was an agent a friend had recommended, named Dick Seff.

"He was working at MCA, and Jim Goldman and I had another show at the time, before *A Family Affair*. We were playing it for MCA agents David Hocker and Audrey Wood. We really bombed out, but we didn't know it. David and Audrey went out to the elevator, and Dick came back and said, 'I've got to tell you guys that they stopped talking about your show the minute they got in the elevator, so it doesn't look good. But I think you're really very talented, and *please*, if there's anything I can ever do for you, if there's any other project, come to me, because I think you've really got something.' So when *A Family Affair* came along, we did go to Dick, and Dick was really responsible for making it happen. He got his cousin, Andrew Siff, to produce it."

Kander's next show was a collaboration with Ebb called *Flora, the Red Menace*, which opened May 11, 1965, and played for eighty-seven performances. But Liza Minnelli achieved a Tony Award and stardom as the heroine, a fashion designer who joins the Communist party at the urging of her boyfriend. After *Flora*, Minnelli also forged a permanent alliance with Kander and Ebb.

"I didn't have to do any research for *Flora* because I was there," says Kander. "I was very young during the thirties, but I remember the sounds well. *Cabaret*, on the other hand, was a show I researched a lot. For *Cabaret* I listened to German jazz of the twenties, old German records, German cabaret acts, and popular music. German jazz of the twenties was a very rigid kind of rhythmic thing. The Germans took American black jazz and turned it into something altogether different. So I listened and listened and then put it away and forgot about it. That sort of seeps into your unconscious.

"It was the same with *Zorba*. I listened to lots and lots of Greek folk music and then forgot about it. As far as *Chicago* of the thirties, that was still different—jazz, jazz of that period. Not listening specifically to the great jazz people, but I listened to an overall kind of performing style. A lot of piano stuff from the twenties."

All three shows benefited from Kander's thoughtful musical approach. *Cabaret*, the grimly affecting tale of an English cabaret singer in a sordid German nightspot, opened November 12, 1966, and ran for 1,166 performances. *Chicago*, which began Broadway life June 1, 1975, told an equally unsavory story of a murderess whose cunning attorney builds up public sympathy for her and gets her acquitted. It was billed as "vaudeville" and had Gwen Verdon and Chita Rivera, plus a pungent Kander and Ebb score, to keep it going for a successful 699 performances.

Zorba opened November 17, 1968, and had a more modest run—305 performances. But "Hal Prince did a masterful job of staging," says Kander. "The style was fresh and it was Hal's concept."

Whatever the subject matter, Kander and Ebb have enjoyed an efficient and profitable partnership. A defined work plan helps, according to Kander.

"We always write the first song first. I don't think it's necessarily the most important song, but the opening of a show tells you something about what you're going to do. I can't say it more clearly than that. It gives you some sense of the language and style you'll be working in."

When he's doing a show, where does he work?

"I go to Fred's house. He likes to stay at home, and I like to go out, so it's ideal. We work in the mornings, generally. Funny thing, when I go home, I think about the work a little bit, sure, but it doesn't hang over me. But Fred

Anthony Quinn in a scene from *Zorba!*
The 1968 musical received a Tony nomination for Best Musical.

will worry over a piece—maybe because I go out, and he stays in the same environment."

Initial ideas tend to come from Fred, Kander says, "but lyrically I have a certain amount of input. Fred is peppier than I am, so he will often get me going rhythmically."

Creating a show—vocally, orchestrally, lyrically—is often a backbreaking, agonizing process, in the opinion of many acclaimed writers. Kander's attitude on that subject is unusual.

"I've got to say something that sounds really arrogant. I don't mean it that way. Writing is never hard, even if it takes a long time. Freddy and I never *don't* have a good time when we're writing. We may write junk and tear it up and then write it again, but the act of writing is never depressing. Everything afterward is hard as hell. But even when there's trouble out of town, and concepts change, or songs and dances change, the *act* of writing is not difficult."

Kander's love of writing, shared by Fred, stands them in good stead during emergencies.

"When we were working out of town with *Chicago*, the ending of the show had two songs in it for the girls, and they just didn't quite work. We liked them. Anyway, Bob Fosse, the director, and Stuart Ostrow, who was working with Fosse and assisting him, came to us much more politely than they usually do and said, 'Would you mind going off and reconsidering the ending and thinking of another song for it?' They were terribly apologetic. We said we'd try. And Fred and I didn't even look at each other. We left and went to the hotel to where the piano was and laughed, because it was as if they had sent us to Florida for a vacation. We were allowed to go off and write, and we wrote a song called 'Nowadays,' which took us very little time to do, and which we loved. We spent the entire day away and made it look hard.

"Even so," Kander admits, "collaboration is the most difficult aspect of our business. By that, I mean collaboration involving the director, producer— everyone in a key position. If the collaboration is working well and the director, who should be the captain of the collaboration, is sending you off in another direction or suggesting another direction to you, it won't seem like a terrible thing to do. If you're in a situation where you and the director do *not* agree on where you're going, then it must be murder. As a matter of fact, I don't think I've ever really been in that situation. I'm trying to think of an example where somebody made us do something that we literally did not want to do, but I can't.

"I have a wonderful relationship with Michael Gibson right now," says Kander, "and it's really fun because we talk when we're doing a show together. Michael has terrific ideas on his own, but we'll talk in the morning at eight o'clock and write music on the telephone. If anybody walked into the room, they'd think, 'What is this person *doing*?' but Michael might say, 'I hear a drum here, a clarinet there.' Then both of us would be quiet for a second—we're several hotels apart, after all—and I'll say, 'Yeah, that sounds nice, but what if we . . . ?' And he'll say, 'That's a good idea.' Not that he doesn't do the orchestrations; he really orchestrates them. He doesn't surprise me, though. What I get from Michael is really what I intended, rather than someone coming in and improving me."

Basic concepts do change radically, even when the collaboration is harmonious. This happened with *The Act*.

The Act, which opened October 29, 1977, and ran for 233 performances, presented Liza Minnelli as a movie star who decides to rejuvenate her career via nightclub performing. Out of town reviews for the show were unfavorable until certain fundamental changes were made and the tide turned in New York.

"We had set out to do something that the audience refused to accept. We were trying to tell the story of this woman's life. At the same time, the songs that she was singing in her act were non sequiturs. They were not supposed to relate, and we thought we were very smart doing that. We could say we didn't want them to relate, but the audience refused to accept it. When Gower Champion came in, he made that clear to us, and he was absolutely right. He said, 'Fellas, you *have* to connect it.' So it was for the best. The concept of an earlier show of ours, *The Happy Time*, changed in a way that saddened us, though. Gower also directed that. We were in California, which was the wrong place to be for that, because people were saying, 'You can't have Robert Goulet be a failure,' literally. Gower lost confidence in what that book was about, and Dick Nash had written a really beautiful script. We ended up changing it in ways I didn't like."

Kander explains why he doesn't orchestrate his own music.

"For one thing, I'm not as good as Ralph Burns and Michael Gibson. The other reason is—you'll find this, oddly enough, with people like Bernstein—you cannot stay home and orchestrate and be at rehearsal and write. What you can do is supervise, to the extent you feel it's correct."

Kander concentrates on what he calls *riffs*, regardless of the collaborator.

"Inside musical figures," he agrees. "They go along with the basic tune. I think that way, as an orchestrator, but it's not a conscious thing. The worst thing that Fred can do to me is to say I write terrific vamps. If he says, 'Give me a terrific vamp,' I freeze. But, for instance, the vamp for 'New York, New York' is a part of the tune. There are vamps in *Cabaret*, too, and *Woman of the Year*. I want them to be there, but I don't sit down and say, '*Now* I'm going to write that.' When I do, I get tense."

Kander's creative vamps are recognized and admired by other professionals. "A wonderful guy, Ron Melrose, who has done the dance arrangements for a couple of shows of mine, gave me a present once, an opening night

Shown right are
David Wayne *(left)*
and Robert Goulet,
two stars from Kander
and Ebb's 1968 musical
The Happy Time.

In 1980, Kander and Ebb composed the score for yet another Broadway hit, *Woman of the Year*. Shown above are *(from left)* co-producers David Landay and Lawrence Kasha with Raquel Welch and Debbie Reynolds.

present, a thick piece of music he had written out. It was all my interior melodies, all vamps. I guess they do happen frequently."

What about overtures?

"I haven't had a lot of overtures in shows. For instance, for the opening of *Cabaret*—the stage had to be the darkness with Joel Grey coming out. In *Zorba*, the opening—in the original 1968 version, Hal's version, which I dearly loved—had the sounds of these instruments behind the curtain and the sounds of the crowd. When the curtains parted, there was this very smoky place, and little by little the music came out of that."

Kander notes that he's much happier being a composer than a librettist.

"I think being a librettist for a musical is the worst job in the world, because it's always his fault. He's losing the best stuff he's written to the composer. If he writes a lyrical moment or a dramatic moment fully enough, chances are it's going to set off an idea with a composer or a lyricist to say it another way, and in a musical it's the *music* that will dominate."

Yet, paradoxically, reviews give the score a line or two and concentrate on libretto.

"The critics are not musicians. And they tend to separate things, such as 'The lyrics are fine, but the music wasn't,' or vice versa—as if the two had never met. And it's strange, particularly with Fred and me, who don't make a move without each other. We've been together for twenty-two years now."

Regarding critics, Kander says, "I think critics are the enemy by definition, and there's no way of getting around it. I think some critics are better than others."

Has a critic ever helped him rewrite a number and improve it?

"Yes and no. When you're out of town with a musical, and you get five reviews that all point to that moment in the second act, then you have to figure it out. But I've never had a critic say anything that illuminated anything for me. I do feel pretty good about critics when we finally get to New York. Fred and I differ on this. I really don't have to read the reviews. I do have to know whether they were good or bad, but I don't feel compelled to read a bad review. I need to know if the *Times* was really lousy, but then I won't search it out from the garbage to make sure I read it. Sometimes they say things you remember for the rest of your life.

"I have an example of that, actually. I'm sure we all do. But after *The Happy Time* opened, I went on a holiday—I had a wonderful holiday—and I came back and the plane was delayed in Antigua. There was a *Time* magazine there, and I thought 'Ugh, this critic hates your work and has said so.' Well, the plane delayed and delayed, and I still kept circling the newsstand, and finally I said to myself, 'I'll open it and turn to the Table of Contents, and if it says "Theatre," then I won't buy it.' So I opened the magazine, and there was the part that said Table of Contents. And for that week only, I think for my benefit, the magazine had tried out a new format where they put capsule reviews of everything on the Table of Contents page. Right above where it said 'Contents,' there was a sentence that said, in blazing letters: 'SONGS SO UNDISTINGUISHED THEY SCARCELY DESERVE TO BE SUNG OUT LOUD.' I really had to laugh, because I'd spent two hours torturing myself, doing it to myself."

The Happy Time, which opened January 18, 1968, and ran for 286 performances, was a lighthearted view of a French Canadian family. Kander's songs, such as the lilting "A Certain Girl," "Tomorrow Morning," and "I Don't Remember You," were among the show's principal charms.

The Rink paired two Kander and Ebb favorites—Liza Minnelli and Chita Rivera—in a touching drama of a mother and daughter, long estranged, who clash again and eventually reconcile. The setting of a family roller rink, on the verge of being sold, added a haunting, intriguing mood.

"Freddy and I, once a show opens, even if it's a success, feel it's over when it's running. We don't like to go back to the theatre. But both of us independently, night after night, found ourselves watching *The Rink*. People always get up at award shows and make speeches, saying this show or that was such a loving experience. Usually they've forgotten. But this was the real thing, an extraordinary experience for the people involved. It was the most complete realization of what our intentions were, of any production we've done."

When asked what types of shows he thinks will be commercially successful in the future, Kander says the current state of the theatre puzzles him.

"A few years ago I'd have said the theatre is going in all kinds of directions, which was very exciting to me. But somehow or other, I think it's been diminished musically rather than enhanced.

"The odd thing, though, is that a hit show is jammed. But—let's see if I can get this out—musical theatre has always been wonderful entertainment. But then, around 1970, people started writing about it in very *serious* terms, that it was America's great gift to the theatre world. Maybe it's a shame that we ever found that out. I think musicals are taken much too seriously. It used to be that composers had the range to do anything. I went to see *Leave It to Jane* last night. It was wonderful, just wonderful. It was kind of concert-staged. They did the whole book, and it made me nostalgic for a time I've never lived in—not because I wanted to write that way, but because I wanted to have the *freedom* to write that way. *Pacific Overtures* was such an intellectual work. Not that there's anything wrong with that, but if that's all you're allowed to do—" He pauses. "You can't pin down what's acceptable and what isn't acceptable in the theatre."

Kander elaborates on other productions he found particularly appealing in the past. His favorite show, other than ones he and Ebb have written, is *She Loves Me*, Bock and Harnick's romantic adaptation of *The Shop Around the Corner*. He also loves Jerome Kern.

Fred Ebb *(left)* and John Kander.

Joel Grey won a Best Supporting Actor Tony in 1967 for his performance as the Master of Ceremonies in *Cabaret*

"The fact that he has that incredibly open melodic style and still retains sophistication is marvelous. This sounds dumb, but I like Kern kind of in the way I like Wagner—not on the same plane, but both of them were incredibly melodic writers. Anybody whose fingers have twisted themselves up playing 'All the Things You Are' knows their accomplishment. Such a wonderfully simple melody, and all that's going on underneath it—amazing."

As for personal favorites in his own catalogue, Kander cites "My Own Space" from *The Act*. "It has a wonderful lyric by Fred. Another song I like from that is 'The Only Game in Town.' And a song from *Flora, the Red Menace*, called 'A Quiet Thing.' "

Can Kander pin down where he sees himself in the future?

"I can only do what I do today and hope somebody produces it. I think being a young writer today is murder. Freddy and I were lucky we came along in the last big wave of writers who were able to get produced all the time. We are at a certain point in our career, and most producers, if we have a project, are going to look at it seriously and say, 'Well, they have a good track record.' "

 Liza Minnelli in a scene from *The Act*. The 1977 musical presented Minnelli as a movie star who decides to rejuvenate her career via nightclub performing.

His track record in the movies has been good too—he recently scored the Oscar-winning *Places in the Heart*—but there are discouraging aspects.

"I'm not terribly good unless I have someone who's very encouraging. Robert Benton, who directed *Places*, is terrific to work with. But I started to do a film once, and Lionel Newman, the music head of 20th Century-Fox, was the overseer. And I backed out of it, because Lionel had already made the statement to one young composer, 'Well, if you're going to live here, I'll help you, but if you're going to live in New York, I'll see to it as much as I can that you don't work in this business.'

"Fred would think I'm being too romantic, I think, but I feel it's true—the theatrical community in New York is really very small as opposed to being out in Hollywood, where everything is stretched for miles, and there isn't that much of a sense of community within that business. Here in New York, with all the crazy things that go on, all the competition, there's some kind of supportive substance that comes from being part of the theatrical community. It doesn't have to do with whether you're a big success this year or not. It doesn't have to do with what parties you go to. It has to do with the fact that you've been accepted as a professional, once you've proven you *are* a professional. Then people and the community accept you as part of itself.

"What I'm saying is, in Hollywood they ask, 'What are you doing now?' In New York they ask, 'Who are you?' "

Who is John Kander? How would he like to be remembered?

"I never thought of this before, but I think I'd like to be remembered as an emotional stirrer, whether the emotions are happy or tender or sad. But emotions that have impact, feelings that don't just wash over you and do nothing."

CHAPTER SEVENTEEN

HENRY KRIEGER & TOM EYEN

"I HOPE YOU LIKE ANIMALS," says Henry Krieger, leading us through his apartment on Charles Street in Greenwich Village. En route to the sofa, we encounter two dogs and two cats, companions and audiences when Krieger composes music for such shows as *Dreamgirls* and *The Tap Dance Kid*.

It's not surprising that Krieger is an animal lover. He has a quality of warmth and kindness that permeates the room. His hazel eyes and open smile invite visitors to relax, feel accepted and welcomed.

Most of all, Krieger conveys tranquility and inner peace, rare attributes in a person heavily involved with the world of Broadway.

"I haven't gotten confused," he says, in a quiet, humble voice. "I don't mix up my career and my day-to-day life. I have a lot of friends in the neighborhood. I have four pets I love, and I walk my own dogs. Essentially, I think the secret of being truly happy, of having real success, is remembering that you're a human being with very basic, simple needs, and life is very simple if it's good."

Life wasn't always this good for Krieger. The family lost everything in the stock market crash, and his father had to give up his first love, the violin, to concentrate on making ends meet. "But he continued to play for pleasure. My mother sings for pleasure. She, my sister, and I used to harmonize together. When I was about seven or eight, my parents got us a used piano, an upright."

Krieger grins. "I studied piano for only a minute, though. I studied with a Frenchwoman who said, in a heavy accent, 'Now you *must* read the notes.' I couldn't read or play, so I wound up learning better French from her than piano. That was the end of formal lessons."

He played by ear, however, and was aware from the start that he wanted to be a composer. "I didn't know if it would be theatre or pop. I just knew I was determined, in some way, to be in the entertainment business. I hoped it would be writing songs."

Rather than dream aimlessly, Krieger took action. "The first thing I did was to write an album worth of songs and record it. It was never released. My best friend at the time, John Cohen, financed the album. God bless him, he's no longer with us. I dedicated my work in *Tap Dance Kid* to him."

The death of his friend was a crushing blow, but Krieger persevered.

"I went to work at a radio programming outfit. We selected the repertoire weekly—ten or twenty records for radio stations in places like Sitka, Alaska; remote places in California, Michigan, and New Mexico. That was interesting, but after a while I got bored and worked in a catering place. When that palled, I worked for a rent-a-car agency."

All these jobs were stopgap solutions. Not knowing specifically how to proceed, Krieger placed an ad in the *New York Times*, saying "Situation Wanted—Young man interested in entertainment field job."

It was a long shot, but a press agent named Richard O'Brien, who handled Dick Cavett, Joan Rivers, and Woody Allen, answered the ad.

"When you do things without thinking, 'What am I going to get out of it?' you *do* get something in return. Because things circulate. I had a wonderful time in 1969 and 1970 representing these people for Richard. I took Rodney Dangerfield out to lunch with a press person. What a funny man!"

Dangerfield, Rivers, and Allen brought humor to Krieger's life, but hit rhythm-and-blues singer Jerry Butler brought music.

"They called him the 'iceman'; he was anything but. I eventually went out on my own, with Richard's blessing, and represented Jerry as a PR man for about a year. As confidante too."

Jerry Butler, who wrote and recorded the hit song "Only the Strong Survive," wasn't specifically a theatre writer, but he taught Krieger the vital elements of songwriting. "He said, 'First of all, a song is a *story*, and you need a through line. You need to be simple, to say as much as possible in as few words as you can. And you need *images*.' "

Krieger showed Butler his songs. "He was always generous, helpful, supportive."

Singing also featured prominently in Krieger's own personal plan. He had always considered himself a talented performer. Between 1973 and 1975, he sang at the now-closed Tin Palace between Second and Third Avenue in Manhattan, and The Blue Room at the Mercer Art Center on Mercer Street.

"I sang to support myself, after giving up PR work," says Krieger. "And I started to get a following at La Mama. That's how I met my partner and lyricist, Tom Eyen. I played my music for him, and he was cool—very, very remote. Enigmatic. He checked up on me, called people we both knew. Tom and I got together at my house, and again he was enigmatic, warm in a cool way. We had a lovely afternoon, and I didn't hear from him for four months."

Fortunately, Eyen contacted Krieger again. "The phone rang, and I was feeling down, like nothing was happening, and he said 'Hello, are you ready to work?' I didn't even know who it was, but I was so desperate for work that I said, 'Great!' And from then on, we've had a very happy partnership. He's a wonderful man. If anybody has taught me anything, it's Tom. I'll say it: he's my mentor."

Mentor Eyen and his protégé commenced work on their first show, *The Dirtiest Musical*, their adaptation of *The Dirtiest Show in Town*.

"Nell Carter had a song," Krieger recalls. "It was in the first act, and it was called 'Can You See?' It clobbered the show, stopped it like a sledgehammer—like *fifty* sledgehammers. The place was packed every night. And Nell stopped that show sixty percent through the first act. I said to Tom, 'Isn't it wonderful?' and Tom answered grimly, 'Wake up and smell the coffee. It's a tragedy.' And I said, 'What are you talking about? They love it.' Tom told me. 'Rule Number One: You don't stop the show in the middle of the first act. You stop it at the *end* of the first act. Otherwise, after you stop you have to start all over again. It's become a performance. Like a little show within a show, and that's totally counterproductive.' "

Krieger was miserable, until Eyen assured him "It's a good show. It's just that you can't possibly have this construction work on Broadway. We're being too good in an obscure place. Let's put that number at the end of the second act."

And that, says Krieger, was his first lesson in play construction. Interestingly, that lesson also contributed to the evolution of *Dreamgirls*.

"*Dreamgirls* had a lot to do with Nell Carter's showstopper. When Tom and I saw how effective we could be together, we thought, 'Why don't we use Nell in a different way? Why not talk about the lives of three backup singers?' It was an exciting idea."

"We did a workshop with Nell at Joe Papp's Public Theatre and developed a score in 1979. Initially, we named it *Project Number Nine* and then *One Night Only*, a song title from the show. Joe liked the workshop, but just then Nell decided she wanted a career in television. She had finished *Ain't Misbehavin'*."

Disappointed, Krieger and Eyen kept hoping for her return; Nell guaranteed them she'd be back in April. "Darling," Krieger told her, "this is January!" So he and Tom asked Joe Papp, who wanted to delay things for Carter, to return the property. He agreed, offering his blessings.

"So we waited a year, and Nell's Hollywood career solidified." When it became clear to Krieger and Eyen that Carter wouldn't be able to do *Dreamgirls*, "We took it to Michael Bennett and his partner, Bob Avian, and they liked it. So we did another workshop with Michael. That's how it started."

Financing for *Dreamgirls*, according to Krieger, was relatively easy to arrange, an unusual situation in modern musical theatre. "Michael called producer David Geffen and asked him to our final workshop. David is an absolute genius, he's wonderful," Krieger enthuses, "and David said, 'I want to finance the whole thing myself,' which made all the other people jump up—ABC Entertainment, Metromedia, the Shuberts, who were already in. That created a nice partnership with the Shuberts and David Geffen that continued through *Little Shop of Horrors*. We were very fortunate."

The composers' good fortune continued when a replacement was found for Nell Carter: Jennifer Holliday. The Houston-born singer had first created excitement on broadway with *Your Arms Too Short to Box with God*. Influenced by her favorite singers, Patti LaBelle, Gladys Knight, and Aretha Franklin, Jennifer—whose soaring voice had formerly thrilled members of her hometown church, Pleasant Grove Baptist—proved an ideal instrument for Krieger's melodies.

In the show, she played Effie, one of three black girls in a Supremes-type group called the Dreams. The manager of the Dreams informs Effie near the end of the first act, that she is being replaced—in the group and in his bed—by a more glamorous substitute. This provokes a wailing, heart-rending burst of song, "And I Am Telling You I'm Not Going," which became one of the great musical moments in theatre history.

The rest of *Dreamgirls*, which opened on December 20, 1981, charts Holliday's fall and eventual comeback. Audiences were with her every step of the way, and so were critics such as T. E. Kalem of *Time* magazine, who declared, "Holliday has devastating vocal firepower and a stage presence that could crumble reinforced concrete." *Dreamgirls* ran nearly four years, closing October 11, 1985.

The Krieger and Eyen songs that solidified Holliday's stardom were written by both men in the same room, and the team still finds this arrangement effective.

"I know lyricists and tune writers often work separately, but we work together a lot," says Krieger. "Tom and I sit at the piano, and we start with a lyric and experiment. I'll say, 'Could you make this slightly shorter?' and he'll make these incredible cuts, very quickly. He's unbelievably facile. "Or," Krieger continues, "I'll write something, and he'll say, 'It's not building. You're in too low a register. Try it again.' And I'll go up. Because he's *hearing*; he's a musician too, in his own way. And it works both ways: 'Give me a longer line, a different syncopation.' We just have a great rapport."

That rapport produced the smash hit from *Dreamgirls* "And I Am Telling You I'm Not Going."

"Tom gave me the lyric. He said, 'Just *do* it. Don't come out of the room till it's done.' And I sat in the room by myself and turned blank. Nothing. Then I played an E-flat chord, and I said, 'and I am telling you,' and it came to me, the next chord." Krieger demonstrates enthusiastically on his piano, reliving the breakthrough, "And the song wrote itself. After hours of pain it poured out; it announced, 'Here I am!' "

Krieger acknowledges the importance of "I Am Telling You" in *Dreamgirls* but considers the most important song in any show "the song that reveals the character of the main protagonist, or the character of the show itself, in the most accessible and participating way for the audience—which is to say, where the audience can relax, suspend anything they've brought with them, whatever their personal lives are about at that time. So for me, the crucial song is the song that reaches my audience in the most complete and loving way."

Dreamgirls was a stimulating experience for Krieger and Eyen, and so was working with Michael Bennett.

"I found Michael very energetic, in charge, supportive of me. Michael as director of the show gave us the spectacle, the grandeur, the finite detail.

"He's remarkable," Krieger continues. "He masterminded all these talented people—scenic designer Robin Wagner, lighting designer Tharon Musser, costume designer Theoni Aldredge—in a really professional and greatly theatrical way. He gave it pacing."

Occasionally there were disagreements. "We had a song, 'I'm the New Girl,' which is in my nightclub act. A wonderful musical comedy song. It was just before 'And I Am Telling You I'm Not Going.' Michael said, 'It doesn't belong in the show.' He was right," Krieger admits, "But he said, 'It's a love song; it doesn't work.' I replied, 'You're right to take it out,' but I was in a contentious mood that day, and when he said, 'It's a love song,' I argued, 'It's a bitchy song.' Tom jumped in and said, 'Let's go shopping.' Michael was fuming, and I was very naughty. I wasn't really that angry, but I was also saying, 'You're *wrong*.' I didn't mind the song being taken out. I minded it being taken out for the wrong reasons."

But Tom Eyen maintained his perspective and gave Krieger advice that could benefit any Broadway writer in the middle of an artistic disagreement: "Let's save our fights for when they're really important."

The show's first stop was Boston. "We changed a lot there. We had one duet called 'I Found You,' which was cut out. The two characters who sang it—well, we decided they shouldn't be in love after all. 'One Night Only' was removed from the show for about a week or so because Michael had a feeling the chords were too somber and Hebraic. We substituted 'It's Gonna Be My Time,' but people loved the old song and wanted it restored. Michael acquiesced, and 'One Night Only' came back."

The Hebraic flavor Bennett referred to was intentional on Krieger's part. "The Jewish people and the black people come from an area that is now

Africa. The Middle East is right next door to Africa. There's a tendency on this planet to have certain regional characteristics. The Orient has many different peoples. Japanese people are extremely different from Chinese people. However, there *are* also certain prevailing currents that are shared. And I think the Hebraic feeling has a correlation to some of the black musical impulses. It's essentially a direct line to the soul. Soul has been very trivialized in our time. *Soul* is a very important word, though, and I think the Jews and blacks have certain shared experiences. That's one of the reasons why slaves in America identified closely with the stories of Moses and God delivering the children of Israel from bondage."

Dreamgirls has a soul and freedom of emotion and movement that was based on constantly varying rhythms. "This is a different form from the traditional. It's an offshoot, a mutation, a hybrid. And what we based it on was rhythms. The very first thing you hear when the curtain's about to go up is bom, bom, bom, cowbell, 'ladies and gentlemen!' And for the whole night there's some sort of underpinning rhythm, underscore. It never stops."

Frank Rich of the *New York Times* agreed, saying "It's a show that seems to dance from beginning to end." He added, "Mr. Bennett has fashioned a show that strikes with the speed and heat of lightning."

Ultimately, Krieger felt his overall goal was achieved. "I tried, maybe not consciously, but I felt a different musical tone for each personality. I deal with personal essences. I try to be not exactly a mirror, because a mirror gives you back exactly what's there, but like a painter."

Krieger's next experience was equally fortunate and fulfilling.

"*The Tap Dance Kid*, which I wrote with lyricist Robert Lorick, was something I began before we went ahead with *Dreamgirls*. A terrific woman named Evelyn Baronet produced the 'After-School Special' movie of *The Tap Dance Kid*, and she asked, 'Would you be interested in doing the music for this?' At the time Tom was writing 'Mary Hartman, Mary Hartman,' and I said, 'Maybe so.' Then, when *Dreamgirls* appeared to be happening, she wanted to continue, and I went forward with it. It took a lot of hard work to get that show financed, unlike *Dreamgirls*. And it's such a strange little show. A dangerous career move to do two black shows in a row."

Considering the risk, there must have been something else about the property that appealed to Krieger. Why did he agree to do *The Tap Dance Kid*?

"The material seemed so human, so universal, I felt audiences would respond. The ingredients were there. It was an honest story about children who wanted to be taken seriously as human beings before they were twenty-one, twenty-two, twenty-three. I had previously written three seasons of 'Captain Kangaroo' and enjoyed it, because it allowed me to write *up*, not *down*, to children. It was also my first good-paying job, a job that helped me to support myself with music. Then things kind of opened up."

Krieger feels strongly that most music written for children patronizes

A scene from *Dreamgirls*.
The 1982 musical received
a Tony nomination
for Best Musical.

Deborah Burrell,
Loretta Devine,
and Sheryl Lee Ralph
sing a number from
Dreamgirls.

Krieger *(top)* with lyricist Robert Lorick.
The two men collaborated on *The Tap Dance Kid,*
which won the 1985 Tony Award for Best Choreography.

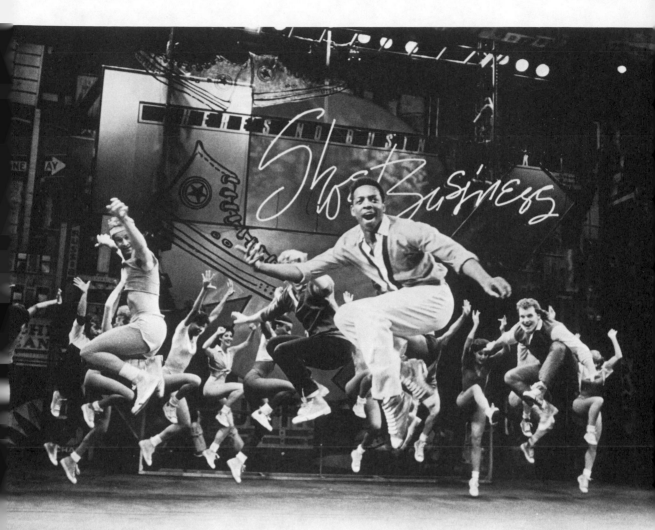

Pictured right is Hinton Battle,
star of Krieger's musical *The Tap
Dance Kid*, with the chorus in a
number called "Fabulous Feet."

Tom Eyen.

them. "I want to communicate with them and not be silly. I write about things that matter to them, just as they would matter to a grown-up like me. One song was called 'My Dog.' It goes,

> My dog gets up in the morning,
> My dog has breakfast with me,
> My dog, he's a silly one,
> But one in a million,
> He's always ready for fun . . . my dog.

"Children," Krieger reiterates, "are human beings. The fact that they were black was beside the point."

He's now writing a show called *Revenge* with Tom Eyen. "I'm already promoting it. I play two songs from *Revenge* as a teaser in my act."

Two shows playing simultaneously on Broadway, during the most difficult and precarious period in its history, is an admirable feat. Krieger is aware of this.

"My great triumph is that my life has evolved to a point where I'm allowed and able to do these things. It's something I thank God for. Not to sound too religious, but I thank God all the time. I pray every morning, and tell Him, 'Thank you for letting me do this.'

"I'd just like," he concludes, "in as many different ways as I can, to bring joy."

As we were preparing to leave, Krieger's collaborator, Tom Eyen, stopped by for a few minutes. The gifted lyricist volunteered further thoughts on *Dreamgirls.*

"It's a popular piece—contemporary and well done in all departments. I wasn't attracted to the project at first. I really kind of grew into it through my early life in New York, working in the sixties Off Broadway with Diana Sands, Nell Carter, Leata Galloway, and Marion Ramsey. These are the models for the characters in *Dreamgirls.*"

Eyen could have played up the glamorous Diana Ross–like character who usurps the Florence Ballard–like character, but he chose not to.

"Making the loser a winner is a lot more interesting than making the winner a loser. And I've always been drawn to the theme of commercial versus noncommercial, beauty versus beast, the acceptable versus the freak. This all comes out in *Dreamgirls.*"

Eyen sums up the secret of the success enjoyed by the songwriting duo: "The chemistry between me and Henry is like fire and air—complementary and dangerous, which is good for creativity."

CHAPTER EIGHTEEN

ALAN JAY LERNER

ALAN JAY LERNER TELLS AN AFFECTIONATE AND ILLUMINATING ANECDOTE about his father. Although the elder Lerner rarely volunteered direct approval of his son's achievements, he did speak up after the opening of *Brigadoon* in 1947. A neighbor commented to Mr. Lerner, "I just read the reviews of *Brigadoon*. Your son is certainly a lucky boy." "Yes," Lerner's father said, "It's a funny thing about Alan. The harder he works, the luckier he gets."

Lerner is known by his peers as a perfectionist, a man who strives constantly to bring beauty, wit, and humanity to his lyrics and librettos. We observed that trait when our show, *Copperfield*, was being prepared for Broadway in 1980. It had book problems, and with only ten days scheduled out of town in St. Louis, there was no time to fix them satisfactorily. Lerner, a friend of our producers, Mike Merrick and Don Gregory, came in to help us during New York previews, offering encouragement and direction as we labored to solve the more serious mistakes.

The problems were never completely overcome, but we learned an astonishing amount from this graceful, urbane, witty writer. Even though the production's run was brief, our score was nominated for a Tony, and we believe Lerner's advice and support had much to do with it.

The man who gave theatre one of its few genuine masterpieces, *My Fair Lady*, was born on August 31, 1918, in New York City. His family's wealth (Lerner's father founded the highly successful Lerner Shops) only fueled

Lerner's ambition to carve a personal creative identity of his own. He studied piano and attended the Juilliard School of Music, then honed his craft with two Hasty Pudding shows as a Harvard student. He concentrated afterward on radio scriptwriting.

In 1941, Lerner moved to West 44th Street to the Lamb's Club, a famous old theatrical establishment. "That's where I met one of the all-time great lyric writers, Larry Hart. I was close to him for three years, until he died," says Lerner. "I never knew a man so lonely."

Alan Jay Lerner met Frederick Loewe in 1942. Loewe, desperate to find a lyricist for a show he was composing that was scheduled to open in Detroit, approached Lerner at the Lamb's Club. He had earlier admired some Lerner-written sketches for a Lamb's Club revue and made a direct, businesslike proposal: "You are Alan Jay Lerner? You write good lyrics. I am Frederick Loewe. I have something to say to you."

The show, which surfaced October 1942, as *Life of the Party*, made Lerner and Loewe certain they had a future together. *What's Up*, which opened in November 1943, only managed 63 performances; but *The Day Before Spring*, which came to Broadway November 22, 1945, played for 165 performances and netted the pair good reviews.

Good reviews and good box office greeted *Brigadoon*, which played 581 performances after its debut March 31, 1947. Named by the Drama Critic's Circle as Best Musical of the Year (the first musical to receive their accolade), *Brigadoon* told the fanciful tale of a Scottish village that only comes to life once every hundred years, and the two strangers who unwittingly stumble into it. Lerner and Loewe wrote some of their greatest, most enduring standards for the show: "Almost Like Being in Love," "Come to Me, Bend to Me," and "Heather on the Hill."

Paint Your Wagon, which followed November 12, 1951, was less successful, though the score matched *Brigadoon* in quality with "They Call the Wind Maria" and "I Talk to the Trees." Lerner captured the Americana flavor effectively, and the story of gold prospectors offered a good nail on which to hang songs.

It wasn't, in the end, Americana that catapulted Lerner and Loewe to greatness, but British drawing room romance. In 1952, Lerner was working on a screenplay for *Brigadoon* when producer Gabriel Pascal, who owned the rights to Shaw's *Pygmalion*, invited him to lunch.

"He asked me to write the lyrics for *Pygmalion*. I remember him swearing that Fritz and I were the only writing team he had contacted about doing it. I didn't contradict, though we knew he had already approached Rodgers and Hammerstein, among others."

Lerner and Loewe dug in, intimidated at first by Shaw's characters, "who would not stop talking." More difficult to handle was the fact that Shaw's original play lacked romance—Professor Higgins educates Eliza and then pairs her off in an epilogue with Freddie Eynsford-Hill.

In 1981 Lerner's smash-hit musical *Brigadoon*
enjoyed a revival on Broadway
and was nominated for two Tonys.

"You can write a love song," says Lerner. "But how do you write a *non*-love-song?"

Further discouragement came from Oscar Hammerstein, who assured Lerner that the problems inherent in *Pygmalion* were insurmountable.

"During this time, other composers were asked to try *Pygmalion*—Comden and Green were one of the teams. Somehow 1952 became 1954, and I lost faith in myself. I didn't know what to write, and I wasn't satisfied with what I had written."

Lerner and Fritz Loewe separated, temporarily, and Lerner contracted encephalitis, which turned into spinal meningitis. After Lerner recovered, he and Loewe returned to the *Pygmalion* project.

"Fritz and I considered the possibility of adding new characters to the play," says Lerner. "We eventually rejected the idea. We made a decision. Shaw showed Higgins as a man with a passion for the English language. He believed language to be the principal barrier separating class from class. This was the fundamental premise that could be dramatized by words and music."

Another roadblock appeared when Lerner and Loewe realized that they were composing a score without owning the rights to the property.

"Fritz just said, 'We will finish the show without rights, and when the time comes for them to decide who is to get them, we will be so far ahead of everyone else they will be forced to give them to us.' "

The team approached designer Oliver Smith, who had already served as designer for *Brigadoon* and *Paint Your Wagon*. Cecil Beaton agreed to do the costumes.

"The first person I thought of to star as Higgins was Rex Harrison," says Lerner. "We naturally avoided mentioning that the rights were still not ours. Harrison was skeptical but curious."

References to *Pygmalion* began to appear in the papers, and Mary Martin's husband, producer Richard Halliday, contacted Lerner and expressed an interest in *Pygmalion* as a vehicle for his wife.

"First we played the songs for Richard and he loved them. Then he brought Mary to my mother's apartment and Fritz and I played five numbers: "The Ascot Gavotte," "Just You Wait, Henry Higgins," and three we didn't use—"Say a Prayer for Me Tonight," "Lady Liza," and "Please Don't Marry Me." Mary and Richard made no comment.

"I didn't hear from either of them, and a week later I called Richard. His reaction shook me to the core. He told me what a *sad* night it had been for them both. It seems Mary had said, 'How could it have happened? Those dear boys have lost their talent.'

"Those dear boys have lost their talent," Lerner repeats incredulously. "And these were the first people to hear anything from *My Fair Lady*—though it wasn't called *My Fair Lady* yet."

Lerner admits he was devastated by Mary Martin's reaction to their songs, but Loewe accepted the verdict philosophically, and they set their minds to finding another actress for the role of Eliza Doolittle.

Fortune smiled when they caught Julie Andrews's performance in a Broadway production of *The Boyfriend*. "We began to imagine how exciting it would be to have a girl of eighteen play the part. That was the age Shaw specified in his play."

It took a while to persuade Rex Harrison to portray Higgins. He remarked, none too subtly of two of the songs: "I hate them."

"We realized he was right," Lerner says. "The songs were too slick. Skin deep. Word games."

Harrison also hesitated because he wasn't a singer. "He thought we were mad," says Lerner, "but we *knew* he was Higgins. We also knew he could sustain the role without making it too romantic or sympathetic, as Leslie Howard had done in the film version of *Pygmalion*."

The songs began to flow. "Wouldn't It Be Loverly?," Eliza's expression of longing for creature comforts, came early, followed by "Why Can't the English?"

"Best of all," Lerner says, "we contacted Moss Hart to direct. We were so delighted when he agreed to hear the score."

To the vast relief of all, Hart accepted their offer.

"Moss was irreplaceable," says Lerner. "I still wonder how the gods could have robbed us—robbed the world—of such a precious human being. Such a great talent. He always knew the goal at the far end of the road. He worked with us; he had an unerring eye for casting. He had a superb sense of construction. He *understood* everyone's problems and needs—actors', producers', writers'." Lerner shakes his head.

Meanwhile, the search for a choreographer intensified. Gower Champion declined, despite his enthusiasm for the score, because he wanted more money. Michael Kidd was considered, but his blunt denunciation of one of the songs, "You Did It," angered Hart. "*No*," Hart said, after the meeting, leaving no room for discussion.

Hanya Holm was the final victor. "She had choreographed a musical called *The Golden Apple*, and she understood the needs of the play right away."

But other minor problems plagued the project. "Rex wanted every speech to stem directly from Shaw," Lerner says. "When I wrote original lines of my own, he objected. Finally, I decided to tell him every word was directly from Shaw, whether it was or not. That seemed to satisfy him."

Another problem was Julie Andrews's difficulty in mastering cockney. Director Hart closed down the company and drilled her until her accent was perfect.

"Moss admitted, with humor, that it was a challenge rehearsing a girl who had never played a major role in her life and an actor who was singing onstage for the first time," Lerner remembers.

By the time *My Fair Lady* was edging close to opening night, everything on stage was polished, down to the last detail. The title *My Fair Lady* eventually pleased everyone.

"Except Fritz," says Lerner. "He preferred *Fanfaroon*. He also wanted to cut 'On the Street Where You Live.' It was restaged, and Fritz admitted that the new staging turned the tide. 'On the Street Where You Live' wound up stopping the show."

My Fair Lady was a triumph in Philadelphia and New Haven, and when it arrived in New York, anticipation ran high.

"I wouldn't have attended the opening night party even if there had been one," Lerner says. "Self-preservation, I suppose. Nothing hurts more than a festive atmosphere followed by crippling reviews."

Any worries he may have had proved groundless. *My Fair Lady* went on to become a landmark against which all musicals are measured and, in 1964, an Academy Award winner for Best Picture. It had taken eight years to reach the screen, because the bidding, which began in 1962 after the show closed, involved a high price tag of $5,500,000. Jack Warner won the rights over his competitors, and the picture was released triumphantly by Warner Brothers.

Elated by their *My Fair Lady* success, Lerner and Loewe looked around for another Broadway project to match it. They didn't find anything they liked until late 1958.

"We first took an interest in what was eventually *Camelot* when I noticed a book review of *The Once and Future King*. It was an excellent review, and the material seemed filled with possibilities."

The casting was ideal: Richard Burton as King Arthur, Julie Andrews as Guinevere, Robert Goulet as Lancelot.

"Laurence Harvey wanted to be Arthur," Lerner says. "When we didn't hire him, he sent us a bill for his singing lessons. Later on he did a London production and was brilliant."

Burton, however, was "a magnetic King Arthur."

Lerner says, "Both on stage and off, he was the king in every sense of the word. He had a worshipful entourage that followed him everywhere."

Audiences who had loved *My Fair Lady* were primed to worship *Camelot*, but the early version ran four-and-a-half hours.

"It was a bladder contest," Lerner says. "And humor was completely lacking."

Critics were kinder than they should have been. "They wanted to like it, to be constructive," Lerner says. "So we began surgery, cutting wherever possible."

Disaster struck unexpectedly. Moss Hart suffered a major heart attack. He had suffered another ten years before. "The pressures were staggering. We had no director, and no one could figure out how to fix the mistakes. Those debilitating weeks on the road shook our confidence."

Julie Andrews and Rex Harrison record a song from *My Fair Lady*. The highly successful 1956 musical established Lerner and Loewe as songwriters of the first rank.

Richard Burton won a 1961 Tony for Best Actor for his portrayal of King Arthur in the Lerner and Loewe musical *Camelot*.

They shook the foundations of the Lerner and Loewe partnership as well. After an engagement in Toronto, the show was scheduled to open in Boston and a new director was needed. Lerner told Loewe, "I must open it in Boston myself and by that time we'll have a new director." Loewe wasn't happy; he wanted a new director immediately.

"Minor differences became major," Lerner says. "Interviewers quoted us, distorting what we said, aggravating the problem. "Maybe," he speculates, "the problem may have been too much success, because our approach in the past would have been to laugh and go about our business."

"Thank God for Richard and Julie," Lerner says. "They behaved like stars in every sense of the word. Professionals. Gracious, helpful, good-humored. Every moment with both of them was a joy."

When *Camelot* finally had its opening, the *New York Times* complained about second act trouble, after praising the first. The other reviews were mixed, although a large advance sale protected the show commercially.

"What really rescued us," Lerner says, "was performing the score on 'The Ed Sullivan Show.' Richard sang 'Camelot,' and Julie sang 'The Simple Joys of Maidenhood.' Bobby Goulet also appeared to do 'If Ever I Would Leave You.' And, thank God, the public loved the songs and flocked to the box office. We were home. *Camelot* ran for two years on Broadway."

Lerner's only disappointment after the *Camelot* opening was the dissolution of his partnership with Loewe.

"He was sixty," Lerner remembers. "Healthy, energetic. But he fell in love with Palm Springs and the French Riviera. He had enough of New York. It was an overwhelming loss, personally and professionally. Fritz was a balance wheel."

The separation was permanent, except for one brief reunion—1974's motion picture version of *The Little Prince*.

"The result was a terrible letdown," Lerner says. "The director, Stanley Donen, tampered with Fritz's beautiful melodies till you couldn't recognize them. He changed all the tempos, deleted key musical passages." Lerner shakes his head at this directorial ineptitude.

There was no such difficulty with director Vincente Minnelli on the great 1958 Lerner and Loewe film musical *Gigi*, which appeared in theatres just before work on *Camelot* began.

"I had had a lot of enjoyable experiences at MGM," Lerner says. "I did the screenplay for *An American in Paris*, which won an Academy Award. I also wrote *Royal Wedding* for Fred Astaire, which had the song 'Too Late Now.' But *Gigi* was special. First of all, we had Maurice Chevalier, who had been an idol of mine since childhood. And Minnelli is still the finest director of musical films."

Leslie Caron was the ideal Gigi, though her singing voice had to be dubbed, "over her strenuous objections," Lerner says. "She had no clear idea of how

A picture from the 1973 stage production of *Gigi*.
For this adaptation of their 1958 film
depicting turn-of-the-century Parisian society,
Lerner and Loewe contributed four
additional songs.

Two photographs of the
songwriting team of Frederick
Loewe and Alan Jay Lerner.
Within the time span
represented by these portraits,
the two men wrote some of
the greatest music ever to
grace the Broadway stage.

she sounded. But it was not a pretty sound. Dubbing was essential."

Lerner quotes Arthur Freed as saying, "Leslie took it hard." Caron supervised her "ghost" voice, Marni Nixon, until Nixon was nearly hysterical.

The preview audience displayed hysteria of a different kind—appreciation. Memory of that applause compensated for an early, negative review from *Time* magazine.

"Fritz was in an oxygen tent at the time," says Lerner. "When I read that notice, I wished I was there with him."

Time magazine was forgotten when *Gigi* won the 1958 Academy Award for Best Picture. Maurice Chevalier collected an honorary statue, and *Gigi* captured Best Song. Minnelli won as Best Director.

On November 13, 1973, *Gigi* opened as a Broadway musical, starring Alfred Drake, Agnes Moorehead and Daniel Massey. Four new songs were added, and the show won Lerner and Loewe a 1974 Tony for Best Score.

In addition to Lerner's three masterworks—*My Fair Lady*, *Camelot*, *Gigi*—he has written other well-regarded theatre pieces. One of them, *On a Clear Day You Can See Forever*, a musical about reincarnation, opened October 17, 1965. The show ran for 280 performances on the strength of such superb Lerner-Burton Lane songs as "What Did I Have That I Don't Have" and "Come Back To Me."

Coco, with music by André Previn, began its Broadway run December 18, 1969. Starring Katharine Hepburn, the show drew large audiences for 332 performances. "Hepburn *was* Coco," Lerner says. "Even though the real Coco Chanel didn't want Kate because she was too old!"

As for *1600 Pennsylvania Avenue*, a collaboration with Leonard Bernstein: "You remember the *Titanic*?"

The occasional dark stretches never mattered to Lerner. "I write not because it is what I do, but because it is what I am. Not because it is how I make my living, but how I make my life."

CHAPTER NINETEEN

TIM RICE

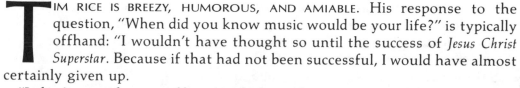

TIM RICE IS BREEZY, HUMOROUS, AND AMIABLE. His response to the question, "When did you know music would be your life?" is typically offhand: "I wouldn't have thought so until the success of *Jesus Christ Superstar*. Because if that had not been successful, I would have almost certainly given up.

"I don't consider myself particularly a theatre person. I mean, I enjoy writing for it very much. But I don't think I ever said, 'I must go into theatre.' I thought it would be nice to write, and it happened that I wound up in the theatre. But there was never a driving feeling that I had to."

It's highly unlikely that the versatile lyricist of *Jesus Christ Superstar*, *Evita*, and *Joseph and the Amazing Technicolor Dreamcoat* would have allowed himself to be defeated by momentary obstacles. Rice's love of writing can be felt in all his work, and his love of rock and roll has made that kind of music an integral part of Broadway.

"Rock music is now thirty years old or whatever," says Rice. "And I think theatre has to absorb, tip its hat to, rock and roll. I think musicals like *Chess* and *Evita* certainly acknowledge the existence of other areas of music. But I think a show written today that doesn't acknowledge that something happened in music when Elvis Presley and the Beatles came along—not to mention the most recent people—won't find a big audience. Because, let's face it, people can be considerably older than I, and I'm forty, and have been brought up on rock music.

"I certainly think," Rice continues, "the audiences that I found for my shows are all people who were brought up on records, probably more than the theatre. So I think you've got to acknowledge the role of rock."

Rice is an authority on the subject. He co-authored the best-selling *Guinness Book of British Hit Singles*, regarded as the definitive coverage of the British record charts. He's also a widely known broadcaster who appears frequently on TV, armed with a thorough knowledge of pop music.

He doesn't feel that rock should take over the theatre, however. "No, theatre could never be 100-percent rock; otherwise you might as well make it into a rock concert. I mean, rock is rock, and theatre is theatre. But just as rock borrows from theatre, I think theatre should borrow from rock."

Rice's discussion of lyricists who influenced him reveals the importance of both rock and theatre in his development as a songwriter.

"I suppose I was influenced a bit by such great lyric writers of the theatre as Alan Jay Lerner, whose records were lying around the house when I was a kid. But I didn't really listen to an awful lot of lyrics. I suppose the ones I listened to most were pop records, people like Jerry Leiber and Bob Dylan."

Rice's musical career began to develop when he met a talented young composer named Andrew Lloyd Webber.

"I took a book to a publisher in 1965, a book about the history of the record charts. The publisher rejected it but suggested I meet Andrew, who was a young composer he was acting as agent for at the time. I said I was interested in all sorts of writing; I had actually recorded a pop song, for which I had written words and music. So the publisher set up our meeting."

The team clicked immediately. "It was one of those things. He wrote some good tunes, and I had some quite good ideas."

With their dissimilar backgrounds, Webber and Rice were an unlikely team of songwriters. "I never went to the theatre as a kid. I think one of the reasons Andrew Lloyd Webber and I got quite lucky," Rice continues, "is that he had all these heroes of the theatre and I didn't. The combination of Andrew's being an expert and very much steeped in theatre from an early age, and my being more interested in rock music and records—I think that combination of ignorance and experience probably helped us to be original."

Originality eventually paid off, but success wasn't instantaneous for the Webber-Rice team.

"We tried hard to get our first show on. It was called *The Likes of Us*. We took it to agents and people, but it never got on."

Joseph and the Amazing Technicolor Dreamcoat began when Webber and Rice were asked by Alan Doggett, head of the Music Department of Colet Court School, to write a musical piece for his schoolboy choir. The first performance took place on March 1, 1968, at the school.

The *Sunday Times* in Britain saw the show and wrote favorably about it. Decca Records decided to turn the musical into a recording in the summer of

1968. The album was released January of 1969 to critical but not public acclaim. Commercial success came with its American release. A West End production followed in 1973, followed by two other West End runs, after which *Joseph* came to Broadway and repeated its successful pattern.

"The show sort of grew from there," says Rice.

"The show was in a permanent process of being rewritten—well, not rewritten, extended—from day one."

The work was worth it. *Joseph* contains delightful examples of the comedic and charming Tim Rice approach, such as the moment when Joseph's brothers sing:

> These dreams of our dear brother
> Are the decade's biggest yawn
> His talk of stars and golden sheaves
> Is just a load of corn
> Not only is he tactless, but he's
> Also rather dim
> For there's eleven of us and only one
> Of him!

Jesus Christ Superstar, which opened October 12, 1971, on Broadway, solidified Webber and Rice's international fame. Based on the last seven days in the life of Jesus of Nazareth, it was considered controversial when the album first appeared and attracted millions of record buyers. Producer Tom O'Horgan was eager to turn it into a Broadway rock opera, and it appealed strongly to the masses, running 720 performances. Ben Vereen won a Theater World Award for outstanding new talent as Judas.

Rice persevered with *Jesus Christ Superstar* because "I just thought it was a good story. I'd always wanted to write a piece about Judas. This comes back to what I was saying earlier about writing, rather than writing particularly for the theatre. I had always had this vague idea at school about writing about Judas Iscariot, who I felt was an interesting character, somewhat maligned at times. By the time I was in a position to write something about Judas, I was working with Andrew. After the success of *Joseph*, I suggested to Andrew that maybe we had proved you can use the Bible as a source of material with good results, and without causing too much offense; I suggested we have a go at *Superstar*. The title of *Superstar* came a little bit after the initial idea, which as I said was really to tell the story of Jesus through the eyes of Judas."

The next project tackled by Rice and Webber was the life story of Eva Peron, the colorful dictator from Argentina.

Rice explains: "I heard a radio program about her and thought, '*Here is a really good melodramatic story that is also true and would suit musicals.*' In

Above: Bill Hutton in a scene from *Joseph and the Amazing Technicolor Dreamcoat*. Although the show's first performance took place in a British school in 1968, *Joseph* didn't reach the Broadway stage until 1982, when it was nominated for Best Book, Best Score, and Best Musical Tony Awards.

Right: Ben Vereen as Judas in *Jesus Christ Superstar*. The rock opera tells the story of the last seven days in the life of Jesus of Nazareth.

order to do a *big* musical, I think you need a big subject, and we were keen to write another big musical. I think Eva Peron was a character who lent herself wonderfully to it. I didn't know much about her before I heard the radio program; but the more I thought of her, the more I read, the more fascinating I found the whole Eva Peron saga."

Evita proved to be a well-developed show, and Rice feels it came closest to attaining his initial vision among his first three hit shows.

"I'm never quite sure if I *have* an initial vision. Initially I tend to see things in true form. Perhaps I'm not explaining myself very well, but I tend to see things literally; therefore, I saw the story of Evita unfolding like a movie, rather than something theatrical. I tend not to think of theatrical effects at the time. I just write it. But, in retrospect, I think to date *Evita* has probably been the production where the theatrical presentation most matched the feelings I wanted to get over about the subject."

Rice realized his movie visualization of *Evita* by using film in the stage production, a resource unavailable to former generations of songwriters.

"We used a fair amount of film in *Evita*, but I think that was justified; because with a real person who existed on film, the footage was actually quite educational. Seeing the real Eva Peron there filled in a few gaps. But I don't think we overdid it; at least I hope not.

"I've seen very few shows in which film has been used, actually. I think it's a pity if you use it too much because the one good thing about theatre, presumably, is that it's *live*. And if you're going to depend too much on video and film, then you tend to defeat the point of doing it in the theatre."

Another Webber and Rice innovation was getting shows to the stage via record albums.

"*Superstar*—well, we couldn't find anybody to put *Superstar* on the stage, and we decided to do it on a record instead. We found somebody who was actually quite interested in making a record of it, and by mistake we stumbled onto a very good way of getting a show on: to make a hit record first. We repeated that with *Evita*."

Considering the long gestation period for these shows, how much rewriting was done?

"A few rewrites. For *Superstar*, virtually none, which was probably a mistake. In *Evita*, we made a few changes, nothing dramatic. We altered one or two songs.

"Basically," says Rice, "we've been quite lucky in that the pieces I've been involved with have almost been right from the start of the production. And this is really one of the reasons for doing it on record. Because when you do it on record, and you get a hit, then it becomes hard for the most powerful director to say, 'Well, I'm sorry; we're going to make major alterations.' You can tell him, 'No, you can't,' because the public knows the work as it is."

If he had the chance now, would he add or subtract from *Evita* or *Superstar*?

"I wouldn't change an awful lot. I mean, I'm not claiming they're perfect works, but I think I'm not really one to dwell on regrets so much. I think you can go on forever trying to improve things. Basically, if a show works at the time, then by and large you tend to be satisfied with it. There are a few lines here and there, more in *Superstar* than in *Evita*, that I might change; but for what the pieces were meant to be, I think they work quite well."

They work well due to Rice's collaborative approach, which is to get a tune first. "My normal method is to provide the plot, which my collaborator or collaborators would make comments about and possibly alter. Then they would provide a tune that I hope illustrates the story line I've given them. And I would then write lyrics to the tune. I generally write lyrics to the tune rather than try to write random lyrics.

"We don't write a song and then say, 'Where should we shove it in?' We write a song knowing exactly what we're trying to do, so either the song works at that point or it doesn't. And if it doesn't work, it should certainly be abandoned."

Although *Evita* and *Jesus Christ Superstar* were released as albums before being staged, when Rice works, he thinks of the show's needs first, not the record market. "I think if you do slant—if you're too cynical and commercial about it—it won't work. 'Don't Cry for Me Argentina' was a huge pop hit. But I think if we sat down to make that piece of music and that scene something for the pop charts, we could never have written such a strong song. It would never have been called 'Don't Cry for Me Argentina.'

"I suppose we figured that 'Another Suitcase in Another Hall' from *Evita* would be big. It was quite a hit in England but never became an international standard like 'Argentina.' We certainly didn't expect 'Argentina' to be, until after the record was released, and then everybody said, 'Hey, that's the one.' *Superstar*? I think we figured 'I Don't Know How to Love Him' would be the biggest hit out of context.

"I think it's a mistake to aim for the pop charts. Your aim should be to get the whole piece right, and if it's good, I think you'll find that automatically you'll get one or two numbers that work in the pop field—which I love. I have to say that the thrill of a pop hit is fantastic. It's almost more exciting than opening night.

"But a hit record is something that you get only if you pay attention to the whole show. I mean, a great pop album like *Sergeant Pepper*, which is chock-full of hits, is not a great show. It's no criticism of the Beatles, but the music was not written to be a great show."

Rice never saves unused songs, ballads or otherwise, from one production to use in the next. "I wish I could. But it's difficult for lyricists to do this, because lyrics tend to be much more pertinent to the particular situation than music. No composer, of course, will agree with this. But it strikes me that Andrew has done that on more than one occasion—if you write a great

Evita, based on the life of Eva Peron, received 1980 Tony Awards for Best Book and Best Score. Of the subject choice Rice explains, "I heard a radio program about her and thought '*Here* is a really good melodramatic story that is also true and would suit musicals.' In order to do a *big* musical, I think you need a big subject."

Rice with Andrew Lloyd Webber. Rice put his lyrics to Webber's music for *Joseph and the Amazing Technicolor Dreamcoat*, *Jesus Christ Superstar*, and *Evita*.

tune and it doesn't work in one show, why not use it in the next one? But it's difficult. If *Evita* had been a flop, we could never have used the lyric 'Don't Cry for Me Argentina' in a musical about chess. But Andrew could have used the tune in any number of situations. As a lyricist, I feel it's jolly unfair; but it's terribly hard for us lyricists to shove our words into another show. Of course, a love song is different. But as far as I'm concerned, I would actually start fresh every time. I think if you spend your time trying to save yourself work by dragging in old lyrics, you end up doing more work than if you had written something new in the first place."

Rice's career has followed an upward curve, but he, like all writers, has experienced disappointments. "I don't have any one thing that I can say, my goodness, that was a *great* disappointment."

There's hardly a songwriter alive who doesn't care at all about critics' reactions, but Rice rejects the notion of sitting down and writing in a way sure to please critics. "It's certainly not an aim, because you can't really please them. Obviously, you're concerned about whether the reviewers will like what you do, but on the whole I've had pretty rotten reviews of nearly everything I do. Yet my shows don't seem to be unpopular with the public."

When asked about his hopes for the future, Rice reflects on his show *Blondel*, the tale of a 12th century minstrel who searched for his imprisoned King Richard I. Rice's collaborator on this musical was Stephen Oliver, composer of 20 operas including *Tom Jones* and *The Duchess of Malfi*. "Which doesn't mean Andrew and I have broken up," Rice adds. We're just pursuing separate projects at this point.

"I was a bit disappointed when *Blondel* didn't do better in the West End. I'd like very much to do some rewriting on the show, get it going in the *Joseph* direction. *Joseph* started off like *Blondel*—in schools—and *Joseph*'s first West End run was not very successful. But I think *Blondel*, with a fair amount of work and rewriting, has the potential to become successful in the same way *Joseph* has. I hope my greatest triumph will be when I eventually prove it was quite a good show, and we'll be doing it again somewhere with a greater success."

A long run seems likely for "Chess," another hit album which was transferred to the stage in the fall of 1985. A million-selling single "One Night in Bangkok" has emerged from this project, co-written by Abba members.

"I love records and theatre," Rice concludes. "It gives me great satisfaction to combine both worlds."

CHAPTER TWENTY

MARY RODGERS

MARY RODGERS, DAUGHTER OF RICHARD RODGERS, is the composer of 1959's *Once upon a Mattress.* Her work in it prompted Brooks Atkinson of the *New York Times* to applaud "a vigorous musical intelligence" and add that "the score has taste and gaeity and comes out of musical richness."

In a field dominated by men, she is one of the few important female Broadway composers still active, as her 1978 Best Score Tony nomination for *Working* demonstrates.

Rodgers loves her craft, calling it "the most fun thing in the world," as she nods toward the grand piano in her Central Park West living room. A petite, graceful woman, Rodgers is completely down to earth.

Mary Rodgers was born in New York on January 11, 1931, and pursued her musical interests at Wellesley College and the Mannes College of Music.

Her father, she claims, was "a little embarrassed about my writing at first. I was writing really terrible popular music and lyrics. But then I began doing children's songs. He listened to them and said, 'Those aren't so bad. Maybe you ought to keep that up.' From that point on he was fairly encouraging.

"I was very strictly brought up, and I was a very rebellious child, so when

I said I wanted to go to Juilliard, my parents packed me off instead to Wellesley, where I was quite bored. But I continued writing. I contributed. I wrote almost all the Junior show, for example."

How did people react to her being Richard Rodgers's daughter?

"I think it could have been a problem if I had thought about what people were saying behind my back—I'd have found it very demoralizing. But I chose not to contemplate what they were thinking. And because music was the only thing in the world I loved to do, I didn't pay attention to that aspect. I think being Richard Rodgers's daughter got me through any door, or to see any producer or whatever, but that doesn't get you hired. People are not stupid. They are not going to hire you and fall on their own faces. So I think what was much more difficult and germane to this discussion is that it was very difficult to be a woman. People tend to think in terms of, well, she couldn't be any good. Her music is bound to be *feminine*. Obviously, if it is good, it is good. And music doesn't have a sex."

What was the skeptics' definition of feminine music?

"Pretty. I enjoy writing pretty music. But I can also write gutsy music. My music was melodic, especially when I played it myself. I was lucky if it even sounded pretty, because I was such a terrified performer that I'd usually end up apologizing.

"I have a feeling there are so few women composers," Rodgers continues, "because the actual act of playing the piano has always been considered essentially masculine. And women aren't brought up to believe that composing is what they can do. I happened to grow up in a household where that's what anybody did, and I forgot to think about it in terms of a sex role. I did it because it was the only thing I could think of to concentrate on, and I really loved it."

Rodgers's love of music urged her to push onward to musical comedy. Her first major show was launched when she teamed up with lyricist Marshall Barer and created *Once upon a Mattress*, based on the fairytale "The Princess and the Pea." It was launched in an amateur production at Camp Tamiment, in Pennsylvania's Pocono Mountains.

Though written in only three weeks, according to Rodgers, *Mattress* was delightful entertainment. Carol Burnett gave a superbly comic performance as Winifred the Woebegone, a gawky scatterbrain who has to prove she is a true princess in order to wed Prince Dauntless. She also has to overcome the sabotaging efforts of the prince's possessive mother, Queen Aggravain.

The show encountered the usual problems on its way to fairy-tale success., but Rodgers was encouraged when Jean and Bill Eckart, who had originally been designers, said they were interested in becoming producers and launching *Once upon a Mattress* beyond Tamiment.

"They saw the first production of *Mattress* and asked Marshall and me if it could possibly be expanded, and we thought it could. We said yes, on the

Rodgers teamed with lyricist Marshall Barer to create *Once upon a Mattress,*
a musical based on the fairytale "The Princess and the Pea."

Once upon a Mattress received a 1960 Tony nomination for Best Musical.

theory that you always say yes and find out later if you can really do that. They asked us to do the score for George Abbott, who also said yes, contingent on our being able to write the book, expand it, and add songs. We had six weeks to get it done. That was the only real problem then.

"The next problem was a song called 'Very Soft Shoes.' I wrote it at Tamiment, and Marshall made me rewrite it eleven times before it suited him."

Working with the great George Abbott was a feather in Rodgers's cap. What insights did he offer?

"Basically not much. I don't think he's a very sophisticated man musically. He either likes something or he doesn't. And I think he likes fairly obvious stuff. I think the greatest insight we gained from dealing with George was not to mess around—he was the captain of the ship. Whether he was right or wrong, at least there was somebody minding the store, and it was a great comfort."

Rodgers also found comfort in the consistency of her work routine with Marshall Barer.

"Lyrics always came first. Marshall would get up at the crack of dawn and go walking on the golf course or something, and if he wasn't back by nine, I knew the day was shot. Either he had something right away he could give to me or not. He'd hang around long enough to see if he thought I was going in the right direction, and if he was satisfied, he'd disappear and write the rest of the song and come back at lunch with a bridge. But if he wasn't back by nine, that meant he was having a terrible time and he was stuck."

Rodgers admired Barer's musical intuition. "He's tremendously musical. He played a little piano, but he had a stupendous sense of rhythm, and he was very clear about what he wanted. When he handed me a lyric, he would mark stress beats and bar lines, and he knew exactly what he was after down to the last dotted line. It was interesting to work with him and enormously helpful.

"The biggest problem was when you didn't like a lyric of Marshall's. Now here is something that pertains to the sex of the composer. It was a problem for us. When I got better at writing lyrics myself, and I knew more about the theatre in general, I wouldn't slavishly sit there because Marshall was a male and nine years older than I was and had been around longer. I couldn't just accept everything he gave me. I began to know enough to argue with him, and say, 'I really don't like this too much.' I don't write so quickly and easily—as, say, Jule Styne does—that I can afford to say, 'Oh, well, that song doesn't work. Let's throw it out.' It really pains me to work hard on something for a long time and then have to throw it out. I therefore find it very difficult to accept a lyric I don't like. And it became a rather subtle sexual battle, I think, because Marshall felt he should be boss because he was the boy."

The collaborators did, however, agree that the sound should have a flavor of early England. "But it was just my version, Mary plus early England. I didn't do any research."

Rodgers writes complete piano parts, "but beyond that I didn't work with the arranger at all. I wish I had learned how to orchestrate when I was at college. It's been very frustrating at times without it. There are times I heard a thing sound wrong in the pit, and I could tell it was wrong, but I couldn't tell them why or how to fix it."

She feels control at the piano, where she does all her work, unlike some composers who often write away from their instrument.

"I do exactly what I learned from my father. I use all my ten fingers for the background and sing the tune. Both hands are the accompaniment."

Her opinions on the casting of *Once upon a Mattress* were respected, "although George was the boss. We accommodated each other. But we had a terrible time with Jane White, who was by far the best performer for the part she played. George was worried, though—it had nothing to do with not liking blacks, but this is medieval England. She was going to look very weird up there, and George didn't think we wanted to distract the audience with this black lady, even though her acting was wonderful. Her singing voice was wonderful too, although we hadn't written anything for her at that point. We had to persuade her to go get a white makeup and come back and reaudition, which was hard for her because her father was Walter White, the founder of the NAACP! It's really like saying, maybe you convert a Hitler youth to a Jew. Her biggest worry was how she was going to get from her apartment to the makeup man at the theatre without being seen by anybody. She didn't want to be seen by any of her friends."

When *Mattress* opened on Broadway in 1959, Rodgers was praised for her "fund of cheerful melodies" by critics. A Tony nomination resulted.

Rodger's talent and professionalism were much more sorely tested by the pressures of *Hot Spot*, a show about the Peace Corps. Her lyricist was Martin Charnin, who later did the words for *Annie*, and collaborated with her father on Danny Kaye's 1970 *Two by Two*. The star of *Hot Spot* was Judy Holliday.

Stars are sometimes a handful to cope with, and originally the producers of *Hot Spot* decided they didn't need one and searched for an unknown actress.

"They chickened out, and decided to go for a known star, and Judy Holliday was their first choice. Then she got sick and was not available, and we started auditioning other people. We found one wonderful performer, not a beautiful girl, but she had this *terrific* voice. She learned two songs of Marty's and mine, and she was great. She would have been marvelous as this Peace Corps person, but she was turned down. That was Barbra Streisand. Getting along with Streisand would have been a lot easier than working with Judy, who ended up playing the lead eventually. *Hot Spot* was done toward the end of Judy's life, and she was crabby.

"I think she was pretty unhappy. I don't know what she was like on *Bells Are Ringing* or anything else. But I got to know her a little because she had a son who was the same age as my oldest boy. She and her mother were always shipping him over to us when we were doing a group thing on Sunday, like Radio City or something. The mother would get on the phone and say, 'Can Jonathan come too?' So we ended up with another one."

As time went by and tensions tripled, Holliday unloaded the conductor and choreographer. In the midst of chaos, Rodgers and lyricist Martin Charnin persevered.

How did she meet Charnin?

"He was in the original company of *West Side Story*, and he had written some stuff that Steve Sondheim had heard and liked. When I was looking for a collaborator, Steve suggested that Marty and I get together. We worked briefly on the Jackie Gleason show. We also did a show for U.S. Steel with Woody Allen, which was fabulous because U.S. Steel said to BBD&O, the ad company, 'We'll give you ten thousand dollars to give to some writers. Let them write an hour TV show, and if we like it, we'll put it on, and if we don't, they can keep the money.' So we wrote something insanely iconoclastic and offbeat, figuring we had nothing to lose. We put the songs on tape and performed for all these U.S. Steel executives. At the end of our little audition, they said 'Thank you very much,' and Marty and I collected our ten thousand dollars. The show never got on, but we had a very good time."

After *Hot Spot*, Rodgers wrote the music in January 1966 to a hilarious satirical takeoff of *Mad* magazine, called *The Mad Show*. Jo Anne Worley and Paul Sand were among the cast members who enlivened the evening. Air pollution, politicians, and atomic energy were some of the production's targets, and Rodgers's melodies (with lyrics by Marshall Barer, Larry Siegel, and Steven Vinaver) kept the zany humor bubbling.

Things looked rosy after that success, until Rodgers tackled a musical version of Carson McCullers's *Member of the Wedding*.

"It really broke my heart," says Rodgers. "I worked on it for three years, and it was my best stuff, and it never got on. And I thought, 'It took me *three years*, and I don't have three years. I have five children and a husband and a fairly active social life and some charitable work that I get involved with on occasion. I just don't have three years of time and emotion and money to squander on something that may never get on, and if it does, it may get trashed in one night.'

"Steve Sondheim told an editor friend of his that I would be right to do a children's book for her, since I had written children's songs. Out of that came *Freaky Friday*. It was perfect timing because I was really fed up at that point."

Freaky Friday—a comedy about a mother and daughter switching places for a day—was purchased by Walt Disney Studios and became a hit film.

Yet Rodgers's first love is the theatre, though she admits that "a lot of rock and a lot of *Grease*—those weren't the sounds I was used to making, and they weren't the sounds I wanted to make."

She agrees with most Broadway writers that the theatre is in a difficult transition period, but adds, "I think it's encouraging that the ASCAP workshop, the BMI workshop, the NYU musical theatre program are useful to new writers. We are, all of us, working in one way or another on the East Coast, listening to kids, advising them, being part of that educational process. There are lots of people who want to write. I think the scariest thing is the lack of understanding of what a libretto is. We have few, very few people to teach that craft, and the only way newcomers can learn what works is to study what has worked in the past."

Rodgers is emotional about helping writers support themselves through early creative stages. Her empathy stems partly from the fact that her own son Adam, 18, is an aspiring and gifted composer.

She also feels that shows, by new or seasoned writers, have achieved their aim if they make a viewer care about the music, truly love it.

"So little is generally mentioned about the score in reviews of musicals," says Rodgers. "They talk so much about the book, the sets, the production values. I suppose it's because they don't know how to write about music. They're like a friend of mine, who doesn't write music and responds to nice, hummable, obvious stuff. I may not like it, but she can grasp it right away."

Music can be hummable without being obvious. Rodgers cites *Brigadoon* as a melodic but exceptional score. "I loved *My Fair Lady*, and I loved *Guys and Dolls*. Frank Loesser had such a lot of vigor; he was so adventuresome."

Women, Rodgers feels, must be adventuresome, but no more adventuresome than men. "They just have to want to do it. There's nobody keeping them out, especially now. I'm not a very political feminist. I have worked ever since I was 20 in one way or another, and I've earned money, but I think this is as easy a time as there ever was for women to succeed in the theatre. Nothing is really succeeding right now, so if a young woman is going to have a hard time, it's not because she's a female. I don't think there's anything more a woman needs to do. My regret is that I didn't get better educated, but I'm better educated than a lot of men I know."

Rodgers objects to the tag *feminist* being pinned inappropriately on women by male reviewers.

"Gretchen Cryer and Nancy Ford's last show, *Hang On to the Good Times*, was called by critics a feminist show. *I'm Getting My Act Together* might have been a feminist musical, but this one wasn't. It was a revue, vaguely feminist, I suppose, and they are certainly known as feminists because of *Getting My Act Together*. But when you're working on a book show, unless you've decided to write about women's problems, there's no reason your sex is going to show."

Rodgers is very definite about the type of material she prefers to write about. "I'm not very interested in writing abstract stuff. I need the story. I like the story, and I've never written music, written anything, unless there was a project to write it for, which I think is something I picked up from my father. He never wrote anything either unless there was a reason to do it."

She is certainly clear about the reason she writes music. "I don't know why anybody, male or female, wouldn't want to. Writing music has an immediate emotional impact on you as you're doing it, which propels you into writing the next note and the next chord. I could write music for twenty hours a day and not be bored or unhappy."

CHAPTER TWENTY-ONE

CAROLE BAYER SAGER

CAROLE BAYER SAGER, who wrote the lyrics for Broadway's *They're Playing Our Song*, the Grammy-winning "That's What Friends Are For" and the Oscar-winning *Arthur*, is witty and natural. When asked to define the Sager style, she quips, "Well, it's short with dark hair and not bad. . . ." Then she laughs engagingly and completes the answer. "Do I have a style? Well, I do, yes. It's direct, simple, honest, I think. I write songs that deal with feelings and emotions. They're not very poetic in their imagery. I wish I was more like that. But I do think at their best they're romantic and accessible and have a certain—I hate this word—vulnerability to them. I don't know. It's easier to define the style of composers than of lyricists. It's easier to recognize their musical themes running continuously through the music."

Sager began shaping her songwriting style at fifteen, while she was a student at New York's High School of Music and Art. Her first hit arrived in 1966, and numerous others followed, including "Midnight Blue," recorded by Melissa Manchester, and the Carly Simon smash she wrote with Marvin Hamlisch, "Nobody Does It Better."

Nobody did it at all—words or music—in Sager's family.

"Music and lyrics were an entertainment my family enjoyed. But there was not any great musicality that I know of on either side of the family. I did grow up on 57th Street and 7th Avenue in Manhattan, though, directly across the street from Carnegie Hall, so that, in a sense, the neighborhood emphasized music more than my immediate family."

She always liked lyric writing, starting with "little notes to my parents, and poems. So, as I say, growing up in New York City, going to Music and Art, with so many outlets, writing felt natural. I mean, it's not like growing up in Omaha and wondering how you can meet someone. I was very lucky in that way. There were channels, and at the time, being fifteen, writing songs was highly unusual." She laughs. "Today that's practically a has-been. Ten-year-olds have hits."

Sager was inspired by Carole King, also a teenager and launching a spectacular career at the time with such standards as "Will You Still Love Me Tomorrow?" and "A Natural Woman." "Before that I loved Oscar Hammerstein. I loved Broadway shows, and seeing musicals was my favorite thing."

Scores she loved include *Promises, Promises*, written by her husband, Burt Bacharach.

"Before Burt was one of my favorite persons in the whole world, *Promises* was one of my favorite scores. *Gypsy* is another one. I loved the scores of *Gypsy, West Side Story, My Fair Lady*—they don't write them like that anymore. *Brigadoon. Finian's Rainbow.*"

As a young songwriter, however, Sager's main focus wasn't Broadway shows. She was signed as a staff writer to Screen Gems–Columbia Music, with eyes trained on the pop charts.

"It was run by Don Kirschner, and I was on staff at twenty-five dollars a week—that's what they started me at. I remember, when I went to fifty, I thought success was just around the corner—I had really arrived."

The idea of Broadway arrived via another staff writer, George Fischoff.

"He very much wanted to write a Broadway musical, and although he'd had some pop hits, 'Lazy Day' and 'Ninety-Eight Point Six,' his dream was to write that musical. I think in order to appease George, they let him try to write songs for *Georgy Girl*. It was a property they owned the film rights to and which Fred Coe wanted to produce. George chose me in 1968 for this musical which we retitled *Georgy*. I was very young and very grateful to have a shot at it. It was half financed by the very company I was signed to as staff writer. So that's how it happened—we did some auditions and the money came very quickly. Too quickly, I'm sure they all think now. Those poor investors."

Georgy proved a frustrating experience. "I was a novice working with Fred Coe, the producer, Peter Hunt, the director, who had just won the Tony for *1776*, and Tom Mankiewicz, the scriptwriter. But I had strong opinions about what the show should be. I wanted the pop singer Melanie to play Georgy—she could act and sing the songs like Georgy would. But she didn't get the part. And I wanted a Jimmy Webb string line and a strong rhythm track and suddenly we had horns. The musical director said it was all right, never mind how it sounds in Boston, it will sound wonderful at the Winter Garden. It didn't; it sounded the same as it had in Boston."

Georgy closed after five performances at the Winter Garden and Sager was, in her words, "really a wreck."

How, having experienced a Broadway letdown with *Georgy* and a triumph later on with *They're Playing Our Song*, does she sustain herself emotionally through ups and downs?

"I sustain myself through faith—the belief that I'm doing what I'm supposed to be doing, the belief that good things eventually find their way, the joy of doing. You see, if you just do it for the result, and that result is a letdown, then everything's awful. But if you've enjoyed what you've done, and the result is not what you hoped for, it can't take away from the enjoyment of having done it. The thing that I try to do is not have a lot of expectations, because then I set myself up for disappointment. Rather, I just enjoy the creativity of the work, and everything else will take care of itself."

The joy of theatrical achievement compensates for any letdowns, Sager feels. "Live people on a stage. Checks each week if it's a hit. The *liveness*— that's the main thing. Every night it's there—live, nourishing, fresh."

Sager's second chance at live theatre grew out of meeting Marvin Hamlisch.

"I met Marvin in 1974 because A&M Records wanted me to put lyrics to a song Marvin had recorded and was releasing as an instrumental. It was the theme for an ill-fated television show. I remember telling him that it was silly to put this out, since the show was already canceled, and why didn't we write a song for something that had more life ahead for it? I knew Aretha Franklin wanted to record. So I gave him a try at 'Break It to Me Gently,' and he wrote a beautiful melody. I knew at that moment there was good creative chemistry. I was also very impressed with Marvin's facileness. I mean, beyond his talent was such speed with which he operated that it was kind of like holding on to the tail of a jet. So it was fun. Not that holding on to the tail of a jet is fun for me. I'm not thrilled about flying."

The creative chemistry led to an Oscar-nominated hit in 1977, "Nobody Does It Better" from *The Spy Who Loved Me*. By now personally and professionally involved, they set to work on a show about a songwriting couple. It was a two-character play, but each had three singing alter egos. *They're Playing Our Song*, produced by Emanuel Azenberg and directed by Robert Moore, opened February 11, 1979. The show caught on immediately with the public, who liked the amusing love story and such numbers as "If He Really Knew Me," and "Falling."

Sager exposed her own fears in "Falling":

I'm afraid to fly
And I don't know why
I'm jealous of the people
Who are not afraid to die

Sager wasn't frightened about the challenge of *They're Playing Our Song*, however. Librettist Neil Simon and Marvin Hamlisch helped to make her feel totally secure.

"It was one of the smoothest rides I've ever taken," Sager recalls. "I've said a number of times that to be able to work with Neil Simon and Marvin Hamlisch—well, I always felt so very protected, and wow, this was almost a free ride in that they're both so masterful in their areas. I just knew they would protect me and not allow me to do anything that wouldn't be right for our show."

They're Playing Our Song exhibited a freshness and immediacy that had much to do with the personal nature of the plot—the depiction of the real-life Sager-Hamlisch love affair. But Sager feels the show's success stems from its universal theme.

"Altogether, I think *They're Playing Our Song* was popular because it was fun. I think people like to be entertained. I think they could identify with the love story. I also think career women could identify with the problem of two people who live together and who are also both working.

"That's a kind of contemporary theme, and Neil Simon has such a wonderful way of handling complex problems with light humor, universal humor. And when he hits on something, it's usually a home run. Marvin and I wrote a light, contemporary score to match Neil's book. Lucie Arnaz and Robert Klein were wonderful. It all worked."

Sager goes on to generalize about what a good Broadway musical—a show that works—should be.

"Something done real well. Something that people can identify with on a mass level, from all walks of life, all geographical levels. Something that just has a message of sorts or something that entertains or uplifts or provokes. Something that lasts, something that feels good. Something that sells and continues to sell.

"My definition of a musical that works, a good musical, is when I don't come out of the theatre saying, 'I can't *believe* we spent a hundred dollars to see that!' My definition of a good musical also is, one, I really wish I wrote it, and, two, I admire and care about the people—where I've had a good time or I've been moved. When I've liked the songs.

"Maybe the best definition is that I've forgotten I write musicals too, and I'm transformed—taken somewhere else. Where I'm no longer a lyricist watching another member of my craft do their thing; and in some way, unfortunately, judging it. I'm just a member of the audience, and I'm going right with it, and I believe it all. I'm taken away. That's great."

According to the lyricist, *They're Playing Our Song* worked because "we read the script a number of times, generally with Neil. And saying, 'What if?' There were a lot of 'what ifs.' "

Another factor that made *They're Playing Our Song* work was Sager's making sure her opening number set the tone of the evening.

Lucie Arnaz and Robert Klein in a scene from *They're Playing Our Song.*

Sager with her husband, Burt Bacharach. Sager says, "Before Burt was one of my favorite persons in the whole world, *Promises* was one of my favorite scores."

"That's vital. The best ones we all know—"Comedy Tonight" from *A Funny Thing Happened on the Way to the Forum*. They should say what type of evening you're going to have, and they should foreshadow the theme of the musical. They should be theatrical. They should be great so that you look forward to more. They should suck you in and keep you in your seats."

We pose our own "What if" and ask Sager what she would do over in the show if she could.

"Oh, if I could do anything over, I'd like them to write about me and Burt. No," she laughs, "I'd want to change that song in the recording studio at the end of Act One, which is just a perfect place to insert a hit because it becomes a hit. It was called 'I Still Believe in Love,' and it wasn't a hit."

They're Playing Our Song was a rock-oriented musical about two hit songwriters, so it's ironic that the songs didn't step out to become pop hits.

"I should have had more pop hits," Sager says. "I tried to, but I didn't do such a great job. Not well enough. That would be the thing I'd want to accomplish with my next show."

As one of today's most successful rock lyricists, Sager views rock and roll as an inevitable force in the theatre.

"It will grow and become more powerful, simply because your theatregoer tomorrow is your rock and roller today. They really have a different sensibility, and they're not going to relate to what our parents related to or what we relate to, because tomorrow's theatregoer has grown up on rock. They're going to have a hard time relating to Sheldon Harnick and Jerry Bock. It'll be easier for them to relate to *Cats* and *Evita* and *Jesus Christ Superstar*.

"I'm all for newness, for innovation, if it's *good*. I'm all for anything that's innovative and breaks ground, as long as it doesn't distract. Or if it distracts, it distracts in the right way that it's supposed to. Then I like it."

Sager's pop songwriting experience allows her to compare that world with writing lyrics for the theatre.

"As a lyricist, the major difference is, on a pop song, I can pretty much write whatever I feel like writing, as long as I keep in mind that someone is going to turn on a radio and want to hear it or want to buy the record. But there's no subject matter. It's on me to come up with the subject matter.

"A film song usually dictates what the song's going to be about. They've given you the title by nature of the film's material, and your first purpose is to enhance that picture. Whether it's a pop hit or radio hit or sells records is secondary to that. And a song for the theatre even more so. You have to advance the story, and you have to move the book along. And if, at any time, the book stops and you have the greatest hit song in the world, then you are simply a big yawn. I mean, if people are thumbing through their programs to see what happens next, then no matter how good that song, you've stopped the action. You want to continue the action in the song, in theatre."

Sager's plans for continuing in the theatre include the possibility of collaborating with Burt Bacharach on a show.

"Burt and I have two properties we'd like to write together. I'm not at liberty to discuss them in print, because they're just such wonderful ideas that every aspiring person who wants to write for the theatre, who reads this book, will run to do the very same musicals. So I can't talk about them."

Will she ever write a libretto?

"I just wrote a novel, *Extravagant Gestures,* so anything's possible."

Sager obviously feels that a creative person should be free to attempt many things, double up on roles.

"Like the composer/director, or the director/choreographer. Sure, if someone's talented enough to do both or three or four or five things, do it. I root for people to succeed, and if someone can choreograph and direct, as Michael Bennett surely can, then he has a greater sense of the whole. If someone can write, choreograph, direct, and star, terrific. As long as the person handling all those roles keeps an objective eye, it's fine. There are no rules. For me, theatre has always been about collaboration. But if you can do everything yourself, then do it. Freedom to be creative is all that counts."

CHAPTER TWENTY-TWO

STEPHEN SCHWARTZ

I 'VE DECIDED NOT TO WORRY WHETHER SOMETHING IS COMMERCIAL and just go on the basis of, 'Is it something that *interests* me and feels like a project I'm eager to work on?' " says Stephen Schwartz. "If you do something, and it has quality, it turns out to be commercial in some form or another."

Schwartz's pursuit of quality has yielded remarkable results. His first three shows, *Godspell, Pippin,* and *The Magic Show,* were smash hits and at one time were all running on Broadway simultaneously. *Godspell* and *Pippin* earned him Best Score Tony nominations; he won a Grammy for the *Godspell* cast album, which he also produced. The innovative *Working* followed, as well as *Mass,* co-written with Leonard Bernstein.

Schwartz was exhausted the day we saw him. As always, he spoke quickly and with great intensity, but his eyes betrayed strain, a strain due to last-minute preparations for a two-week showcase revival in 1985 of *The Baker's Wife.*

"I believe in this show," says Schwartz. "I want people to have a fresh look at it." The earlier David Merrick production, starring Topol, had proven a disappointment, closing in November 1976 at the Kennedy Center Opera House and canceling its trip to Broadway.

Based on a 1938 French film by Marcel Pagnol and Jean Giono, the story dealt with a baker whose wife leaves him for a shepherd.

"I feel it's my best score," says Schwartz. Theatre buffs agree with him, as do the hundreds of actors who utilize "Meadowlark" and "If I Have to Live Alone" as audition pieces.

It's not surprising that Schwartz wants to revive and stand by one of his creations. He has always believed in himself and his achievements since earliest childhood.

"As a kid," he says, "I put on shows, writing songs for puppet shows and the neighborhood children. When I was in high school, I went to Juilliard in the preparatory division and took piano and composition. I started piano lessons in the seventh grade."

He sensed, even then, that the theatre required an overview, an all-seeing creative eye that went beyond music training.

"I decided to go to drama school when I went to college, rather than majoring in music. I think everybody writing for the theatre should take acting, because the processes are so similar. A lot of writers don't understand how to get that internal process going, so they write songs that are nice but not really dramatic. And the key word is *dramatic!*"

Life took a dramatic turn for Schwartz at age 22, when he came to New York to drum up work. "I went around and showed my music to producers, record companies, and so on. One of the places I went was RCA Victor Records. In those days—this was 1968, 1969—RCA was very intimidated by the whole youth market. Just about anyone who was young and walked in their door was offered a staff position. When I came to RCA, I had done two demo records, with me just sitting at a piano. But based on these records, RCA offered me a position as producer in their Artists and Repertoire Department."

He took the job, conceding, "It wasn't a planned career move, but financially it was a terrific thing. It kept me solvent for two years while I was finding my footing. During those two years, I really did learn about the recording studio."

Producing records was an education, but Schwartz's first love remained writing. In early 1970 he received a letter from an Off-Broadway producer, who claimed to have heard an album of a musical Schwartz had written while a sophomore at Carnegie Tech College—*Pippin Pippin*.

"He said he was interested in perhaps doing the show Off Broadway, and would I mind working on it and revising it? I was receptive, of course. But it turned out the so-called producer was only a kid with aspirations. Still, he wound up putting on a backer's audition for some people. We did five or six of the songs, and an agent from International Famous Agency [IFA], Bridget Ashenberg, was there. She had been persuaded to come by another 'agent'— who turned out in the end to be some guy who worked in the IFA mailroom!"

Schwartz shakes his head at the mysteries of show business. "Bridget wound up introducing me to my agent, Shirley Bernstein—that's Leonard Bernstein's sister. And everything started moving from then on. So a fake producer and a fake agent made it all happen. The moral is," and Schwartz grins, dissolving his serious expression, "if you want to get started in this business, meet someone who works in the mailroom."

Shirley Bernstein agreed with Bridget Ashenberg about the merits of the *Pippin Pippin* score (later shortened to *Pippin* by director Bob Fosse) and asked Schwartz to play it for producers Edgar Lansbury and Joseph Beruh. "They were enthusiastic about the story but not particularly interested in the show," says Schwartz. "Meanwhile, though, the producers saw *Godspell* at the Cafe La Mama—an Off-Off-Broadway experimental theatre down in the Village—and liked it. They called me—in desperation I'm sure, because every established writer had turned them down—and asked me to write a score musicalizing the Gospel of Matthew from the New Testament. At the time, *Godspell* had only a few songs, and they had been written by cast members. It wasn't really a musical. I saw the show in March of '71, and they planned to go into rehearsal April 11th."

Schwartz acknowledges, "I was too dumb or too young to know you couldn't do that, so I just said, 'Oh, fine.' And six weeks later we *did* go into rehearsal, and the score was finished. We opened five weeks after that. I had the advantage, of course, of having seen the show at La Mama, so it wasn't a mystery to me. The production didn't change that much. All that happened was the new musical numbers got interpolated. I didn't have to go through the process of discovering the show from scratch, the way one does on a brand-new project."

In spite of the pressure, Schwartz showed versatility and a nimble way with words. In "Light of the World" he spoke with modern tongue-in-cheek:

> You are the salt of the earth
> But if that salt has lost its flavor
> It ain't got much in its favor

"All Good Gifts," on the other hand, adhered closely to a poetic biblical tone:

> We plow the fields and scatter
> The good seed on the land
> But it is fed and watered
> By God's almighty hand
> He sends the snow in winter
> The warmth to swell the grain
> The breezes and the sunshine
> And soft refreshing rain

Godspell proved a smash Off Broadway, running 2,124 performances beyond its opening on May 17, 1971. On Broadway it ran an additional 527 performances after opening June 22, 1976.

Schwartz has a regular work process, which helps him to complete assignments such as *Godspell* quickly.

Doug Henning as himself in *The Magic Show*.

Ben Vereen's performance in *Pippin* earned him a 1973 Tony for Best Actor in a Musical.

The cast, band members, and creators of *Godspell* celebrate the show's first anniversary.

"I always get as much of the lyric idea down as possible. I think music is much easier than lyrics, because lyrics are craft, and music is a sort of emotional response to a situation or a particular feeling. So I handle the lyric first. Also, it's important that I get as much lyric done as possible right away, because once the music is done, that's it for me. I'm trapped in that form."

Schwartz feels less restricted in his approach to finding book writers. "In some cases, writers have come to me and said, 'I have this idea,' and I say 'OK.' In the case of *Pippin*, though, the idea for the show, about Charlemagne's son and his attempts to find himself, and parts of the score existed before we found a book writer. I read a lot of plays and talked to a lot of people who were recommended to me for *Pippin* before I finally found a writer who understood the property, who understood exactly what I was trying to do with it. That turned out to be Roger O. Hirson."

Schwartz and Hirson joined forces effectively to write the story of Charlemagne's son Pippin, who ventures into the world, involves himself with war, women, and revolution, and returns home, opting for tranquil domesticity. Director Bob Fosse added theatrical elements, including a group of clowns headed by Ben Vereen as The Leading Player. Vereen and cohorts commented musically on the action. Fosse was so pleased with Vereen that he expanded his role.

The performance brought Vereen a 1973 Tony Award as Best Actor in a Musical, and Fosse earned one as Best Director. Schwartz's outstanding contributions were underrated, due to friction between Fosse and himself, but he doesn't dwell on the past.

"I keep working on," he says, "and my routine is pretty unvarying. I almost always write in the morning since I'm a morning person. I'm fairly wasted by one o'clock in the afternoon. Anything after that is preparation for the next day. I get away from the actual writing and let the unconscious take over. Things arrive when I'm driving or in the shower."

Schwartz usually writes at the piano, but not always. "Sometimes I write in my head. I don't do what Leonard Bernstein does—which is to write at a score paper. I hate to write music down. I'm still waiting for that machine where I can sit at a keyboard and play what I play, and it will write those notes out. It's difficult for me—for anyone—to write down *exactly* what's played. Just the act of having to analyze each bar kills some of the spontaneity."

Schwartz's determination to keep writing paid off in the form of *Working*, for which he received greater credit than he had for *Pippin*. He directed the show and wrote the book, for which he received a Tony nomination. He also supplied four songs for an overall score that included material by Mary Rodgers, Micki Grant, James Taylor, Craig Carnelia, and Susan Birkenhead. Perhaps that is why he feels closer to *Working*, based on Studs Terkel's comprehensive portrait of the working man, than to any of his other shows.

"I was fondest of it," says Schwartz. "When it was initially unsuccessful in

New York after a particularly difficult preproduction period, I felt crushed. But *Working* went on to become a very successful show all over the country in regional theatres. I came to grasp that, if I do my work well enough, there will be an audience somewhere. It may not hit on Broadway, but somewhere it will find an audience and have a life; that is why one does these things."

Working opened on May 14, 1978, and closed after only 25 performances. Despite the bumpy box office reception, it was superbly directed by Schwartz and contained many fine songs: "Millwork" with music by James Taylor and lyrics by Matt Landers and Graciela Daniele; and Micki Grant's "If I Could Have Been," a summation of the working woman and her aspirations; and others.

Not surprisingly, Schwartz says that it's a song from *Working*, called "Fathers and Sons," that most personally reflects him. "It's about a guy who's looking at both his relationship with his son, who's three, and his relationship with his father. He thinks about all the changes he went through, thinking of his father first as a hero, then as a man with failings, and finally accepting him as a human being. I think all of us go through stages like that with our parents. And in the song, he accepts that, for the time being, at least, he's a hero to his little boy."

The lyric to "Fathers and Sons" sets the premise with sensitivity:

> I've heard a lot of songs say
> "Where are you going, my son?"
> Now I know they're true
> Boy, you never stop to think how fast
> The years run
> Now they're taking you

Schwartz's music and lyrics have given his shows life beyond Broadway. "They've all gathered their own special audiences and have gone on. The records have been favorites of people. The *Godspell* album, the *Pippin* album, *Working*—all have a lot of fans. So I consider that the greatest triumph."

Another triumph Schwartz has experienced is the hit status of songs from his shows, a rare occurrence today. "I know I had 'Day by Day' and 'Corner of the Sky' with the Jackson Five," says Schwartz, "but I really didn't think in terms of the pop market. 'Corner of the Sky' was the philosophy of Pippin— the hero's attempt to find a place for himself in the universe. In the case of *Godspell*, I was writing so fast I was lucky to get the music done. It's funny; you play your scores for people, and they say, 'Oh, that song is going to step out' or 'That's liftable,' but the hits turn out to be the songs you didn't *know* were liftable. No one ever pays attention to the songs you believe have a chance. The song you sort of didn't know about, that's the one everyone listens to."

People *do* like to listen to Schwartz's music, and he names Jule Styne,

Studs Terkel, author of the best-selling book *Working*, with Schwartz. Ask Schwartz to name his best show and he replies that he has the deepest fondness for *Working*, a musical based on Terkel's comprehensive portrait of the working man.

The opening night curtain call for *Mass*.
From left: Gordon Davidson, Leonard Bernstein, and Schwartz.

Rodgers and Hammerstein, Lerner and Loewe, Bock and Harnick, and Stephen Sondheim as composers who have helped him develop his own abilities by example. He notes, however, that "the big change in my style came when I discovered rock and roll. I didn't like rock throughout the fifties, the era of 'Rock Around the Clock.' I found all that boring. It wasn't until the Motown sound and the Supremes and folk influences took over that I got interested. The Mamas and the Papas, Jefferson Airplane—all that was extremely influential."

Yet Schwartz isn't sure about the ultimate impact of rock in the theatre, as much as he loves it. "There seems to be trouble assimilating it. I'm hard-pressed to think of anyone who has successfully used rock in a *book* show yet. I liked *Evita* very much, but that's an opera. *A Chorus Line* has certain pop music elements, but you can't call it a rock score. *Cats* has a lot of nice music, but it doesn't have much of a dramatic structure. You're essentially viewing a pageant.

"Director-choreographers have contributed to that," he continues. "Some are great—like Jerry Robbins and Michael Bennett—but other director-choreographers seem less interested in the content of the words, structure in the story sense. They're more involved with choreographic structure, so we get these extravaganzas and pageants with little emotional resonance when they're gone. A mediocre show done the old way has more of a chance of lasting than a mediocre show done the new way. When you have a director-choreographer, you have to have a great show like *A Chorus Line* to have lasting impact."

Dramatic structure matters enormously to Schwartz, which is why he regards opening songs in any production as vital. "In *Godspell*, we deliberately did a number that was different from the rest of the show. We thought of it as the black-and-white section of *The Wizard of Oz*. We wanted to set up a world and a sound that we could break out of; so when the drums came in and the colored lights and the colored costumes came out, there was a freshness and a relief without going to another place. The opening number, 'Prepare Ye the Way of the Lord,' is a prologue that gets the audience emotionally ready to jump into the rest of the show. Listen, every situation is different, but more than anything, the opening has to just catch you up and throw you into the show. You can do it quietly or gently, but it still has to hook you!"

Ballads are not the most logical way to hook an audience, though most composers are addicted to them, including Schwartz. "All of us love our ballads. Yet ballads are really *tough* to make work in the theatre. Ideally, you should have none at all, but I wind up writing more than I should all the time. If you write 'Send in the Clowns,' you can have a ballad, but too often the guy comes out and sings this pretty song, and everybody says, 'Yeah, that's kind of nice.' Then they look at their programs, and when the ballad is over the show can start again."

Ballad or up-tempo, Schwartz often researches his material. "In the case of *The Baker's Wife*, it was set in France in the thirties. So before I wrote anything, I spent about a month listening exclusively to French records like Edith Piaf, Yves Montand. I played Debussy and Ravel on the piano, just so my fingers would automatically go toward those chord structures, and I would have those sounds in my head. But when I started to write, I didn't pay attention to it, and what happened is what I'd hoped would happen. I went instinctively to certain chords I wouldn't have gone to before I'd done that. It's sort of like an actor's preparation, building up a sense of memory or whatever other exercises an actor does."

Schwartz is spontaneous and intense when giving his view of where the theatre is going. "Anyone who has tried recently to do a Broadway musical knows why you can't do one. There are no producers. The theatre owners have taken over, and it doesn't work the same way with people who are essentially businessmen. It's not that people in the Shubert organization lack artistic judgment. What they lack is artistic *passion!*"

His face colors when he says it. "See, in the old days, people like Leland Hayward would decide to do *South Pacific*. And, by God, he'd get the group, and he'd get *South Pacific* on. In my case, it was Stuart Ostrow who really got *Pippin* on. He got it all together. That kind of thing doesn't exist anymore."

Is money a basic problem?

"Absolutely. Everything costs so much that you can't even get it together in a room with a group of actors to work on something because you fall under these ridiculous union codes and workshop codes. So you don't have a chance to work anything out. Young writers have no chance to do something.

"The unions are greedy and shortsighted. I think management has capitulated to the unions stupidly. I think a good Broadway show these days, a good Broadway musical that *opened* on Broadway, is an accident, an incredible fluke. I know they used to be rare, but they didn't used to be *accidents*."

We asked Schwartz if he thought there was a future for the Broadway theatre.

"I don't see any future for the Broadway theatre unless it simply becomes, which it's sort of becoming now, a place that houses good work done elsewhere. I think people who write for the theatre have to find other places to perfect their material. And then when they get it finished, if someone sees it and says, 'Oh, that's good; I'd like to do that at the Winter Garden,' you say, 'Oh, fine, great.' But to try to *plan* a show that goes out of town and opens at the Winter Garden is next to impossible. You have economic pressures. You're spending too much money. You don't have time to work, and you don't have freedom to experiment.

"The way to do musicals today is to initiate them at some small place or

Charles Strouse accompanies Schwartz in a song from *Rags* at a Juvenile Diabetes Foundation benefit.

regional theatre and develop the project in a series of readings outside of New York—or work in a showcase situation. Even the workshop doesn't make sense anymore because they cost $500,000, and you're so limited in terms of rules that you don't have room to move freely, try things out. It's not like when we did our *Godspell* workshop, when everybody met when they felt like it and said, 'What'll we do today?' It was a much more creative process then. Now it's just like rehearsal without the scenery; that's all it is, just doing the show without the scenery!"

Schwartz feels that critics compound the problem. "It's actually better now than it was a few years ago. There was a time when the criticism was particularly terrible and destructive and discouraged a lot of people from writing for the Broadway theatre. It certainly discouraged me."

In spite of the problems, however, Schwartz intends to continue writing for the theatre. "It's what I know how to do. I wouldn't say I love writing for theatre above all media, but I have an instinct for it. I love pop records and pop music—I don't seem to have the same kind of instincts for it, though, as the people who do it very well and very successfully. I think my talent is essentially a theatrical one, telling a story in dramatic terms or structuring an event where the audience is taken on a whole long journey, as opposed to the short form of records. I'd love to do movies, but I haven't been able to get work; so I have no idea if I'm any good at that or not. I'm here on the East Coast, not in California, which is a handicap. Television? I think it's limited in terms of a musical form. I did *Working* for television, and it was certainly well received; but I can't see writing a lot for TV."

Unlike many writers, Schwartz appears to have a firm grip on the pattern of his future. "I've finally discovered how I have to work, the way I *can* work. What I mean is, there are people who are very taken up by doing a Broadway show, and that's important to them. They like the *process* and the pressures and the way it unfolds, the stars and the meetings. I don't. I hate it, and I can't work that way. What I've found is that I like to work at my own speed over a long period of time on a project that interests me, that I care about, and I like to keep working on it in various forms until I feel it's the thing I saw and meant to do.

"Fortunately, I have had enough success early so I don't have to worry about feeding my family. So, at this point, what I want to do is just go from project to project; do things I'm interested in, things that are meaningful to me."

What means a great deal to Schwartz is directing. He distinguished himself on *Working* and recently directed a work in progress, *Cradle Song*, with music and lyrics by Jan Mullaney and Mary B. Phillips. The show has been optioned for Broadway.

"Directing is important to me," says Schwartz, "and as for writing, I'll probably wind up doing something with an opera form. I don't have long-term goals for myself anymore—I just keep at it."

Schwartz will continue to be a major creative force in the musical theatre, "I feel I can't be defeated by the fashions of the time or by particular critics. It's like Steve Sondheim says in the song 'Move On' in *Sunday in the Park with George*:

> Stop worrying if your vision is new.
> Let others make that decision—
> They usually do

"Don't worry about what other people are thinking. You just keep going on, doing what you do, trying to do as well as you can. Don't worry about anything else. If you can get to that point of view, you're home."

CHAPTER TWENTY-THREE

CHARLES STROUSE

I LISTEN TO A LOT OF POP MUSIC," says three-time Tony-winning composer Charles Strouse. "I recognize that I don't write black music, but I'm very aware of rock, and I certainly would like chart hits."

In suit and tie, leaning toward us over a glass table in his dining room area, Charles Strouse looks like the antithesis of a rock-and-roller. His affable, articulate conversation suggests a teacher, which in fact he is; he has taught an ASCAP theatre workshop for many years and has helped hundreds of students in their pursuit of a theatrical writing career.

"I'm open to everything," says the composer of *Bye Bye Birdie, Annie, Applause,* and *Golden Boy.* "Rock, jazz, classical—I always have been, ever since I began taking piano lessons." His mother was a jazz pianist ("but not a professional one"), and he first started taking music seriously in 1943, at age fifteen.

It's not surprising that the man who wrote the music for *Bye Bye Birdie* would be so receptive to the needs of the Top 40 marketplace. *Birdie* was, after all, the first rock musical. Even though, as Strouse admits, the score compromised between Broadway and pop commercialism, it set the stage for the Andrew Lloyd Webbers.

The stage was set for Strouse's career when he attended the Eastman School of Music. "I wasn't *passionate* about music before," he says. "I became passionate when I got there. I studied orchestration a great deal, and I thought at first of going into abstract or serious music. The popular music came later. For a while, I supported myself playing piano, and then I had a couple of pop songs. One was written with Fred Tobias, called 'Born Too Late.' The Ponytails did it."

Strouse was already preparing *Bye Bye Birdie* when "Born Too Late" was written. "I was very much immersed in Fats Domino, Presley, and all that. And those things influenced 'Born Too Late.' In fact, Fred and I wrote it when we were supposed to be playing poker. Nobody showed up for the game that night, so we wrote it because we had nothing else to do."

"Born Too Late" proved an isolated instance. Theatre became Strouse's focus soon afterward.

"The way I got into theatre was really very simple. After college I was still studying privately with Aaron Copland. I worked with Copland for three years. To support myself at that time, I started playing dance classes—ballet classes—and I always had a propensity for jazz. I also played on weekends in dance bands—very boring jobs, extremely frustrating. Then I met a choreographer named Ray Harrison. He was going up to a summer stock place, and he asked me if I would go up and be the choreographic pianist, which translates into slave labor today. Even then it was slave labor. You just play the same music over and *over* again, for dancers.

"But when I was up there I wrote arrangements, and it was good training. I enjoyed it, and they asked me back the next year. I started writing songs, and in between those two years I met Lee Adams at a party for a mutual friend. That was 1949. I asked him if he wanted to write revues, and we started. We had to write a revue a week, with very good people like Carol Burnett, Don Adams, Dick Shawn. The name of the place was Green Mansions.

"It was—it no longer exists—in the Adirondacks. It was tremendously popular with the younger people, and it had a captive audience. On Saturday nights, instead of having Buddy Hackett or the equivalent of big-name acts, they had the staff put on the shows. At one time all the resorts did that— Grossinger's, the Concord, the whole Borscht Belt. Eventually, the precedent was broken and big hotels started booking name acts—people became very competitive. I guess I was the last of the group that worked at Green Mansions. My predecessors at Green Mansions, you know, were terrific, like Fred Ebb, Jerry Bock, Herman Wouk, Sheldon Harnick, Lee Adams, of course. Neil Simon was at another similar place, Tamiment. I can think of very few around my age who *didn't* do it."

The early 1950s brought Strouse into close contact with another major musical influence, Frank Loesser.

"He was actually a very close friend of mine. I was his associate for about a year—assistant would probably be a clearer word. I respected him tremendously—after all, *Guys and Dolls* is a classic—and because of my dance background, and the fact that I could play better than Frank, who wasn't a very good pianist, I became his alter ego. We spent about a year and a half together, over the period of *Greenwillow*, basically. We had a very open relationship. Frank would write things out—he had a very good sense of organization—and he used to say, 'Play that again.' He'd say, 'Play an A-flat in the bass with that same chord.' You know, that kind of thing. I was able to say, 'Well, let's try a B instead of the A-flat,' and he'd say either 'No, no, no' or 'Yes, yes, yes.' I wasn't married at the time, and I'd work with him till two or three in the morning up at his place. He was very open with me."

Strouse pauses. "I always wanted to emulate his career. It seemed highly enviable to me—it still does—but musically I don't think he was the influence that, say, Bernstein was or Copland, and more than either, Stravinsky, including my work in the pop theatre."

His work in the pop theatre began with revues, co-written by Lee Adams. A producer named Ed Padula heard the material and asked Strouse and Adams to attempt *Birdie*.

"*Birdie* evolved. We wanted to do a thing about teenagers, but the book, a wonderful book, written by a now-deceased author named Warren Little, wasn't acceptable to anyone. We went through a string of five writers, including Mike Nichols and Elaine May, who were number four on the list—and finally Michael Stewart was our choice. We had worked with Mike Stewart in Green Mansions. He later went on to do *Hello, Dolly!*, *I Love My Wife*, and *42nd Street*, but we had to push him through at that time. Nobody wanted him at all. We knew how gifted he was. The evolution continued, and Lee had the idea of making it about a rock and roll singer who gets drafted. Next thing the rock singer became the focus, and it tied in with Presley's well-known draft, and that was that. At the time it was odd—groundbreaking—to do a show on the subject."

The idea of featuring Dick Van Dyke as the rock star's manager was immediately appealing to Strouse, although Van Dyke, like Michael Stewart, was relatively unknown.

"Everybody else wanted a star—they wanted Jack Lemmon. I had virtually offered it to Dick, but we kept pursuing the Jack Lemmon course. All through this, Dick's agent, a man by the name of Dick Seff, a wonderful agent—brilliant man, too—kept pestering us: 'What about Dick Van Dyke, what about Dick Van Dyke?' Everybody hemmed and hawed, 'Yeah, but we need a big name.' Finally Seff *insisted* we see Dick Van Dyke. And we hired him." Van Dyke went on to win a Tony for Best Supporting Actor.

"Eydie Gorme was another contender for *Birdie*. We wanted Eydie—she got pregnant. Then we got Carol Haney."

Carol Haney was a big star at the time and had just done *Pajama Game*. But she was a victim of recurring psychosomatic illness.

"She knew the music well, and she sang incredibly. She was certainly Broadway caliber all the way. The day she was to sing the songs for me, Lee,

The stage was set for Strouse's career when he attended the Eastman School of Music. "I wasn't *passionate* about music before, I became passionate when I got there."

The producers of *Bye Bye Birdie* originally sought Jack Lemmon and Eydie Gorme for the leading roles that went to Dick Van Dyke and Chita Rivera.

and Gower Champion, Lee and Gower came down to her apartment at St. Mark's Place in Greenwich Village. I had worked with her an hour before Lee and Gower arrived. The doorbell rang, and she said, 'I'll get it,' and then, facing Gower and Lee, she gasped, 'I've lost my voice. Oh, my God, I've lost my voice.' She couldn't talk at *all!* I had never seen anything like it in my life. I'm sure doctors see it all the time, but it was obviously an anxiety thing. We sat for twenty minutes. I was very embarrassed, and we kept saying, 'Oh, it'll come back' and Gower said, 'It happens all the time.' She kept apologizing. 'I don't understand—this is ridiculous—I can't talk' for half an hour, and that was the end of it. We were desperate, realizing she couldn't do it.

"Somebody then—I can't remember who—suggested Chita Rivera. We had done a thing called *Shoestring Revue* with her. She was a dancer. It was her first show, and she was supposed to be doing background while everybody else became a star. I was musical director of that, and I was very instrumental in giving Chita songs—not all of them, but I was the guy who said, 'Let Chita sing that one; Chita can do that one.' She came out of *Shoestring* fairly well known. Then she did *West Side Story*, but she had never starred in a show."

The story of *Bye Bye Birdie* was satirical. A popular singer named Conrad Birdie, played hilariously by Dick Gautier, faces induction into the army. Conrad's manager writes a farewell song, to be performed on television by Conrad to a young female fan. Chaos reigns when the fan's boyfriend hits Conrad on the air, and her father attempts to upstage the star. In the end, Conrad does Uncle Sam's bidding. His exhausted manager settles in a small town with his girlfriend and resumes his teaching career.

Birdie had many musical high spots: the zany "We Love You, Conrad," sung by a group of Conrad's fans underneath his window; "Kids" ("Why can't they be like we were, perfect in every way? What's the matter with kids today?"); "Ed Sullivan"; "One Boy"; and the smash "Put on a Happy Face."

"I knew we had something with 'Kids,' " says Strouse. "The message was so universal. I never dreamed it would hit so big, though!"

"Put on a Happy Face" was, in Strouse's words, "more of an entertainment piece than a book piece. It worked perfectly, but only after careful analysis and rethinking.

"We wrote it for another spot. Actually, we'd even started on the tune in Green Mansions. But anyway, we finished it, and Gower did exactly the staging one would expect of him. It was brilliant. Dick got a fantastic hand; Chita was an instant success. But it was Marge Champion, more than Gower, who said, 'No, no'—she had another idea for the song. She was incidentally, a very intelligent woman and a great support to Gower and me in everything. Marge had this idea about doing a tap dance with the kids in the first act, when Birdie is leaving. They decided to try it her way. I was secretly very embarrassed about it. This was my first Broadway show—I was virtually out of music school—and I thought, 'Oh, my God, this is one of the first songs in the show, and it's a *tap dance*—it's like bad MGM.' I was very negative. And the minute it started, everyone just ate it up. Two sad girls, and he sang 'Put on a Happy Face,' and he stopped the show every time. Today that seems typical, but it was very inventive in 1960."

The show that followed *Bye Bye Birdie* proved less successful.

"I had always liked a book—I can't remember the title—about a Slavic professor who came to this country and got Americanized, falling in love with America for the reasons Americans don't like—its vulgarity, its brash-ness, its spirit. But he was a man of peculiar European sensibilities, and his interaction with people on a college campus seemed like a wonderful idea. But we couldn't get the rights. Then, by coincidence, we found a book by Barbara Lewis Taylor called *Professor Fodorski*, which had a very similar character. The plot was different, but it also had to do with football."

All American opened March 19, 1962, and ran 80 performances. The Mel Brooks libretto dealt with an immigrant, Professor Fodorski (Ray Bolger), who came to the Southern Baptist Institute of Technology and inspired the football team to victory. A memorable Strouse and Adams hit "Once Upon a Time," emerged from the show.

Strouse and Adams next adapted Clifford Odets's *Golden Boy* into a musical; turned the Italian hero-boxer, Joe Bonaparte, into a black man named Joe Wellington; and fashioned the show for Sammy Davis's talents. Joe was no longer a musician, as in the 1937 play and 1939 film; but otherwise the libretto concentrated on the same romantic plot between Joe and his manager's mistress Lorna. The newly added racial aspects resulted in an exciting Harlem sequence, entitled "Don't Forget 127th Street," in which the successful Joe returns to his old neighborhood. Another effective scene was the opening, in which fighters trained to rhythmic accompaniment.

"We were always capacity business with Sammy," says Strouse, referring to the show's run of 589 performances.

Who, we wondered, originally thought of doing *Golden Boy* as a black show?

"It was producer Hilly Elkins's idea. He told us he had Sammy Davis to do it, and we said, 'Fantastic,' and he told Sammy he had Clifford Odets and us—nobody had *anybody*, but Elkins really put it together, and I'm proud of him. I've always liked that show. There's a revival planned, and I think it's going to be good. We're writing two new songs for Sammy, and he's going to play the fight manager this time."

Strouse's enthusiasm tells us that he put a lot of himself into the show. He bears this out by continuing, "Oh, I'll tell you, the most personal song in all of my shows is probably "Night Song" from *Golden Boy*. That's the song about a lonely young man in Central Park—in this case he was on a rooftop—looking over the city. I remember being very lonesome and standing out in the park, looking toward perhaps this building.

"I remember the most flattering remark ever made about that song to

Sammy Davis, Jr., and Johnny Brown sing "Don't Forget 127th Street"
in a scene from *Golden Boy*.

me—by a stewardess. We were talking about the theatre. Anyway, she brought up that a song reminded her so of when she was a kid in Harlem, and she mentioned "Night Song." I don't think she knew I wrote it, but to me it was the best compliment ever—as good as a *New York Times* review. I still remember it because that was me as a kid; I had the same feelings."

On March 29, 1966, just a year and a half after the premiere of *Golden Boy*, *It's a Bird, It's a Plane, It's Superman* opened on Broadway. It ran 129 performances. The plot dealt with a gossip columnist, Max Menken, and his launching of an unmask-Superman campaign so he can claim Planet reporter Lois Lane as his own. Produced and directed by Hal Prince, the show had wit and a respectful approach to the cartoon flavor of the material, treating the characters as real instead of burlesquing them. Audiences watched as Superman flew high above the stage, courtesy of invisible wiring.

The next Strouse and Adams show was more successful than *Superman*. *Applause* opened March 30, 1970, and played for 896 performances. An adaptation of the 1950 film, *All About Eve*, it starred Lauren Bacall as Margo Channing, the role Bette Davis had originally created. *Applause* gave Strouse and Adams the opportunity to create witty sophisticated songs, such as "Fasten Your Seat Belts," "But Alive," and the energetic title tune. Their score, which cleverly evoked the world of the theatre and those who work in it, contributed strongly to the Tony the show received as Best Musical. Bacall also earned a Tony for Best Actress.

"It was difficult to get the financing for that. But it worked out, and Bacall really came through. I worked with her a long time myself before she went with a coach, and it was really a question of the right keys. She picked up style; she was *so* good. One of the best songs in *Applause*, to my mind, was "Welcome to the Theatre," a *very* rangy song but what Bacall did was she talked the part, the part that was low. She made everything work—she is an *actress*."

Strouse also enjoyed working with Betty Comden and Adolph Green who wrote the *Applause* libretto.

"They were lyricists themselves, but Lee did the lyrics for *Applause*. There was no conflict, though. We were warned, 'They're very demanding, very difficult,' and we didn't find that at all. They were absolute pros! I'd love to do a show someday with them as lyricists."

Despite the success of *Applause*, Strouse and Adams eventually went their separate ways.

"Lee and I have never formally broken up," Strouse hastens to explain. "We are still good friends. It's that our working habits grew different. We'd grown apart. At one time, toward the end of what I'd call our most fruitful period, he moved to the country, and already that was a big change. I'm a New Yorker, and it doesn't mean anything to me to work at eight in the evening; that was not available to me with Lee. Our lives just pulled apart. I can't name one factor, but two things happened as a result of it. One, I met and wrote with a lot of wonderful collaborators, like Marty Charnin on *Annie*, and I'm doing a show called *Rags* with Stephen Schwartz, and I'm working on another with Alan Jay Lerner. I'm also doing a show with Sammy Cahn, *Bojangles*."

Strouse has found collaboration with all these gifted men stimulating but different in fundamental ways.

"It's all on an emotional level. Varying needs that they have—varying habits of cleanliness. Lee, for instance, is meticulous about his papers and that kind of thing and is a very public person. Alan Jay Lerner is an extremely private person. Alan wants you to write the song right in front of him and will sit with you all day while you're writing it. He got that habit from working with Frederick Loewe, who hated playing piano. Alan used to have to chain him there because Fritz was a child prodigy. He found it a chore to go to the piano and work, so Alan sits with you, though I'm used to writing by myself or writing along with somebody writing a lyric. Marty Charnin: very open and likes to sit with you forever and have you do the song over and over. He likes the song written first, before lyrics."

Strouse is interested in writing lyrics himself, what he refers to as "a strong desire, a lyrical bent. When Lee and I stopped, I started to do lyrics more and more seriously. I'd written a song in a revue for Joel Grey called 'I Lost the Rhythm,' which was my first performed song, then lyrics for different revues here and there. I also did an opera about three years ago called *Nightingale*, for which I wrote all the words myself. It was on a commission, and was very well received—the lyrics too; it got very nice notices in London."

Strouse doesn't start with a title when he writes words. Lee Adams always did. And Marty Charnin, his *Annie* collaborator? What was his overall approach?

"Marty's a puzzle player, a little bit like Stephen Sondheim. He's a visual artist—does a lot of lines and faces and sketches. He likes fitting things, going over them, putting them together."

Four years of effort were spent getting *Annie* onstage, since no producer thought a story about an orphan searching for her parents had a commercial chance. The sentimental tale of Annie's adoption by Daddy Warbucks struck them as old-fashioned and Dickensian. In 1976, producer Michael P. Price booked *Annie* at the Goodspeed Opera House in Connecticut. Mike Nichols saw it and helped to iron out the rough spots. It opened triumphantly on Broadway on April 21, 1977.

"I didn't have to research *Annie*," says Strouse, "because I grew up with Shirley Temple. I always thought *Annie* was just about the best Shirley Temple film ever made, and I was in love with Shirley when I was a kid. The only thing was, I was scared to tackle another comic strip after *Superman* failed. I was totally negative, in fact, but Marty Charnin is a good friend, and we'd always wanted to work together. I was absolutely convinced that doing *Annie* was a dumb idea, and it turned out to be the biggest moneymaker I ever had."

It also had one characteristic in common with all Strouse's shows—an opening number that came about only after others had been discarded.

"The opening songs on my shows have always been replaced," he says. "*Applause* went through three different openings. *Annie* was an absolute hodgepodge of openings. *Annie* had an opening song and scene that was a medley of coughing. We were convinced that *Birdie* was the biggest bomb of all time, and we cut it down. Originally six minutes long, the opening was cut down to two minutes. Everybody thinks 'The Telephone Hour' was the opening, but it was really the second song.

"*Annie* starts with a ballad, and that was the fifth choice. Even now Martin and I tell different stories about this, but I'll tell you the true story. It was my idea. Martin says no, but it was mine. The opening was in mud all the time. It would go from things like Roosevelt and bums selling apples on the street to 'It's the Hard-Knock Life'—all these being various openings, and none of them held any interest for the audience. We had another song in there called 'Annie,' and it opened with that. The show was in Washington, on tour out of town, we were sitting around, and I said, 'Why don't we start with the ballad?' and everybody said 'no' in the beginning. I did worry, 'If it's wrong, what will happen?' But Martin, after the decision to start with a ballad was made, said 'No, let's go ahead with it.' You know, when you make a change like that, it's not just a question of 'We'll try it tonight.' It's orchestrations, set changes, lighting—very expensive. But we did it, and the production built from there.

"So we *finally* wound up with 'Maybe.' I remember it was an idea that I started, and then we got frightened with it—I certainly did. I *knew* it wasn't going to work; I pulled back from it, but it was one of those lucky ideas. The audience just loved the melody and gave us the greatest reception. Incredible."

Strouse felt that the hit song "Tomorrow" was out of style with the rest of the show, even though he hadn't intended it to be a pop song. "Every other song could have, more or less, been written by Harry Warren or one of his contemporaries, with the exception of 'It's the Hard-Knock Life,' but 'Tomorrow' was a tune that could only have been written in the seventies. It had those kind of harmonies—melodic rise and fall—that could only have come from that period. It was really rock-derived, everything about it."

Everything about it also pulled at the audience's heartstrings. "Surprised the life out of me. This little girl came out with a dog. And we were so scared, watching the dog, that he'd behave."

The scene-stealing orphans stop the show with
"You're Never Fully Dressed Without a Smile"
in *Annie*.

Lauren Bacall holds the Tony for Best Musical of 1970. Celebrating with her are the creators of *Applause. From left to right:* lyricist Lee Adams, co-producer Joe Kipness, choreographer Ron Field, co-producer Lawrence Kasha, book writers Betty Comden and Adolph Green, and composer Strouse.

Lenny Wolpe is Ed Koch in Strouse's 1985 musical *Mayor.*

He did, and the show won a 1977 Tony for Best Musical, as well as Best Score for Strouse and Charnin.

How does Strouse rate himself as a composer?

"I feel as though my batting average is average." Strouse says, referring to disappointments such as *Charlie and Algernon*, a 1980 musicalization of the 1969 film *Charley* which had won an Oscar for Cliff Robertson. This dramatic fantasy about a retarded man briefly given super intelligence netted Strouse a Tony nomination for Best Score.

"Maybe it was too offbeat," Strouse speculates. "It's funny—my wife seems to think that all the good ones work because I did everything right—and the bad ones don't, because someone else did something wrong. I can't tell. The biggest successes I've had in my life seem to be really accidental.

"They're all disappointments when they don't work," adds Strouse. "*I and Albert* was a tremendous disappointment to me in London, although it got excellent notices, as fair shows do. I thought it had one of our best scores. I hope it'll be redone some time in America."

Strouse doesn't let occasional disappointments keep him down; in 1985, his new show *Mayor* opened Off Broadway to favorable reviews. The self-effacing composer just keeps honing his craft. "I don't feel by a country mile that I'm where I want to be yet, but I express myself more and more freely through words as I work on them."

That determination is expressed best by the way Strouse defines his basic theme: "a triumph of life over death. My father was chronically ill—had diabetes from a very early age and heart trouble. He also had hardening of the arteries, and we always lived with great fear about him. I couldn't bear unhappy or sentimental tunes because I was always so frightened that my father was dying. So my songs are like 'Tomorrow'—'The sun'll come out tomorrow.' "

CHAPTER TWENTY-FOUR

JULE STYNE

THERE'S A LEGEND ABOUT JULE STYNE, the man who supplied music for *Gypsy, Funny Girl, High Button Shoes,* and *Bells Are Ringing.* When asked by a producer to come up with alternate melodies for a spot in one of his shows, Jule wrote tune after tune, even though the producer loved each one more than the last. To say he's prolific is an understatement. Jule Styne is the kind of composer, they say, who won't take yes for an answer.

"Jule's melodic fertility is extraordinary," says Stephen Sondheim, Styne's lyricist for *Gypsy.* By his own admission, Styne wrote so many hit songs in his heyday that it was "embarrassing." Some of the titles: "It's Magic," "Time After Time," "I'll Walk Alone," "Let It Snow, Let It Snow, Let It Snow," and the Oscar-winning "Three Coins in the Fountain." Yet his first love has always been the theatre.

It's not surprising, then, to learn that his office is located in the back of the Mark Hellinger Theatre. Two flights up, we meet his longtime assistant, Dorothy Dicker, who ushers us into Styne's office.

"Sit down," he says; and as we set up our tape-recording equipment, we confront the legend who is wearing a black jacket, red tie, and red silk handkerchief. In Jule Styne is the echo of a long, distinguished Broadway tradition. The echo sounds more forcefully when we look at the pictures on the wall of *Gypsy; Peter Pan; Gentlemen Prefer Blondes; Funny Girl; Something More; Subways Are for Sleeping, Bells Are Ringing, Hallelujah, Baby!,* and *High Button Shoes.*

When asked why theatre has always been his prime passion, he responds,

"It's in my blood. I'll tell you why. It offers the most important thing, the thing we all fight for, called freedom. It allows me, not the director, not the author, not the writer, to keep what I've written until proven guilty."

Jule Styne is guilty of only one thing—creative genius. He was born on December 31, 1905, and it didn't take long for the genius to surface. At age three, while attending a play, he jumped onstage to sing along with the star, Scottish entertainer Sir Harry Lauder. By nine, he was a piano soloist with the Detroit and Chicago symphony orchestras. He won a scholarship at 13 to the Chicago School of Music, and by 21 he had a hit song, "Sunday." He found time through all this activity to create his own orchestra in 1931, for which he also supplied arrangements.

He loves and admires many composers—Frank Loesser, George Gershwin, Johnny Mercer among them—but he doesn't hear them when he writes. "I like Jerome Kern and all my contemporaries, as every composer should. But I don't listen much to popular music. Once in a while you want to listen to people, but I don't write at the piano, so when I sit at my desk and write, I'm not hearing music. My brain dictates what I should write. And when I'm doing a show, I read the script, and I become involved with the character, and I write completely for that character. I don't know what it's going to come out like. I'll make sure there's a beginning, a middle, and an ending, so people remember the song. Whether they like it or not, they'll *remember the song*. Therefore, I shut out all music. I don't sit down and say I'm going to listen to Dick Rodgers's latest score and see what he's done, or Kern's. I write for the character."

Funny Girl is an excellent example. He couldn't write for Barbra Streisand at the beginning because she hadn't been cast. He wrote it to portray the show's protagonist, Fanny Brice.

"Streisand came after we couldn't get Eydie Gorme and Carol Burnett and several other people the producers wanted to play Fanny. They had never heard of Barbra Streisand."

Then on March 22, 1962, *I Can Get It for You Wholesale* opened. A young newcomer named Barbra Streisand stopped the show playing a secretary named Miss Marmelstein. Streisand was nominated for a Tony. *Funny Girl*'s producer signed her up.

Once they had Streisand, Styne felt that the opening number for her was a make-or-break decision.

"I knew in *Funny Girl*—I said, 'Fellas, when you don't have the greatest singer in the world, you have no story. I'll tell you why. We're dealing with the life of a great singing star, and I've gone around and asked about eighty people if they've heard Fanny Brice sing, and none of them have. So therefore, in your story, you've got to let people know.' And I told Bob Merrill, who did the lyrics, 'Blow it *all* on the first song.' Because if they don't say she's great, it's trouble. And he came up with 'I'm the Greatest Star,' and

I knew that would get them. We made her a star. An unknown was then made a star, and it happened to be Fanny Brice within the confines of the play, in the first song. When she says, 'I'm the greatest star, and no one knows it,' and she held it, everyone said, 'Yes, you are.' She was home after that first song. *Anything* she did was fine after that.

"Now, if it were Carol Burnett, we wouldn't have had to do that. They know she's a star. If it were Ethel Merman, you wouldn't have to think of that. An unknown was going to have to carry the show. We knew she could sing, which is essential. Director Jerry Robbins went down there and flipped out. How many times have you gone and heard a girl you think is great, and you bring people and they don't like her? That's no good. You've got to hit a home run."

He hit a home run with Carol Channing in *Gentlemen Prefer Blondes*. The show, which opened December 8, 1949, and ran for 720 performances, musicalized the romantic escapades of likable gold digger Lorelei Lee.

"The minute I saw Carol, I knew she was it," Styne says. "I went to the writer, Anita Loos, and said, 'I've found our Lorelei.' " Styne didn't go along with the idea that Lorelei Lee had to be a conventional glamour girl (as Marilyn Monroe later was in the 1953 motion picture version). "No, what we need is a comedy actress commenting on a pretty girl," Styne insisted. Casting against type gave the show a fresh, different flavor, adding insight into the character of the heroine.

Channing's charisma was given a chance to flower with two superb signature songs, "Diamonds Are a Girl's Best Friend" and "A Little Girl from Little Rock."

Styne showed his ability to bring the best out of female stars again with Judy Holliday in 1956's *Bells Are Ringing*. Comden and Green provided clever lyrics, and Holliday's role—a switchboard operator who falls in love with a man she hasn't met—gave her ample room to act.

"Judy was a musical *person*," Styne explains. "She was a wonderful actress, so I figured, let her acting ability and the mere fact that she's Judy Holliday make up fifty percent of whatever we write. I figured, Holliday, a great star, had a Charlie Chaplinesque quality, one who could make you cry. 'Let's play on that. She'll handle the rest,' I said. We don't tell her that, and so the first song we wrote for Judy was 'The Party's Over.' It was easy, had a small range. The first song that she sang in the play worked well for her because it set the character. It's very important, like Barbra Streisand on 'I'm the Greatest Star'—she wants a job. That worked. Same thing with Judy Holliday. She sang 'I'm in Love with a Man.' She's sitting alone, and people start caring for her.

"Then, when Judy got more courage, Robbins said, 'Write something in the opening of the second act, of going to a party—make her move a little bit. She can't dance, but we'll make her move a little.' And he made choreographer

Composer Jule Styne and lyricist Bob Merrill work with Sydney Chaplin and
Barbra Streisand on the score to the 1964 musical *Funny Girl*.

Styne and Judy Holliday,
the star of the 1956 musical
Bells are Ringing,
in rehearsal.

Peter Gennaro take a part in the play so he could dance with her. He wouldn't let her dance with anybody else, because anything less would have been disastrous for her. Peter would have a lot of fun with Judy. You were watching Peter, but Judy Holliday was in the number. And we gave her a comedy number, which was right to character, you know, a name-dropping song that was right for her. Like, everyone is dropping names, and she can only think of Rin Tin Tin, till in the end she comes up with Lassie."

Everything didn't go smoothly, however. Judy Holliday wanted what theatrical insiders call "an eleven o'clock number," a number at the end of the evening when the star can make a personal impact.

"She wouldn't come into New York unless she got an eleven o'clock number. Up to that time, Sydney Chaplin had an eleven o'clock number in the show, and he was scoring big with it. She found out, eight weeks on the road, that she didn't have one. It had to be written in two days. I talked to Adolph and Betty. I thought and thought and started eighteen different things. They were all for *singer*-singers, and that wouldn't work. Finally, it had to be comedy. I remembered something George Abbott told me. 'If you're looking for material,' George said, 'material for a comedy number, and you're ever stuck, go back and read the script over to find out the biggest laugh in the show. Take that and make a song out of it. It will work in song form too.' All of a sudden it comes to me that her biggest joke in the show was when they asked her where she worked, and she said she worked at the Bonjour Tristesse Brassiere Company. Bonjour Tristesse fascinated me, because it was ticky-tacky, and I know I'm dealing with an old-fashioned girl. Her ideas, her way of life, the way she dressed and everything, were dowdy. This girl was in 1930, so I figured I'd put her in the Harry Richman period, the Al Jolson period, and it might turn out to be something. The song states the character."

Character is Styne's byword, the term that defines that major difference between the pop songwriter and the songwriter who thinks in dramatic terms. This attention to character made "I'm Goin' Back (to the Bonjour Tristesse Brassiere Company, that Shangri-la of lacy lingerie)" a showstopper.

"At that point in the play, she made a statement, 'I'm going back where I can be me, at the Bonjour Tristesse Brassiere Company.' I said, 'Gee, that's funny.' I had these eight bars, and I played them for Comden and Green, and they fell down. I said, 'Don't write it. Let's see if Jerry Robbins likes it.' Robbins was in bed. I said to Jerry, 'You've got to put your clothes on and listen, because we're having problems with Judy. You're trying to give her different things, and she's not taking it. She's interested in her song. "Finish it," she's saying. "Give me my number." ' We threw in all the jokes, and it was her biggest number in the show. If you stay honest with the character, you're never in trouble."

Ethel Merman with Ruth Mitchell and
Goddard Lieberson behind the scenes of
Styne's 1959 smash-hit musical *Gypsy.*

A young Richard Nixon
appears backstage with Styne
and Merman during the original *Gypsy.*

Angela Lansbury joins with the authors of *Gypsy. (From left)* Jule Styne,
Angela Lansbury, Arthur Laurents, and Stephen Sondheim.

Then Jule Styne adds, "God bless George Abbott. He reminded me of something so valuable."

In terms of character writing, Styne stresses that he didn't write for Ethel Merman specifically when he did *Gypsy*. "No, not at all. Rose in that show was a fiery person, egomaniacal, evil, self-centered. Those things told me what I had to know for writing."

Whether writing for *Gypsy* or *Funny Girl*, Styne recognizes different problems that have to be resolved when dealing with a star.

" 'Don't Rain on my Parade,' in *Funny Girl*, I originally wrote as a tenor sax instrumental. Bob Merrill said to me, 'The cue for the song is right—Don't tell me not to go; I've simply got to.' It was at the end of Act One, and she wanted to go with Nicky Arnstein, and she's warned *not* to go. I didn't want Barbra to start wailing away. I wanted her to sing it the way I wanted it to happen. She couldn't change it because there were too many notes—too many notes for her to fool around. Figuring that, I asked Bob, 'Can you write to this tune?' and I gave the tune to Bob, and in two days he had a wonderful lyric. It was an experience. When she started learning it, though, Barbra didn't want to do it. She did sing it, of course, but she couldn't resist phrasing it differently. She fooled around with the low notes, just to get her endings in."

He grins, remembering. "Like in 'People,' going for changing the note. That's the thing: when you get a great singer, you allow them to do that, and you get something back in return. You know, it's a game of giving in on one thing and getting it the other way. The whole thing is a game. You've got to know when. Same thing with Ethel Merman. 'Ethel, you've got to sing it in C.' 'No, it's too high.' 'Ethel, listen.' So you give in, and in another song she's singing in D, so you get it back."

Styne's willingness to compromise made collaboration with other writers as fruitful as his dealings with actors and actresses. He found it easy and stimulating to work with Stephen Sondheim on *Gypsy*, the 1959 hit.

"When I played 'Some People' for Steve, he said, 'What is that you're playing?' I said, 'It's a double-time thing that a singer named Bea Palmer used to do.' One thing I do remember is, not songs, but singers and style of a period. I was playing in a band in the late twenties, with the Ben Pollack band, and I remember Bea Palmer. She was the greatest singer ever. Pearl Bailey had a lot of her style. This girl was unbelievable, and she used to sing double-time things. I remember her singing 'I'm Comin', Virginia,' and then she'd go on and sing double-time Dixieland. All those double-time things on sixteenth notes and thirty-second notes in the confines of a four-four, you know—all the slurs. I remembered that, and Steve said, 'Gee.' He called me that night and said, 'This is a compelling thing. I think we ought to use it through the whole show.' And we used it, as you know, in 'Rose's Turn.' "

Styne waxes eloquent about Sondheim's talent. "He has great ears. I don't think I can explain how talented he is. He's not a flowery person. He's right to the point. He's honest. He's corrective. He's enthusiastic. You see it in his face, you know. That's where his great sense of musicianship comes in. When I wrote 'Rose's Turn,' Arthur Laurents, the book writer, said, 'Write a medley of all she has seen in the past.' Steve liked the musical intervals in between, a cacophonous thing. When Steve heard it all the way through, he said, 'You only do it once.' So Steve helped me with his musical intuition. He wanted a cacophony, so he put it in the bass trombone's sound. Now look, the audience doesn't know it's a bass trombone, but you feel it.

"The whole thing was on paper. I brought it to him, and it knocked him out. Steve isn't one of those Broadway wise guy types, but it knocked him out. But the number had no ending. At eleven o'clock, I said, 'She's been screaming for five minutes; you'd better give her some applause.' Arthur said, 'That's just the way it will be.' 'Damn it,' I said, 'this woman deserves a hand. Not one place in the whole show does she get one—you're always changing curtains after her. After a big number the curtain changes. You never let her stop the show. Why is that?' But Jerry Robbins said, 'Wait a minute.' Robbins is a guy who *likes* hands. 'Let's try it in one show, Arthur, and see what happens.' Now I've got it written, I've got the ending, and we did it. The show didn't go on for seven minutes after the number—applause, applause, applause. And I said, 'What's better, Arthur, to have a show like that, or to have her quiet? You've got enough drama in your show. They've been crying all night.' "

Styne regards an incident like this as an example of collaboration working toward the best possible result.

"The most important thing is: if you're not a collaborator, you'd better never write a show. Even the guy at the door will offer you a suggestion. You have the scenic designer, you have the orchestra leader, you have the choreographer, you have everybody in the act, and you let them be in the act."

In terms of collaboration, Styne feels that "the lyric writer works with the book writer first. The lyric writer is going to come back and tell you all that took place, and you save a lot of time. When a book writer has to work both at the same time, it's hard. The musicologist isn't going to sit like a dummy, and so when he enters, the concentration is taken off the main purpose. With two people, it's easier staying on the line. Oh, there are times when I believe in eight people at a conference. But at the very start they should get straightened out so that the book writer speaks the same language as the lyric writer—so that all of a sudden, when the songs start, the lyric writer hasn't made another character, so he doesn't start using four-syllable words when he's a two-syllable man. You've got to speak the same. If he's a sophisticated fellow, then he's sophisticated. If he's a romanticist, he's romantic. However the book writer speaks, the lyric writer speaks."

Styne believes the music writer should speak his own language. "Just write yourself," he says. Research, he feels, is needed, if you're doing a period piece like Cole Porter did in *Can-Can*. "Sure, if you've got mazurkas and things like that, you can research."

In his stellar career, Styne has found other brilliant lyricists to collaborate with. Sammy Cahn, for one, his *High Button Shoes* co-writer.

"Sammy's a wonderful pop writer. God knows he does certain things well, his priorities are tremendous, and he wrote a lot of great hit songs. You'll always find one great line in a song of his."

Comden and Green, his collaborators on *Bells Are Ringing*, *Peter Pan*, *Do Re Mi*, and *Subways Are for Sleeping*?

"They're dramatists, because they've written librettos. We wrote *Two on the Aisle*; *Say, Darling*; *Do Re Mi*—had a hit song from that with 'Make Someone Happy.' We had a batch of hits when we did *Bells Are Ringing*. They're special material writers. They love lyrics, and they're also good performers. They've spent time performing and being the darlings of the living room. They wrote some wonderful screenplays too."

Bob Merrill, his co-writer on *Funny Girl*?

"Bob Merrill didn't want to write lyrics. He had another life design: he wanted to be a country gentleman. He wanted to be a film director and a film writer. With lyrics, he said, 'I guess I can do that too.' The first time Bob wrote a song, it turned out to be a smash."

How did it feel to collaborate with a man like Merrill, who could write words and music?

"He was never the composer with me. He never suggested a note or anything. What happened with Bob and me was, I ran into him in Palm Beach and said, 'Do you want to write some songs for *Funny Girl* on spec?' I gave him five tunes, and he came back in about four days with five lyrics. It was incredible. He was, you know, looked on in town as the guy who wrote 'How Much Is That Doggie in the Window?' "

Peter Pan, a Styne collaboration with Betty Comden and Adolph Green, presented a tougher problem than other projects, because the team was called in to help an existing composer and lyricist.

"Leland Hayward was in trouble with *Peter Pan*. It opened with Mary Martin in San Francisco and didn't go so well. Something was wrong with it. I guess it was the score. And Carolyn Leigh. I didn't know her too well, but I had great respect for her lyric writing, and Moose Charlap was her co-writer. I like Moose; he's a cute little guy. I said, 'Let's go up and help them. Let's not rewrite. Let's give them our advice.' Carolyn Leigh was so bitter, she wouldn't take advice. She didn't want to meet. She didn't want to hear anything, and when she did behave that way, I told Moose, 'We're going to rewrite, Moose. Your partner doesn't want to listen.' And we had a big fight with her.

"Poor little Moose. He fought it out. He said, 'Listen, these people have more experience.' There was no time, because we only had a week to prove to Mary Martin that it could be better. So from Monday through Friday night we wrote eight songs. First thing I said was 'Let's attack writing about Never Never Land.' You have to write something that's enchanting, that gives her something to sing. The flying is good. 'I Want to Fly' is good, and the other song, 'I've Gotta Crow,' is good. But give us some warmth. It has got to be some melodic texture, so I went to my German musical education. You say, did you do your research? Well, it's in my mind. And I wrote 'Never Never Land,' a pure Germanic piece. Mary says, 'More, more!' "

Styne thinks, then continues. "In the whole piece, there are two stars, and they didn't sing a song together, which is unbelievable—that they wouldn't have had an encounter, that the wonderful scene wouldn't have been musicalized. It turned out well. We wrote a crazy piece of material for them, and it gave Cyril Ritchard, who played Captain Hook, something to do."

Peter Pan opened in California to respectable notices. Director Jerome Robbins then asked Styne to suggest someone for dance music.

"I brought in Elmer Bernstein. I liked his musicianship. He's full of ambition and fast and he had a good sense of dance. He rewrote all the ballet music."

Occasionally, Styne—like many composers, Cole Porter among them—dips back into his own past.

" 'You'll Never Get Away from Me' in *Gypsy*—that song was used before, on a television show with Leo Robin. It was called 'I'm in Pursuit of Happiness,' and I had no intention of using it in *Gypsy*, except that Steve asked for it. He said, 'Can you get that lyric back? I've always loved that song.' He felt it had a kind of pleasing sound, with Rose moving around, showing her body to Herbie. It had that old-fashioned sound to it. 'It's got that *dip* to me,' he said. So I called Leo, and Leo said sure and gave the lyric back."

The song had a graceful, Fred Astaire feeling. Styne says he intended it that way.

"There are two Fred Astaire songs in that score. I'm such a fan of Fred Astaire; there's a lot of time when I was influenced by him. Fred Astaire has been a great inspiration in my writing. He's the most attractive person that I know in my time on the musical comedy stage. He came from the stage, but even in the movies, all of a sudden, when you're watching him, you think you're in the theatre. All the other dancers, they're out there dancing, but Fred Astaire! There's another Fred Astaire song in *Gypsy*, called 'All I Need Is the Girl.' This guy is supposed to be a lousy hoofer, a show-off, and as I said, the irony of the whole thing is that I'll write the greatest Fred Astaire song. But Jerry Robbins heard it and fell down. He said, 'How can you write this beautiful thing for this lousy hoofer?' Normally, a guy would write a piece of crap, write anything, but Jerry dramatized his dream. He gave elegance to it."

Styne is a perfectionist who wants every song in his shows to sound fresh and contribute to the advancement of the plot. To achieve that, he'll battle for his beliefs.

"A director can't just say, 'Take it out.' Even Jerry Robbins couldn't take 'Little Lamb' out of *Gypsy*."

In "Little Lamb," the lonely Louise, overshadowed by her sister Baby June, sings plaintively to her pet lamb. The moment offered breathing space from the relentless power of Ethel Merman's driving stage mother. Louise whispered,

> Little lamb, little lamb,
> My birthday is here at last.
> Little Lamb, Little Lamb,
> A birthday goes by so fast.

"I told him I'd pull the whole score if the song wasn't used, and it stayed," says Styne. "Later on he came back and told me I was right. In *Gypsy*, also, they buried the orchestra without my knowing it, way down in the bottom. I went to Jerry and grabbed him by the throat, and I was almost going to throw him into the pit. He didn't want to talk to me because I said, 'Raise the orchestra up. Don't you want to hear the overture?' The producers wouldn't listen to me. They sided with Jerry, so on my own I went out and bought twenty-two tall stools. Everybody sat up there. I built them up."

Styne's perfection paid off for *Gypsy*.

"The greatest thrill I ever had was the London opening of *Gypsy*. The great thing was when Angela Lansbury came out. There was a tremendous ovation, maybe twelve or fourteen bows, and she says, 'Tonight doesn't really belong to me. It belongs to Arthur Laurents, Stephen Sondheim, and Jule Styne." The audience stood up, and we had to come forward. We were way back at the bar. And they waited until we got up on the stage and took a picture."

Styne is determined to push for what he knows will work, but he stresses that it's the play, not the trappings, that make the difference between success and failure. Working on *Funny Girl* demonstrated something else, says Styne—that if the show works, it will work; if it doesn't, no light change or set will save it.

"If it doesn't work with one set, it ain't gonna work with no set or two sets. Nothing helps. I'll tell you one thing. When Jerry Robbins came into *Funny Girl* as a new co-director, all he did was change one set because it was ugly, and he said, 'You've got to get a real stove up there. You can't *pretend* that it's a stove. What's up there looks like a cutout.' So they got a real stove in the kitchen and a new set of flags. That was all. If it doesn't work, it doesn't work. I've never seen where scenery or clothes—oh, sure, if you have a rich producer or director or people who want to throw money away—but I've never seen that stuff save anything. You can't hum chords or scenery. It's got to be there."

Styne's instincts about what type of property will work have largely been on the mark. How does he go about picking properties?

"I think today is sad, really sad. We don't have producers in the theatre anymore. What I call a producer is Leland Hayward or Merrick. Merrick is sick now, but he was a producer who went out and dug up properties and secured them. There aren't any now. You have to find your own."

Peter Pan, like *Gypsy, Funny Girl, High Button Shoes,* and *Gentlemen Prefer Blondes,* were properties that turned into high points for Jule Styne. *Say, Darling,* which opened April 3, 1958, and ran for 332 performances, fared less successfully. It was based on Richard Bissell's autobiographical account of his experiences while writing the book *7½ Cents* and the musical derived from it, *The Pajama Game.* Called "A Comedy About a Musical," it featured characters that vaguely suggested real people: David Wayne as the author himself, Robert Morse as Hal Prince, Jerome Cowan as George Abbott.

"The first act was sensational," says Styne. "Then it went to pieces, and we weren't able to change it because the producers didn't have any money. The scenic design was terrible.

"Vivian Blaine wasn't right. She was right for *Guys and Dolls,* but she never really knocked me out. In one movie, *Atlantic City,* she was good. And Johnny Desmond—he's a cabaret performer. Did you ever hear what Johnny Desmond did? I got him a job because he needed a job. He played Nicky Arnstein with Barbra in *Funny Girl.* Do you know what happened the first time Barbra sang? She gets through her first chorus of 'People,' and he walks out and says, 'Let's hear it for this little girl.' He asked the people to applaud in his show. Isn't it unbelievable? It's the truth."

Sugar was another property which left Styne dissatisfied. It opened April 9, 1972, and ran for 505 performances. There were lively songs, such as "What Do You Give to a Man Who Has Everything?" and "Sun on My Face." The farcical premise—two witnesses to a gangland slaying masquerade as musicians in an all female orchestra—had audience appeal.

"I'll tell you about *Sugar.* It's a big stock item. It plays all over. I'll tell you what the trouble was too. *Sugar* was really Billy Wilder saying, 'Hey, this German thing is great fun. Let's get Marilyn Monroe, Jack Lemmon, and Tony Curtis. It was the first real drag show. And it was terribly funny. But Bobby Morse and Cyril Ritchard never got along. The main fault, bless his soul, was Gower Champion. Gower was sick at that time and nobody knew. He did things that, if he were sound of mind, he'd never have done. Here we were, doing a real show. How would girls dance on top of a train? It doesn't figure. So he took the reality out of the play, and it was confusing."

Was Gower replaced?

"No, because David Merrick believed in Gower, and he'd rather have gone down on the ship with Gower. And Gower came up a lot of times for Merrick too."

Sometimes a show is a letdown, no matter how much effort goes into it. Such a show was *Darling of the Day*, adapted from Arnold Bennett's *Buried Alive*. It opened on January 27, 1968, and ran for 32 performances, despite direction by George Abbott and lyrics by E. Y. (Yip) Harburg.

"I thought the score was brilliant—brilliant, brilliant lyrics. Just for the lyrics alone it was great. It failed because of not having the right person and the right director. The star was Vincent Price."

For most songwriters, there are properties done by others that they would have liked to be in on. What are some of Styne's favorite shows?

"*Guys and Dolls*," he says decisively, "because Frank Loesser made musical sounds for each character. Every piece of music he wrote was a pure definition of that character. No one, there isn't *anyone* in the theatre who could write 'Sue Me,' because he allowed for that song to be *that* character. There isn't anyone in the theatre today who could write 'Sit Down, You're Rockin' the Boat.' The tin horn opening fugue is unbelievable. I mean, no one could write it. No one can write a score as well as the score for *Guys and Dolls*, because only his special talent knew to write that particular show. Now, putting it on a higher level, I think the most unbelievable job of music writing—and I say this with deep reverence and envy—the most brilliant job of music writing ever in my life is *Sweeney Todd*. Only a long time from now will people say that. And then a show I found entertaining and very important was *Carousel*."

Turning from the past to the future, we wondered what Styne thought of burgeoning trends in the theatre such as the use of rock music.

"Rock doesn't come off as well on the stage as it does on record, and I'll tell you why. It's not the song but the accompaniment. You can't have that same sound for the girl who died as for the fellow who is getting drunk, or high, or whatever. It's the same pulsating thing. The only way rock can function is if it's in a setting where it belongs. If you're doing a thing of today in a street scene, you play rock. But you can't have a forty-five-year-old man sitting and singing a rock kind of thing. If it doesn't make sense, then don't have anything. Just have the actor sing with a piano or harmonica. But don't have a pulsating thing going on."

Styne wants to see the Broadway musical perpetuated, and he generously shares his experience with newcomers. He takes pride in discovering and nurturing talent, and one of his great glories is Jerry Bock, composer of *Fiddler on the Roof* and *Fiorello!*

"We've got to get him back writing for the theatre," says Styne. "About Jerry—I got him to do *Mr. Wonderful*, and I must tell you I heard fifty song teams at that time. I could have had anybody, but I heard this kid and said, 'Gee, he's got a lot on the ball.' They brought me in a ballad with 106 bars—

Patricia Routledge
and Vincent Price,
stars of Styne and E. Y. Harburg's
musical *Darling of the Day*.

Styne and Carol Channing
in a scene from a benefit
held in the composer's
honor, 1974.

'Mr. Wonderful,' 106 bars. 'You can say it in 32,' I said. 'The shorter you make it, the more chance of a hit song, since it's going to be in the show.' They brought it back the next day and I crossed out everything that was unnecessary. People first writing won't leave well enough alone. There's this fellow in the theatre who develops but never lets you know the song. When you get to bar seventeen, he goes off and gives you something else that has nothing to do with what went before, and it's tough until you get to the end—and you don't know that his beginning can't follow what was there, whether it was good, bad, or too much. You have to cut out all the excess. This kind of help, this kind of teaching, you can teach it to somebody who's basically a songwriter, who knows how to write a song."

Styne has also helped people like Marvin Hamlisch. "He followed me around, and I got him his first job in the movies, in *The Swimmer*, Sam Spiegel's film. Burt Bacharach was playing for singers, I remember. He brought one to the *Bells Are Ringing* audition, and I hated the singer. I walked around in the dark and looked in the pit. There he was. I said, 'Hey, what's your name?' and asked him what he did. 'I play for these girls and write,' Burt told me. And I said, 'Only write. Don't play for these girls. It's not good enough for you.' 'But I have to stay in New York,' Burt said. I offered him a job in a movie that made him a name. I was in London, and Charlie Feldman, the producer, asked me to write *What's New Pussycat?* I saw it on the screen, and I said, 'Charlie, you know I love you—there's a guy in California who can do this stuff and do it good. Burt Bacharach.' Charlie said, 'I've never heard of him,' and I said, 'Naturally you've never heard of him. If you had heard of him, you'd have gotten him, right?' Charlie said, 'Bring him over.' And Burt Bacharach came over and did *What's New Pussycat?* He got an Oscar nomination for that too.

"I get a kick out of helping. That started when I was coaching girls before I wrote songs, coaching girls how to sing. I like to teach, but I don't think I can teach people to write a song. You can't teach someone how to be a dramatist or a good collaborator. You know why? People shouldn't waste their time. It's a luxury to be a songwriter. To say 'I'm a songwriter,' boy, you'd better be ready to starve and everything that goes with it, and then finally the rewards come if you fit."

CHAPTER TWENTY-FIVE

PETER UDELL

I THINK THE THEME THAT RUNS THROUGH ALL MY SHOWS IS HOPE," says Peter Udell, lyricist of *Purlie* and *Shenandoah*. "If we don't have hope, what else is there?"

Optimism has always played an important role in Udell's success. The writer also credits good fortune.

"I was very lucky," he says. "I knew Frank Loesser and worked in his stockroom. While there, I wrote a piece called 'Driftwood,' which got recorded. That impressed Loesser."

Most people have to learn songwriting by trial and error. A few are fortunate enough to find a mentor, someone who can offer specific direction and steer their proteges away from obvious stumbling blocks.

"Loesser taught me fundamentals. He kept reminding me that lyrics are *images*. Frank told me that when he came up with the line 'How would you like to wake up in the morning and find your toothbrush hanging next to mine?' he knew he had learned how to write a song. Not that he was a beginner, you understand. Before that he'd already written little numbers like 'Heart and Soul' and other hits. But when he wrote those words, he understood what lyric writing was all about.

"I think my strongest literary influence was Ernest Hemingway. I don't try to create fancy rhymes. I try to say something *simply*—that's what Hemingway did! He's really simple, right on the money. I'm not interested in intricacy. The idea is this: know what you want to say, and say it. A better way to phrase it: a song is like a sculpture. You start with a big rock, and you knock away until you can't knock away anymore."

Various collaborators helped Udell to develop as a lyricist. He co-wrote a song called "So Happy I Could Cry" with Hoagy Carmichael. "It was a terrible lyric I wrote, but I *never* saw a man work so hard. I remember him saying to me, 'This melody sounds too much like another song of mine, "The Nearness of You."' If Hoagy couldn't get something, he'd throw papers around the room. This was a man in his sixties, and he'd say, 'I've pulled hits out so many times, but I'm too old now, and I can't just sit here until I get it.' But he did; he kept trying. He had pulled the hits out so many times before— 'Stardust,' 'Lazy River,' 'Lazy Bones.' He'd dig in with all his might."

Udell emphasizes Carmichael's tenacity. "He'd call me at four in the morning to change one word of the lyrics. This happened when I was very young. It taught me that you have to be a perfectionist."

Udell's quest for perfection led him to a permanent writing partner. "I wrote with various composers—Lee Pockriss, Gary Geld, Tommy Goodman. I found I was singing the Gary Geld tunes, so I opted to concentrate on the Geld-Udell team. Gary and I realized that music was shifting and publishers were losing their clout. So we went into independent production—the first people to get into that area. We formed a little publishing/record production company called Pogo Productions and signed Brian Hyland. We got into rhythm and blues and had hits with Jackie Wilson. Gary and I had 'Let Me Belong to You,' 'Sealed with a Kiss,' 'Ginny Come Lately,' and a whole lot of other smash hits. Until," and Udell pauses significantly, "the Beatles came along."

Suddenly the rage was the singer/songwriter. The freelance writer became an endangered species when Lennon and McCartney dominated the pop scene.

"The Americans were completely frozen off the air by the British invasion. The scene turned into death."

For this songwriting team, the scene didn't remain gloomy for long. With typical energy and resourcefulness, Udell suggested to Geld that they attempt a theatre piece. Progress stalled for a time when Geld left New York and relocated in Los Angeles. Udell continued to work on different projects and even considered writing with a new partner.

"Miles Lourie, the attorney who later represented Barry Manilow, sent a black composer to my apartment to play me music, thinking of the guy as a possible collaborator for me. The man's style, though, was very *Viennese,* and he wanted to musicalize *Cheaper by the Dozen.* I played him some of my own stuff, material with a strong black influence, and the man was embarrassed. His father was a minister from Kentucky, and the young man had sort of turned his back on his heritage."

Although the minister's son had apparently attempted to cut off his roots,

Udell, outside the theatre with partner Gary Geld.

he contacted Udell six weeks later with a distinctly black property, *Purlie*.

"I read it and knew it was my meat," says Udell. "I'd be able, I thought, to take all the black sounds and country sounds and put them on the stage. I said OK. Producer Philip Rose liked my lyrics a lot, but I knew that this black man wasn't a black writer. Phil, being the Eastern liberal he is, hated to replace him. It was Phil's secretary who thought in terms of the *play*, not personality. 'All right,' she said, 'hire this black man. He'll write a lousy score, and *sixty black actors* will be out of work instantly.'"

Her words made an impact; the good of the show had to rank as first priority.

"Then I had to convince Gary Geld to come in from California. He did, and we wrote *Purlie*, which turned out to be excellent."

Purlie opened on March 15, 1970, and ran for 688 peformances. It had a libretto by Udell, Philip Rose, and Ossie Davis and was inspired by Davis's play *Purlie Victorious*. The title character was a black preacher who fought to free plantation workers from the overbearing control of the plantation's owner Ol' Cap'n. Purlie's other struggle was his effort to raise money to start his own church.

"The book that Ossie Davis, Philip Rose, and I wrote took the original *Purlie Victorious* and kept cutting things we didn't need. And all the lyric concepts came out of my head. Ossie Davis didn't come and say, 'You've got to write a song about "Walk Him up the Stairs." ' The only words I took from Ossie were the words 'great white father.' "

He also warmed to the idea, proposed by book collaborator and director Rose, that the show open in flashback. Critics applauded the rousing funeral service that launched the evening, the excitement generated by a group of gospel singers and dancers.

Purlie's promotion was offbeat. Public relations director Sylvester Leaks didn't concentrate exclusively on white groups for theatre parties. He contacted such organizations as the NAACP and arranged to bus in black audiences from other cities. It was a shrewd box office move.

Even more offbeat was the show's prehistory. "*Purlie* never went out of town," says Udell. "We never had any money from backers. We raised it. My mother-in-law gave me $13,000 in a paper bag, and it allowed us to extend previews long enough to write 'I Got Love.' "

The song, performed with show-stopping intensity by the previously unknown actress Melba Moore, helped to turn the show into a major hit.

Cleavon Little's performance in the title role was rewarded with a Tony Award, as was the brilliant work of Moore. *Purlie*, though nominated, lost out to Strouse and Adams's *Applause* in the Best Musical category.

"I guess I feel we should have won the Tony Award for *Purlie*, and when we didn't, it hurt."

Lack of peer recognition always hurts, but with characteristic energy and determination, Geld and Udell jumped into their next project. *Shenandoah* was based on a 1965 western starring James Stewart. It followed the film's storyline fairly closely, in depicting the divisive effects of the Civil War on a family. The central character was a widower named Charlie Anderson, who suffered through the death of two sons and a daughter-in-law before his tearful reunion with still another son who had been kidnapped by Union troops.

The show garnered numerous awards, including a Best Book Tony for Udell (in collaboration with Philip Rose and James Lee Barrett). John Cullum was honored for his vigorous, spellbinding portrait of Charlie Anderson, and *Shenandoah* (which opened January 7, 1975) had an excellent 1,050-performance run.

Getting the show financed was easier than it had been for *Purlie*. Some of the backing came about in an unusual fashion.

"One of the producers, so the story goes, had made his money in pornography. When he was approached for our show, he said he wanted to do something beautiful. A funny part of the story is that Philip Rose is deathly allergic to blue cheese. He can't have blue cheese; he freaks out. So he went to get the $300,000 or whatever it was, and the backer's wife served a brunch with blue cheese. Somehow Phil got through it."

On the surface, *Shenandoah* is an odd choice for a musical—a melodramatic, frequently tragic tale of a family torn apart by war.

"But it was a clencher," Udell points out, "a powerful antiwar story. It had guts, a biting edge."

Many people compared the show's style to that of a Rodgers and Hammerstein musical. Udell takes exception to the idea. "If you put *Shenandoah* against *Oklahoma*, you'll see there's no relevance to that comparison at all. There are tender, gentle moments, but also a rape and two murders."

A project that followed *Shenandoah* was entitled *Angel*, a musical adaptation of Ketti Frings's *Look Homeward Angel*. Though Geld and Udell wrote another melodic score, critics rated it inferior to their earlier efforts.

Richard Eder of the *New York Times* conceded that one of the songs, "Feelin' Loved," had "an original ripple to it and may do well," and there were other appealing numbers, such as "If I Ever Loved Him" and "Drifting." But the book—a family saga dealing with a writer, his dying brother, and his security-hungry mother—was dismissed as sentimental and melodramatic.

Udell was crushed. "I really wrote *Angel* for my dad," he explains. "Actually, I had written sixty to seventy percent of the music when Gary came in to make musical sense out of my hodgepodge. He wrote some beautiful, sophisticated harmonies, and also some tunes, but basically the tunes were mine."

Was he happy with the final result?

"Well, there was a good, universal story. The negatives of the show were a couple of very bad numbers in crucial points. It could have been short-ened—especially the opening number I wrote, which is terrible and which I wanted out.

"There's a joke about this miner, who's walking in the desert and comes across another guy trying to get his bull to move. He says to the miner, 'I can't get my bull to move. Can I borrow that shovel over there?' The miner says, 'Sure.' He takes the shovel, goes up to the bull, and hits him right on the head. The miner, puzzled, asks, 'Why did you do that to the animal?' and the guy replies, 'The first thing you got to do is get his attention.' That's the definition of an opening number. If you knock them dead in the first six minutes, you have the next twenty-five minutes gratis. You have to grab their attention and entertain them."

Having written both major disappointments and major successes, Udell admits that there's no formula to writing a hit show.

"People pay a big dollar, and they want to see *magic*—that's what you've got to give them. You've got to come up with story values, wonderful songs, good pacing, lighting, exciting sets, choreography. Choreography is more than just dancing. It's movement from one place to another where it just flows.

"A musical is not like a movie. A movie is entertainment. You lay your five dollars down, and you couldn't care less who sits next to you; it's irrelevant. When you go to a theatre, several things happen. There's a reaction that happens between you and the actors on stage and also between you and those you're sitting next to."

He explains further. "I remember when I went to see *Company*, and *Purlie* was playing up the block. There were four people on the street, two couples, and one guy says to the other, 'Hey, that show *Purlie*? I saw it before it opened. It really took off after the Tony Award.' The other guy says, 'What did you think of it?' and he answered, 'When I saw it it was half full.' *That* was his comment! It was very important to him that the theatre be jammed. I think Shaw said, 'The quickest way to sell a ticket is to tell somebody they can't have one.' I probably murdered the quote, but that's the idea."

What, in Udell's opinion, makes a really good show?

"One that is entertaining, as I've said. One that's meaningful. And one that gives you insight, along with a feeling of catharsis. Shows that do that—shows I'm jealous of—include *The King and I*, a lot of Rodgers and Hammer-stein shows, *West Side Story*, *Fiddler*. I saw a show by Gretchen Cryer that I liked a lot, *Shelter*. Why the hell that show closed I have no idea."

It's often difficult for songwriters to judge their own work. Has he accomplished, thus far, what he set out to do?

"Of course not. Sometimes I feel I've never written a good song. Other times I love my songs a lot. But on the other hand, I'll also say, 'Gee whiz, I wish I'd written a melody as beautiful as 'Send in the Clowns' ' or whatever."

An early rehearsal for *Shenandoah*: *(left to right)*
Phillip Rose (director-producer),
Bob Tucker (choreographer),
Gary Geld (composer), and Udell.

Rhetta Hughes *(left)* and Ruth Brown in a scene from *Amen Corner.*

Occasionally, a show fails in spite of a good score and book. *"Comin' Uptown* fell into that category," says Udell. "The lighting was awful. It was lit like a vaudeville show. We also failed to sign Gregory Hines right away, and we didn't have a chance to go out of town. You can't just come to New York and expect things to be in shape. It happened with *Purlie*, but that's a rare occurrence."

Coming Uptown, which opened December 21, 1979, was an all-black version of Dickens's *A Christmas Carol*. The familiar story of Scrooge's reformation through love benefited from some fine songs, including "Have I Finally Found My Heart" and "What Better Time for Love." But critics found it sentimental and over-produced, and the show closed quickly.

Broadway has undergone many changes recently, which makes success or failure difficult to predict. Where does Udell see the theatre going today?

"I wish I knew. I see computers, fancy lights, fancy electronics, dazzling things. They're like toys, and they're wonderful, but they're only toys! The creativity has to come out of your head. Right now we're all enthralled by toys."

In spite of his concern over the current state of Broadway, Udell remains full of optimism about future projects. He closes with characteristic humor: "I don't know what God is doing, but he's spending too much time with Webber and Rice!"

CHAPTER TWENTY-SIX

RUPERT HOLMES

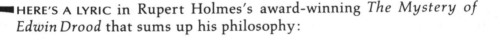

THERE'S A LYRIC in Rupert Holmes's award-winning *The Mystery of Edwin Drood* that sums up his philosophy:

> Don't try to think
> what move might be the best
> Use the heart that beats within your breast
> Never rest
> Don't quit while you're ahead

Only a man with this positive and determined attitude could have fashioned such an amazingly varied career. Holmes wrote book, words, and music for his Tony-winning musical, and beyond that, he created the haunting orchestrations. A jazz saxophonist, classical clarinetist, and rock keyboard player, he has to his credit seven albums and three hit singles as a recording artist, including the Number One "Escape" ("The Pina Colada Song"). He arranged, wrote and coproduced Barbra Streisand's album *Lazy Afternoon.*

Seated in his office on West 74th Street in Manhattan, surrounded by Sherlock Holmes posters—posters that reflect his love of mystery stories—the lanky Rupert Holmes reminisced about his musical childhood.

"I come by music naturally," says Holmes. "My dad played in big bands. He taught at Juilliard when he was seventeen. Later on he conducted the string section of the NBC Symphony in a semiclassical radio series. I still have records of it."

Holmes absorbed and welcomed all musical influences. "From age four, I remember listening to Jimmy Lunsford, Duke Ellington, Mozart, a lot of Ravel, Debussy, Blossom Dearie. And tons of Leroy Anderson. That was my own particular thing because every matinee movie on TV always used Leroy Anderson's 'Syncopated Clock.' "

His receptivity to all types of material stemmed—and still does—from the viewpoint that there are only two types of music: good and bad.

"Duke Ellington said that," Holmes explains. "Also—for some odd reason—I never realized that everything I was hearing was not contemporary. It seemed like one time-continuum of music, from a Sy Oliver 78 to Mozart's *40th*, the Everly Brothers, and Teresa Brewer."

In addition to what he learned from his father, Holmes became thoroughly familiar with Episcopal hymnal music through his devout mother.

"Ralph Vaughan Williams, Mendelssohn, Handel—just gorgeous. Purcell, Malcolm Arnold . . . my father, who's Jewish, felt the same way. He can't hear a brass band play "Onward, Christian Soldiers" without falling to the floor. And my brother affected me too—he's a passionate opera singer. I heard Verdi and Puccini and absorbed them by osmosis."

Training outside the home took place at the Manhattan School of Music.

"I never had to show up for the music-history classes because I'd been taught all this stuff as a kid. I couldn't believe people had to learn themes from symphonies and stuff. I just had trouble remembering what album they were from."

It was natural, given his extensive background, for Holmes to arrange his own work.

"If I'm the producer of the record or my own albums, I always do the orchestration. The thing is, when I was growing up, I didn't know whether I wanted to be a lyricist and a writer or whether I wanted to be a composer or an arranger, and I really went into songwriting because it let me have my cake and eat it too. I wanted to tell stories . . . I didn't mind making them rhyme, and I loved writing music. But I also sort of had in mind that I'd write for orchestras. I studied a little bit to do that. I found, early on, that when I wrote songs—well, you as a composer know where the strings have got to come in, or you know a song will not work unless it has a specific counterline to it. The counterline is often almost more important than the song. And in the beginning I would bring in songs and people wouldn't do the arrangement the way I heard it. It wasn't the way the song was supposed to be and it didn't work, because the song was conceived with those embellishments in mind."

Although Holmes refers to the Manhattan School of Music, "I really learned just by doing a lot of god-awful charts for people, for almost no money. I praise God for Henry Mancini and his book *Sounds and Scores*. I don't know what I would have done without that. It was wonderful if you just want to learn *clean* writing."

Along with musical development, Holmes nourished his literary appetite with mysteries, a taste that made his attraction to Dickens' *Edwin Drood* inevitable.

"I was a mystery buff from age ten or eleven because of a TV series: *Ellery Queen, Detective.* He was the first hero I'd ever seen who wore glasses, and since I was cursed with these, he appealed to me. I was Four Eyes except when I went to 3D movies; then I was Six Eyes. Anyway, I picked up *The Mystery of Edwin Drood* thinking it was going to be an Agatha Christie, one of those No-one-can-leave-the-manor, the-bridge-is-washed-out, one-of-us-must-be-a-killer . . . that sort of thing. My father explained that it wasn't like the stuff in *Alfred Hitchcock Magazine,* that it was more of a gothic novel. And it didn't resolve, because Dickens died of a stroke halfway through the writing."

Holmes smiles, recalling his fascination with the piece.

"I had a mental image of Dickens writing and falling over dead, and it was a very bizarre image for me; I was intrigued with *Drood* from then on. I think that maybe the reason we like mysteries is that life is a completely baffling Why, Who, and How done it, and we never get the answer and we can't relay it to someone else. At least in a mystery you create; you take your universe, tear it apart with terrible crises, and at the end of the book everything is resolved. So I've always loved that, and I love unsolvable mysteries because they tantalize me."

Years later Holmes encountered *The Mystery of Edwin Drood* at an Amtrak bookstand and reread it. He immediately sensed its musical possibilities.

"John Jasper, he's an organist, and Rosa Bud is his music pupil, and scenes of little street chants are quoted in the book. And Jasper hearing strange music when he has his opium visions . . . I thought, you could do modern stuff there at that point. It just seemed like a lot of things I loved in English music and American music, pop, even rock, classical music . . . all of these things could be flooded into the book. So I started to try and write *Drood* as a musical LP. It was somber and too ponderous, and I set it aside."

Drood was shelved for ten years, until Gail Merrifield, head of the New York Shakespeare Festival theatre department, saw Holmes performing at Dangerfield's in New York.

"I was doing mainly comedy and music. She and her husband, producer Joe Papp, were aware of my earlier albums, and knew that I tended to write narrative-type songs—story songs. They told me I was writing miniature theatre, and wouldn't I like to try writing something longer than three and a half minutes? The timing was right, because I'd done seven albums and I felt it was time to make a commitment to something wider in scope. When she asked what I wanted to do, *Edwin Drood* came immediately to mind."

Betty Buckley as Drood *(left)*, Patti Cohenour and John Herrera *(foreground)* and cast in *The Mystery of Edwin Drood* for which creator Holmes wrote words, book and music.

Holmes approached the initial layout of the project as a term paper.

"All your life you have to write term papers because teachers tell you to, and that makes them a drag. You gotta hand them in. But I had never tried writing a term paper that wouldn't be graded, that was just to clarify my own thinking."

He didn't realize, when doing the early pre-work, what enormous energy, time, and turmoil would be involved.

"It was a horrendous gamble. Three, four, five years of your life, and three guys in New York have upset stomachs or it reminds them of their mother or doesn't remind them of their mother, and suddenly that's it!"

Another problem was staying true to Dickens, when Dickens had supplied only a partial blueprint.

"I had no way of justifying where I was taking *Drood*. I couldn't adhere to the author's intentions, since I didn't know what they were. I decided to make the show Victorian vaudeville. I would frame it, so I wasn't writing *The Mystery of Edwin Drood*, I was writing about a hammy, perhaps seedy musical company whose gall exceeds my own."

Holmes was fortunate to find Wilford Leach, a director who shared his vision.

"It was the perfect juxtaposition. He was perhaps the *only* director who could have helped me the way I needed to be helped at that point, because he wasn't judgmental; he didn't say, 'This is what it must be and you must align yourself to it.' It was, instead, 'Let's try it.' We still don't really think of it as a *set* work, and that's the joy of it. I continually get to tinker with the show, which is amazing."

Drood, happily, lends itself to "tinkering," because it asks audiences to guess the ending Dickens left unwritten, and vote for the person they believe to be Drood's murderer. Holmes has written different material for all the endings.

"Depending on who the killer is, everyone has different lyrics and some different pieces of music."

The music for the show, according to Holmes, is not rigidly English, because "I didn't want to bore Americans with a whole two, two and a half hours of English music. That would be an awful lot for them to swallow. And I didn't want to ignore the harmonies that have crept into our vocabulary in the last twenty, thirty years. So what I tried to do was imagine that I had been catapulted back in time to that period. But knowing what I knew of Richard Rodgers and George Gershwin and Ravel and the Beatles, I said, Okay, if I was going to write in that period and not be burned at the stake for writing Devil music, what would I write—but still not forgetting what I'd been doing for the last ten, fifteen years of my career. After the opening number, my music, for a while, is stuff that almost could have been done in 1890. Very Gilbert and Sullivan. And slowly I start to deal in a few extra harmonies, till we get to 'Moonfall,' which is really quite lush. After that, I felt free to write in any period I wanted. Because the ice had been broken. But I eased the audiences into it."

Now that Holmes has eased himself into a Broadway career, are there any other works planned?

"Yes, I have a new musical. As a matter of fact, there's a song from it that's become a smash hit for the Jets, 'You Got It All.' A '40s musical. I can't tell you too much about it—not to be coy, but what if I changed it all? I want people to judge what I finish. But it'll involve the other major influence in my life, the big-band era."

Ironically, Holmes finds it easier to write for the theatre than for the pop market.

"In earlier eras, songwriters were allowed the liberty of high language, whether writing for records or the theatre. But in the pop market today, you can't write 'I'm wild again, beguiled again, a whimpering, simpering child again.' You say 'Na na na.' We're supposed to do what songwriters have always done, but we've got to make it sound like conversation, which technically eliminates sixty percent of the rhymes we could use in the past. I found writing the score of *Drood* . . . not easy, exactly—it was tough work—but in ways it was infinitely easier because my vocabulary was expanded a hundred times.

"When I write a song for records, I must take whatever it is I do and make it accommodate the world as it is right now—1987. It can't sound like two years ago; it's got to sound just like where everyone is at this moment, or a month or two ahead. In theatre, you *make up* a world and the songs are for that world, and that's the joy. You don't have the same pressure, the pressure to fit into a modern program format."

Pressure does exist, however, to integrate songs naturally into a musical show, make them enter conversationally and sustain the illusion of realism.

"The trick," Holmes believes, "is to think of the first line of your song as the *third line*. As though you've said the first two already. Make sure the first line is not the starting line, so it doesn't seem like an author's announcement."

Incorporating songs seamlessly into the plot was unheard of until Rodgers and Hammerstein accomplished it with *Oklahoma!*, and Richard Rodgers is still one of Holmes's favorite composers.

"Actually, Rodgers and Hart are my favorite songwriters," says Holmes. "I could read the lyrics of Larry Hart without the music and have a great evening, and I could listen to the tunes without the lyrics and feel the same. *My Fair Lady* is the most charming musical I've ever seen, and the orchestrations by Bennett are staggering. *West Side Story* is an astounding work. Now, I don't want to make the point too hard, because everyone else is making it, but there should be room for everything on Broadway. Sondheim's done wonderful things, but Aaron Copeland once said he didn't want to be Sibelius. I mean, I love Sondheim and his work, but I hope that

The *Drood* company kicks up their heels in "Don't Quit While You're Ahead." The musical, which composer Rupert Holmes wrote as "Victorian vaudeville," won five Tony awards in 1984.

The Chairman *(center)* and the Suspects: Joe Grifasi, Howard McGillin, George N. Martin, Patti Cohenour, George Rose, Cleo Laine, John Herrera and Jana Schneider. The audience votes the ending.

his shows, combined with a lot of English imports, are not confusing us too much about why people liked Broadway in the past, and what we can *do* on Broadway. *Drood* is my very first work. I'd never written for theatre before, and I plan to write some more if they'll let me. And I'd love to be called a traditionalist. I'd love to have even less concept on my next show. In fact, I'd like to have a book that tells the story."

Whatever approach Holmes takes, aspiring lyricists, composers, librettists, and orchestrators will see freshness, imagination, humor, flexibility, and best of all, the unexpected.

CHAPTER TWENTY-SEVEN

ROGER MILLER

FROM THE BEGINNING I felt a kinship to Mark Twain," says Roger Miller, composer/lyricist of *Big River*, which netted seven Tonys in 1985 for Best Musical, Director (Des McAnuff), Score (Miller), Book (William Hauptman), Scenic Design (Heidi Landesman), Lighting Design (Richard Riddell), and Featured Actor (Ron Richardson). "Twain's language—the way he portrayed Huck Finn—was written the way my people in western Oklahoma talk. We always tried to be very *aware* of Twain. We didn't want to destroy the flavor."

Miller's integrity is obvious in the down-home country flavor of his score. In "Hand for the Hog," he says:

> Well, I always heard but I ain't too sure
> That a man's best friend is a mangy cur
> I kinda favor the hog myself
> How about a hand for the hog

Miller also identified with Huck Finn's adventurous spirit. As a former ranch hand and rodeo man, he understands the universal need in people to live with a sense of freedom.

"I used to have a friend," Miller says, "a guitarist in my band, who didn't want to know anyone for more than six months. When I was a teenager I would leave home to wander around, mostly to hear music. I'd hitchhike to

Amarillo—that was 120 miles from where I lived—to hear Bob Wills and the Texas Playboys. . . . I guess there's this gypsy in all of us."

From the beginning, Miller had an off-center approach to lyrics—the result, he claims, of his "kinky mind. I look at a word and start playing with it." Early hits such as "You Can't Roller Skate in a Buffalo Herd," "King of the Road," and "Dang Me" have a humor and freshness that arises from a "criminal mentality."

He laughs, and explains further, "I like things to flow, to be *loose*," and points to such numbers in *Big River* as "I, Huckleberry, Me" and "Muddy Water." There is no trace of old-fashioned Broadway slickness, no jarring inner rhymes or alliterations.

Miller's Southern background is as far away from Broadway as one can get. His father died when he was a year old, and he went to live with an uncle in Erick, Oklahoma. The house had no electricity until Miller reached the eighth grade. Nor did he enjoy the use of a telephone until age seventeen.

"But we had a radio, so we could hear 'Grand Ole Opry' every Saturday night," he says.

Not surprisingly, one of his early influences was the lengendary Hank Williams. Inspired by Williams—and by Sheb Wooley, a relative who composed the bizarre "Purple People Eater"—Miller picked 400 pounds of cotton to make the eight dollars he needed to purchase a guitar.

"The theatre wasn't my burning desire," Miller says. "After the army, I went to Nashville. I worked there as a fiddler, guitarist, and singer with country bands."

He remembered his roots when deciding to score *Big River* simply, with country band rather than theatre orchestra.

"And the sound track was exact," he points out. "My record producer Jimmy Bowen wanted to do an exact version. The orchestra was beefed up just a little, but otherwise it was exact."

Did he think of pop hits when composing the score?

"Some of the songs were commercially constructed. The whole world hasn't pounced on them yet, but they will."

Miller's confidence comes from a sense of comfort with the overall production of the show, and the knowledge that he took on more responsibility than most composers would attempt.

"I had final approval on all casting," he says. "Still do. It was a great experience, sitting down and explaining to everyone what the songs should say. I stamped and clapped it out. If I couldn't play it on guitar, I'd shout it.

"I did flavoring," he continues. "I would put in and take out. I had hands-on all the way through it."

Watching the show today, would he change anything?

"Not a thing," he answers—an unexpected response considering the number of writers who suffer when they finally see a show mounted. "I still enjoy the show. I love to see the audiences cry—and laugh. Especially the children."

Miller's interest in theatre was triggered by association with producer Rocco Landesman. Landesman, a professor in Theatre Arts at Yale, became a fanatic Millerphile in the mid-60s.

"He was a little nutty on the subject," Miller says, "but I'm grateful."

Landesman's first production was a country musical, *Pump Boys and Dinettes*. He approached Miller about doing a theatrical project in 1982.

"Struck me as ridiculous back then," Miller chuckles. "But he kept after me. He kept insisting that *Huckleberry Finn* was the perfect vehicle."

At the time, Miller had seen very few Broadway musicals—an exception was *How to Succeed in Business Without Really Trying*—but he had already developed an admiration for Rodgers and Hammerstein and Jerome Kern.

"George M. Cohan was also one of my heroes," he adds.

Once enlisted, Miller became totally involved with the *Big River* score. Asked what he had found most difficult about the process, he says, "Getting up in the morning"; but then he turns serious and reflects.

"It wasn't easy. I'd wander through the woods a lot, near my home in Santa Fe, thinking. And I didn't have a specific schedule of working. But my mental processes are geared to *life*. I didn't study other people consciously, but I'm aware of them. That intuition helped."

Did he write the songs in order?

"Just wrote them pretty much at random," he says. "I had my mind in the story and the music. It was clear to me, so when I wrote nineteen pieces of music, we used eighteen. I just looked to see where there were holes, and filled them with music.

"One thing I knew for sure," he continues: "I didn't want dancing to interfere with my lyrics. I wanted the songs to stand on their own."

What songs does he regard with particular pride?

"I like 'River in the Rain.' Rocco has the lyrics on his wall. Also 'Free at Last' . . . and 'Leaving's Not the Only Way to Go.' "

This title can also apply to the up-and-coming theatre writers who feel that today's theatre offers little opportunity and want to abandon it for films and television.

"As I see it," Miller feels, "theatre is wide open for people who are really interested. True, the record industry has been enticing all the young talent. It has a faster payoff. But I'd like to *urge* a lot of young men and women to look at theatre. Theatre needs young ideas, new talent. It's a great experience to be able to be creative and see your show come to life."

The joy of sweeping the Tonys is another peak experience that Miller treasures.

"I was surprised . . . but not shocked. Put it this way: *pleasantly shocked*. It was a nice feeling, because I've never been involved with something where so much good work was put into it."

Daniel Jenkins and John Short as Huckleberry Finn and Tom Sawyer in *Big River,* the 1985 Tony winner for Best Musical.

Ron Richardson and Daniel Jenkins as Jim and Huck singing "Muddy Water" from *Big River.*

Bob Gunton, Daniel Jenkins, Rene Auberjonois and Ron Richardson *(rear)* in song from *Big River*. Composer Roger Miller adapted Twain's *Huckleberry Finn* for Broadway.

Miller is in favor of a theatre that encompasses all influences and doesn't become overwhelmed with any specific musical identity, be it rock, country, or classical.

"I don't think rock or country will dominate," he says. "Theatre has its own style and standards. I don't think rock is the answer for theatre, really. There's a place for it . . . like in *Grease* . . . but it shouldn't become a regular diet."

The only regular diet should be creativity and a truthful approach to the situations, Miller feels, an attitude he shares with two of his favorite modern composers, Marvin Hamlisch and Stephen Sondheim. "You should always be *pure* to the piece," Miller insists.

These conclusions were drawn over a lifetime of living, much of which brought the composer great personal pain. "I don't drink much anymore," he says. "I don't do any dope, and I don't hang out." Nor did he choose to finish off his life in honky-tonks or as a burned-out vagabond.

"But through good times and bad," Miller concludes, "I still held on to everything that made me what I am."

And the traits that make Miller unique—his idiosyncratic vision and fundamental honesty—are what turn *Big River* into an authentic reflection of the novel. Other composers have tried to conquer *Huckleberry Finn*— Alan Jay Lerner and Burton Lane (for a motion picture to star Gene Kelly and Danny Kaye), Kurt Weill and Maxwell Anderson (for a Broadway musical). But Miller persisted, energized by Rocco Landesman's belief in him.

He admits, "Stepping back from the music business for a few years, I kind of bottled things up. I didn't have a place to shoot my arrows. Then Rocco came by. I took aim and fired my best shot."

Miller, the onetime "king of the road," recognized that Twain's Mississippi River might well be today's highway, and his instinctive understanding of that relationship gives *Huckleberry Finn* powerful modern relevance as a musical play.

STEPHEN SONDHEIM

N O BOOK ON MUSICAL theatre would be complete without an examination of Stephen Sondheim's life and work. Mr. Sondheim was unable to meet with us, but we formed a vivid, fully rounded portrait of him through comments from his various collaborators and colleagues. The following are some of those comments, and what they specifically reveal about Sondheim, as individual and as artist.

It's not that I haven't achieved recognition . . . but people think of this as the Sondheim era.

Marvin Hamlisch

Hamlisch's opinion is shared by nearly everyone who cares about the world of theatre. Stephen Sondheim has written words and music for ten innovative shows: *A Funny Thing Happened on the Way to the Forum* (1962), *Anyone Can Whistle* (1964), *Company* (1970), *Follies* (1971), *A Little Night Music* (1973), *The Frogs* (1974), *Pacific Overtures* (1976), *Sweeney Todd* (1979), *Merrily We Roll Along* (1982) and *Sunday in the Park with George* (1984).

In addition, he wrote the colorful, incisive lyrics to Leonard Bernstein's music for *West Side Story* (1957), Jule Styne's music for *Gypsy* (1959), and Richard Rodgers' music for *Do I Hear a Waltz?* (1965).

Four of Sondheim's shows *(Sweeney Todd, A Little Night Music, Follies,* and *Company),* have won Best Score Tony awards. These masterworks, plus *Pacific Overtures* and *Sunday in the Park with George,* captured the New York Drama Critics Award for Best Musical. *Sunday in the Park with George* also received a Pulitzer Prize for Drama, along with eight Drama Desk Awards (including Best Musical) and two Tonys.

Sondheim has written offbeat film scores for *Stavisky* (1974) and *Reds* (1981); additional lyrics for Leonard Bernstein's *Candide* (1973), and incidental music for Broadway's *Twigs* (1971), *Girls of Summer* (1956), and *Invitation to a March* (1961).

The Sondheim era is a result of steady, prolific output and unfailing creative brilliance.

> At the head of the list of people I admire has to be Sondheim, because of his extraordinary talent, his extraordinary adventurousness, and his extraordinary integrity.
>
> *Sheldon Harnick*

Adventurousness and integrity are the words most often applied to Sondheim, even by his detractors. He refuses to fall back on time-proved security blankets. Old masters like Richard Rodgers wanted their songs to become hits, and knew that constant reprises would fix a melody in the mind of the audience. Sondheim feels that arbitrary reprises are false, unless they serve a particular dramatic function. His whole thrust is toward character, toward illuminating the complex, contradictory inner drives of his heroes and heroines.

A good example of this occurred during *Gypsy.* One of Sondheim's lines in the lyric of "Small World" was "Funny, I'm a woman with children," and collaborator Jule Styne gasped, "No man will be able to record it." Sondheim resisted changing the line to fit record-market requirements, because those words, in context, added so much to the characterization of Mama Rose.

His adventurousness is also brilliantly demonstrated by subject matter. Most people think of *West Side Story* as a mainstream musical of the old school. In actual fact, its grim, even sordid depiction of juvenile gang violence divided the press when the show first opened in 1957. It was a bitter pill to many, and not a box-office smash until the popularity of the Academy Award–winning movie version in 1961. Nor was *Gypsy,* which centered on a ruthlessly ambitious stage mother, a sentimental vehicle from the Rodgers and Hammerstein school.

Company—the story of a thirty-five-year-old bachelor and his unhappily married friends—cast a cynical light on marriage. In the closing song, "Being Alive," the hero reluctantly concedes that commitment is better than loneliness. Yet "Being Alive" was Sondheim's concession to producer Hal

Mandy Patinkin as Seurat paints Dot, played by Bernadette Peters, as he sings "Sunday in the Park with George."

Prince, a last-minute replacement for an earlier, more negative number that Prince disliked. Entitled "Happily Ever After," it said:

> Someone to need you too much
> Someone to read you too well
> Someone to bleed you
> Of all you don't want to tell
> That's Happily Ever After
> In hell

This lacerating honesty also dominated *Follies*. *Follies* concentrated on former showgirls meeting in the condemned theatre where they once played, reliving and finally discarding outdated dreams of youth. *A Little Night Music* gently but satirically highlighted the subtle intricacies of romantic involvement in turn-of-the-century Sweden. *Pacific Overtures*, Sondheim's experimental Kabuki musical—which featured only male Oriental actors—examined the Westernization of Japan.

Most daring of all was Sondheim's *Sunday in the Park with George*, a musical study of pointillist painter Georges Seurat, and a show that bypassed conventional narrative to debate the nature of artistic creation.

Like his most frequent producer, Hal Prince, Sondheim doesn't, in the words of *Newsweek*'s Jack Kroll, want to "maim old Mames or doll up Old Dollys."

> What has happened, I think, in the past decade or more, is a real retrogression in the American musical theatre toward infinitely more commercial work. One of the great exceptions is Steve Sondheim. He bucks the current tide, admirably. But there aren't many who do.
>
> *Leonard Bernstein*

Sondheim claims that he chooses his projects primarily because the subjects interest him, not because he is trying to change the face of the American musical.

What interests him is unusual source material. Most Broadway musicals are based on old movies, established classics, or the lives of famous people. Few composers and lyricists would turn to Plautus (*A Funny Thing Happened on the Way to the Forum*), Aristophanes (*The Frogs*), Ingmar Bergman (*A Little Night Music*), and the art of Seurat (*Sunday in the Park with George*).

Sondheim also avoids tacked-on happy endings, even when rosy, off-into-the-sunset fade-outs, like reprises, could help the financial prospects of his shows. "*A Little Night Music* was more successful than *Company* and *Follies* because it had a truly happy ending," he admits.

This propensity for realism doesn't minimize his admiration for Broadway greats who worked in different ways. As Sondheim sees it, Harold Arlen and

Jerome Kern were extraordinary for "their harmonic language." He applauds Cole Porter's playfulness and Yip Harburg's "antic imagination." He also has great respect for the "conversational, colloquial language" of Frank Loesser and Dorothy Fields.

At the same time, however, he doesn't want to repeat what his predecessors have already done and risk boredom. He differs sharply from mentor Hammerstein by drifting toward "sentiment as opposed to sentimentality." He adds, "I love to write in dark colors about gut feelings."

Nowhere is this penchant for dark colors more obvious than in the choice of *Sweeney Todd—The Demon Barber of Fleet Street* as a Broadway production. Based on *Sweeney Todd*, a play by Christopher Bond, it had as its "hero" a psychotic barber given to slitting throats and turning his victims into the substance of meat pies. Star Angela Lansbury admitted, "I never, ever realized how put off people would be by the blood . . . and I'm a very squeamish person." But it gave Sondheim an opportunity to create music that resembled the background score of a horror film. He relished using electronic sounds and a loud, crashing organ.

When Sondheim announces how much he enjoys writing about "neurotic people, troubled people, people with conflicts," he speaks for the state of the world today. He explains: "What 'neurotic people' means to me is people with conflicts. I don't like to write about oversimplified people unless it's for something like farce, like *Forum*. Songs can't develop uncomplicated characters and unconflicted people. You can't just tell the sunny side and have a story with any richness in it."

This candor accounts for his ever-growing impact. The man who once called himself "essentially a cult figure" has made a recent transition to widespread acceptance—an acceptance further aided by Barbra Streisand's Number One *The Broadway Album*, which features six Sondheim songs.

Even those who say they want dancing girls and fairy-tale plots are being drawn in by Sondheim's multilayered characters and lyrics. Nothing looks clear now, and a mad dash for the protection of '50s music and fashions won't make it any clearer. Sondheim's attempt to understand the *motivations behind* relationships, his attempt to locate reasons why we've landed in such a confused state, make him a mirror of modern turmoil, a spokesman for the '80s.

> He has great ears. I don't think I can explain how talented he is. He's not a flowery person. He's right to the point. He's honest. He's corrective . . . great sense of musicianship. When I wrote "Rose's Turn," Arthur Laurents, the book writer, said, "Write a medley of all she has seen in the past." Steve liked the musical intervals in between—a cacophonous thing. When Steve heard it all the way through, he said, "You only do it once." So Steve helped me with his musical intuition. He wanted a cacophony, so he put it in the bass trombone's sound. Now, look, the audience doesn't know it's a bass trombone, but you feel it.
>
> *Jule Styne*

Mandy Patinkin as Seurat sings "Color and Light."

This statement about Sondheim's remarkable musicality highlights one of his greatest gifts: he thinks in orchestral terms. He has little patience with so-called composers who dash off lead sheets with chord symbols, leaving the arrangement to others. Jay Morgenstern, now president of Warner Brothers' Print Division, recalls working with Sondheim at Tommy Valando Music.

"He went over every note," Morgenstern says, "every chord. Sometimes this perfectionism took a year to complete." Few composers are that obsessively thorough, that committed to weeding out every mistake before their music goes to press.

Sondheim has never considered himself primarily a lyricist. The man who numbers Prokofiev, Ravel, Rachmaninoff, Britten, and Copland among his influences began piano lessons at age seven, and later majored in music at Williams College. Winning the Hutchinson Prize, a two-year fellowship, enabled him to study with avant-garde composer Milton Babbitt. He was one of the few students Babbitt taught privately.

This richly detailed education gave him the tools to think of songs as *plays*, as character studies, with instrumentation a key factor in heightening characterization. Spotlighting the bass trombone was a brilliant way of pointing up the anguish and rage Merman/Mama Rose felt at the finale of *Gypsy*.

Because of Sondheim's feelings about doing words and music, he submitted himself to star Ethel Merman in both capacities. Merman vetoed the idea, insisting that Jule Styne handle melody. The *Gypsy* experience convinced Sondheim that he would be satisfied only doing words and music from then on, and he maintained that attitude when asked by Hal Prince to supply lyrics to Jerry Bock's *Fiorello!* music. ("Thank God Steve turned it down," says eventual choice Sheldon Harnick.)

Styne's admiration for Sondheim's ability to "get right to the point" and be honest and corrective stems from early training with Oscar Hammerstein, father of Sondheim's close friend Jimmy. Hammerstein took the budding young composer under his wing and analyzed his first high school musical, *By George*. Pronouncing it "the worst thing I've ever read," he went on to assure Sondheim that he had talent, and then taught him the basics of theatrical writing. These lessons included the need for simplicity, the importance of content, how to tell a story and make songs relate to character.

Armed with practical direction "from a highly professional, rule-conscious man," Sondheim developed his own style. In comparing his two mentors, Hammerstein and Babbitt, he says, "They represented two different fields. One was theatre, the other music. What I was learning from Milton was basic grammar—sophisticated grammar, but grammar. It was a language, whereas what I learned from Oscar was what to do with language."

Milton Babbitt recalls, "Steve wanted to improve himself in every conceivable way," an ambition that resulted in relentless perfectionism.

This perfectionism makes him strive for grace and purity of tone in his lyrics.

"Rhyming must seem fresh but inevitable," he says. "You try for surprise, but not so wrenchingly that a listener loses the sense of the line."

A line, in his opinion, should flow, and he winces at the memory of "So Many People," composed in 1954 for his unproduced *Saturday Night*. The song contains a lyric line that sits awkwardly on the melody: "For so much less than/what I had planned" breaks up a prepositional phrase.

Alliteration, he feels, is acceptable, but only if it's subtly used and has a natural sound.

Writing *backward* is an approach Sondheim finds helpful. "You have a climax, a twist, a punch, a joke. You start at the bottom of the page—you preserve your best joke for the last; the ideas should work down toward it in ascending order of punch."

Most crucial, he keeps a separate folder with notes on the characters, their personalities and backgrounds, what they wear, what cars they drive, how they furnish their homes.

Yvonne De Carlo, who brought down the house in *Follies* with "I'm Still Here," recalled Sondheim's work process while starring in a 1984 Atlantic City run of *Can Can* (Note: Al Kasha directed De Carlo in the show):

"He took me aside and asked dozens of questions," she says. "He wanted to know everything about this woman . . . what she, as a Hollywood star, had been through . . . her marriages, her career problems, the way she faced aging. He took lots of notes, and he interviewed other people in the show as well. He really did his homework!"

Note-taking, rewriting, polishing, adding—none of these priorities are given short shrift. Observers remember Sondheim struggling over *Sweeney Todd*'s vocal arrangements right up to opening night. Just prior to the *Gypsy* opening, he decided that "Some People" needed a verse because the dialogue that preceded the song was on a high pitch and the song started low. He went to Ethel Merman, although she had earlier announced she would learn new material up until a week before opening night, and nothing afterward. When asked to do the additional verse, she refused—a source of permanent frustration for him.

> I could have said, "I'm going to write an operatic musical," and I can also do that. But not as well as people like Steve Sondheim.
>
> *Jerry Herman*

Most composers eventually decide what they can and can't do and produce variations on this basic style. Sondheim, on the other hand, appears to feel he can attempt anything. This adventurousness, praised by Sheldon

The cast of *Sunday in the Park with George* during the first-act finale, "Sunday."

Harnick, can sometimes make people feel, as Len Cariou (Tony winner for *Sweeney Todd*) did, that Sondheim is "going over the edge."

If "going over the edge" means periodic avoidance of conventional melody, Cariou is right. This avoidance is deliberate, because Sondheim is superbly capable of writing memorable tunes when the occasion calls for it—"Send in the Clowns," "Not While I'm Around," "Losing My Mind." But *Arts and Entertainment* journalist Robert Viagas gets to the heart of Sondheim's genius when he says, "Melody is not his goal. Some emotions are simply not melodic: rage, jealousy, frustration. Yet they can be sung, and Sondheim's achievement is to have found a musical language to express a whole spectrum of feelings through song. To be able to break free of melody when a dramatic situation demands it—that opens the door to an infinitely varied kind of musical drama."

By opening that door, Stephen Sondheim is signaling all up-and-coming composers that yesterday's conventions can be redefined, and that no limits should ever be placed on creative imagination.

APPENDIX
TONY NOMINATIONS & AWARDS

Burt Bacharach

1969 Nomination, Best Musical, *Promises, Promises*

Leonard Bernstein

1953 Best Composer, *Wonderful Town*

1957 Nomination, Best Musical, *Candide*

1958 Nomination, Best Musical, *West Side Story*

1969 Special Award

Jerry Bock

1960 Best Musical, *Fiorello!*

1960 Best Composer, *Fiorello!*

1964 Nomination, Best Musical, *She Loves Me*

1965 Best Composer, *Fiddler on the Roof*

1967 Nomination, Best Composer, *The Apple Tree*

1971 Best Score, *The Rothschilds*

Sammy Cahn

1966 Nomination, Best Musical, *Skyscraper*

1967 Nomination, Best Lyricist, *Walking Happy*

Cy Coleman

1963 Nomination, Best Musical, *Little Me*

1963 Nomination, Best Composer, *Little Me*

1966 Nomination, Best Musical, *Sweet Charity*

1966 Nomination, Best Composer, *Sweet Charity*

1974 Nomination, Best Score, *Seesaw*

1977 Nomination, Best Score, *I Love My Wife*

1978 Best Score, *On the Twentieth Century*

1980 Nomination, Best Musical, *Barnum*

1980 Nomination, Best Score, *Barnum*

Betty Comden & Adolph Green

1957 Nomination, Best Musical, *Bells Are Ringing*

1961 Nomination, Best Musical, *Do Re Mi*

1968 Best Lyricists, *Hallelujah, Baby!*

1970 Best Musical, *Applause*

1978 Best Book, *On the Twentieth Century*

1978 Best Score, *On the Twentieth Century*

1983 Nomination, Best Book, *A Doll's Life*

1983 Nomination, Best Score, *A Doll's Life*

Hal David

1969 Nomination, Best Musical, *Promises, Promises*

1968 Nomination, Best Lyricist, *The Happy Time*

1969 Nomination, Best Musical, *Zorba*

1976 Nomination, Best Score, *Chicago*

1978 Nomination, Best Score, *The Act*

1981 Best Score, *Woman of the Year*

1984 Nomination, Best Lyricist, *The Rink*

Micki Grant

1973 Nomination, Best Book, *Don't Bother Me, I Can't Cope*

1973 Nomination, Best Score, *Don't Bother Me, I Can't Cope*

1978 Nomination, Best Score, *Working*

Marvin Hamlisch

1976 Best Score, *A Chorus Line*

Sheldon Harnick

1960 Best Musical, *Fiorello!*

1964 Nomination, Best Musical, *She Loves Me*

1965 Best Lyricist, *Fiddler on the Roof*

1967 Nomination, Best Lyricist, *The Apple Tree*

1971 Nomination, Best Lyricist, *The Rothschilds*

Jerry Herman

1962 Nomination, Best Musical, *Milk and Honey*

1962 Nomination, Best Composer and Lyricist, *Milk and Honey*

1964 Best Musical, *Hello, Dolly!*

1964 Best Composer and Lyricist, *Hello, Dolly!*

1966 Nomination, Best Musical, *Mame*

1966 Nomination, Best Composer and Lyricist, *Mame*

Rupert Holmes

1984 Best Score, *The Mystery of Edwin Drood*

1984 Best Musical, *The Mystery of Edwin Drood*

1984 Best Book, *The Mystery of Edwin Drood*

John Kander

1967 Best Composer, *Cabaret*

1968 Nomination, Best Composer, *The Happy Time*

1969 Nomination, Best Musical, *Zorba*

1976 Nomination, Best Score, *Chicago*

1978 Nomination, Best Score, *The Act*

1981 Best Score, *Woman of the Year*

1984 Nomination, Best Composer, *The Rink*

Henry Krieger & Tom Eyen

1981 Best Book, *Dreamgirls* (Eyen)

1982 Nomination, Best Score, *Dreamgirls*

Alan Jay Lerner

1957 Best Author, *My Fair Lady*

1966 Nomination, Best Composer, *On a Clear Day*

1970 Nomination, Best Musical, *Coco*

1974 Best Score, *Gigi*

1979 Nomination, Best Score, *Carmelina*

Roger Miller

1985 Best Score, *Big River*

1985 Best Musical, *Big River*

Tim Rice

1972 Nomination, Best Score, *Jesus Christ Superstar*

1980 Best Book, *Evita*

1980 Best Score, *Evita*

1982 Nomination, Best Book, *Joseph and the Amazing Technicolor Dreamcoat*

1982 Nomination, Best Score, *Joseph and the Amazing Technicolor Dreamcoat*

Mary Rodgers

1960 Nomination, Best Musical, *Once upon a Mattress*

1978 Nomination, Best Score, *Working*

Stephen Schwartz

1973 Nomination, Best Score, *Pippin*

1977 Nomination, Best Score, *Godspell*

1978 Nomination, Best Book, *Working*

1978 Nomination, Best Score, *Working*

Stephen Sondheim

1957 Nomination, Best Musical, *West Side Story*

1959 Nomination, Best Musical, *Gypsy*

1962 Best Musical, *A Funny Thing Happened on the Way to the Forum*

1965 Best Music and Lyrics, with Richard Rogers, *Do I Hear a Waltz?*

1970 Best Musical, *Company*

1970 Best Lyrics, *Company*

1970 Best Music, *Company*

1971 Best Musical, *Follies*

1971 Best Music and Lyrics, *Follies*

1973 Best Musical, *A Little Night Music*

1973 Best Music and Lyrics, *A Little Night Music*

1976 Nomination, Best Musical, *Pacific Overtures*

1976 Nomination, Best Score, *Pacific Overtures*

1977 Nomination, Best Musical, *Side by Side by Sondheim*

1979 Best Musical, *Sweeney Todd—The Demon Barber of Fleet Street*

1979 Best Score, *Sweeney Todd—The Demon Barber of Fleet Street*

1981 Nomination, Best Score, *Merrily We Roll Along*

1984 Nomination, Best Musical, *Sunday in the Park with George*

1984 Nomination, Best Score, *Sunday in the Park with George*

Charles Strouse

1961 Best Musical, *Bye, Bye Birdie*

1965 Nomination, Best Musical, *Golden Boy*

1970 Best Musical, *Applause*

1977 Best Score, *Annie*

1981 Nomination, Best Score, *Charlie and Algernon*

Jule Styne

1957 Nomination, Best Musical, *Bells are Ringing*

1960 Nomination, Best Musical, *Gypsy*

1961 Nomination, Best Musical, *Do Re Me*

1964 Nomination, Best Musical, *Funny Girl*

1964 Nomination, Best Composer, *Funny Girl*

1968 Best Composer, *Hallelujah, Baby!*

Peter Udell

1970 Nomination, Best Musical, *Purlie*

PERMISSION ACKNOWLEDGMENTS

PHOTO CREDITS

Photo on page 5 courtesy of ASCAP. All other photos in Chapter 1 courtesy of Burt Bacharach. Photos on page 16 courtesy of the Institute of the American Musical, Inc.; photo on page 17 courtesy of the Didier C. Deutsch Collection. All other photos in Chapter 2 courtesy of Leonard Bernstein. Photo on page 33 (top) by Friedman-Abeles, courtesy of the Didier C. Deutsch Collection; photo on page 33 (bottom) courtesy of the Institute of the American Musical, Inc.; photo on page 34 (top) by David Gahr. All other photos in Chapter 3 courtesy of Jerry Bock. Photo on page 42 courtesy of the Didier C. Deutsch Collection; photo on page 46 courtesy of Jule Styne Productions. All other photos in Chapter 4 courtesy of Sammy Cahn. Photo on page 55 (top) courtesy of ASCAP; photos on page 58 by Friedman-Abeles; photos on page 59 courtesy of the Didier C. Deutsch Collection; photo on page 60 (top) by Bert Andrews. All other photos in Chapter 5 courtesy of Cy Coleman. Photo on page 65 (top) courtesy of the Institute of the American Musical, Inc.; on page 65 (bottom) courtesy of Columbia Records, from the Didier C. Deutsch Collection. Photo on pages 70–71 by Martha Swope, courtesy of the Didier C. Deutsch Collection. All other photos in Chapter 6 courtesy of Betty Comden and Adolph Green. Photos on page 81 (bottom) and 82 by Sy Friedman. All other photos in Chapter 7 courtesy of Gretchen Cryer. Photo on page 88 courtesy of Hal David; photo on page 94 (top) courtesy of Dionne Warwick; on page 94 (bottom) by Friedman-Abeles, courtesy of Stanley Green. Photo on page 100 (bottom) courtesy of the Didier C. Deutsch Collection; photo on pages 12–13 by Martha Swope. All other photos in Chapter 9 courtesy of Fred Ebb. Photo on page 112 by Bob Ullman; photo on page 117 by Susan Cook. Photo on page 123 (top) by Friedman-Abeles; photo on page 126 by Thomas S. England. All other photos in Chapter 11 courtesy of Micki Grant. Photo on page 128 by John Vidol. All other photos in Chapter 12 by Ilene Jones. Photo on pages 144–45 by Martha Swope. All other photos in Chapter 13 courtesy of Marvin Hamlisch. Photo on page 152 by Margery Gray Harnick; photo on page 167 by Friedman-Abeles. All other photos in Chapter 14 courtesy of Sheldon Harnick. Photo on page 173 by Werner J. Kuhn; photo on page 176 (bottom) courtesy of the Didier C. Deutsch Collection; photo on page 182 by Friedman-Abeles; photo on page 185 by Martha Swope. All other photos in Chapter 15 courtesy of Jerry Herman. Photo on page 190 by Beryl Tobin. Photos on pages 196 and 204 by Martha Swope; photo on page 199 (top) courtesy of RCA Victor Records. All other photos in Chapter 16 courtesy of John Kander. Photos on pages 213, 214, and 215 by Martha Swope. All other photos in Chapter 17 courtesy of Henry Krieger and Tom Eyen. Photo on page 218 by Jerry Bauer; photo on page 221 by Martha Swope; photo on page 225 (top) courtesy of CBS Records; on page 225 (bottom) courtesy of ASCAP, originally provided by Seymour Kravitz and Company; photo on page 227 courtesy of the Didier C. Deutsch Collection; photo on page 228 (top) by Arthur Zinn, courtesy of RCA. All other photos in Chapter 18 courtesy of Alan J. Lerner. Photo on page 234 (top) and photo on page 237 by Martha Swope. All other photos in Chapter 19 courtesy of Tim Rice. Photos in Chapter 20 courtesy of Mary Rodgers. Photo on page 255 (top) by Joy Thompson. All other photos in Chapter 21 courtesy of Carole Bayer Sager. Photo on page 262 (top) courtesy of Berly Lansbury; photo on page 266 (top) by Thomas S. England. All other photos in Chapter 22 courtesy of Stephen Schwartz. Photos on page 276 (bottom) and on page 278 (top, left) courtesy of the Institute of the American Musical, Inc; photo on page 278 (top, right) by Bill Mark; photo on page 286 (top) courtesy of RCA; photo on page 286 (bottom) by S. Visalli. All other photos in Chapter 23 courtesy of Jule Styne. Photo on page 288 by Rita Katz; photo on page 292 (bottom) courtesy of ASCAP; photo on page 295 courtesy of the Didier C. Deutsch Collection; photo on page 299 by Martha Swope; photo on page 300 (bottom) by Martha Swope, courtesy of David Mayhew of Henry Luhrman Associates. All other photos in Chapter 24 courtesy of Charles Strouse. Photo on page 309 by Friedman-Abeles; photo on page 310 by Martha Swope. All other photos in Chapter 25 courtesy of Peter Udell. Photo on page 312 Courtesy of Rupert Holmes. All other photos in Chapter 26 by Martha Swope. All photos in Chapter 27 by Martha Swope. All photos in Chapter 28 by Martha Swope.

INDEX